Society

OF

INQUIRY ON MISSION

AND

THE STATE OF RELIGION.

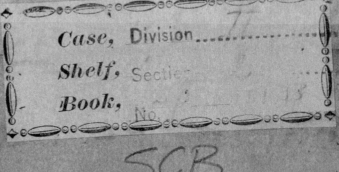

MEMOIRS

OF

Mrs. Abigail Bailey,

WHO HAD BEEN THE WIFE

OF

MAJOR ASA BAILEY,

FORMERLY OF LANDAFF, (N. H.)

WRITTEN BY HERSELF.

SHE DIED IN BATH, N. H. FEBRUARY, 11, 1815.

TO WHICH ARE ADDED SUNDRY ORIGINAL

BIOGRAPHICAL SKETCHES.

EDITED BY ETHAN SMITH, A. M.
MINISTER OF THE GOSPEL IN HOPKINTON, N. H.

"Behold, and see, if there be any sorrow like unto my
sorrow." JEREMIAH.
"Many are the afflictions of the righteous; but the Lord
delivereth him out of them all." DAVID.

BOSTON:
PUBLISHED BY SAMUEL T. ARMSTRONG,
Theological Printer and Bookseller, No. 50, Cornhill.
....
1815.

DISTRICT OF MASSACHUSETTS—*To wit:*

District Clerk's Office.

BE IT REMEMBERED, that on the fourth day of December, A. D. 1815, and in the fortieth year of the independence of the United States of America, SAMUEL T. ARMSTRONG, of the said District, has deposited in this office the title of a book, the right whereof he claims as Proprietor, in the words following, *to wit:*

"Memoirs of Mrs. Abigail Bailey, who had been the wife of Major Asa Bailey, formerly of Landaff, (N. H.) Written by herself. She died in Bath, (N. H.) February 11, 1815. To which are added sundry original Biographical Sketches. Edited by Ethan Smith, A. M. Minister of the Gospel in Hopkinton, N. H.

"Behold, and see, if there be any sorrow like unto my sorrow." *Jeremiah.*

"Many are the afflictions of the righteous; but the Lord delivereth him out of them all." *David.*

In conformity to the act of the Congress of the United States, intitled, "An act for the encouragement of Learning, by securing the Copies of Maps, Charts, and Books, to the Authors and Proprietors of such Copies, during the times therein mentioned;" and also to an act intitled, "An act supplementary to an act, intitled an act for the Encouragement of Learning, by securing the Copies of Maps, Charts, and Books, to the Authors and Proprietors of such Copies during the times therein mentioned; and extending the benefits thereof to the Arts of Designing, Engraving, and Etching, Historical and other Prints."

WILLIAM S. SHAW,

Clerk of the District of Massachusetts.

ADVERTISEMENT.

THE manuscripts, containing the following memoirs, were found among the writings
of Mrs. Abigail Bailey, who died in Bath,
N. H. Feb. 11, 1815. On perusing them,
some of her friends had a desire to see them
in print. To obtain advice, relative to the
expediency of publishing them, the writings
were presented to a minister of the Gospel,
and to another gentleman of public education.
These gentlemen, after perusing the manuscripts, felt a strong desire that the public
might be benefited by them. The writings
were then, by the joint advice of these gentlemen, and some of the friends of the de-
ceased, transmitted to me, with a request,
that, if my opinion coincided with theirs, relative to the expediency of their being published, I would transcribe, and prepare them
for the press. On reading the manuscripts,
I was of the opinion, that they are richly
worthy of being given to the public. They
present such a variety of uncommon, and

interesting events, in a kind of strange connexion; such singular providences; and such operations of faith and fervent piety, under a series of most pressing trials; that I truly think but few lives of christians, in modern days, have afforded such rare materials for instructive biography.

My personal acquaintance with Mrs. Bailey, during some part of her trials, and for years after, gave me the fullest confidence in her strict veracity, integrity, and singular piety.

In her memoirs, the intelligent reader will find, strikingly exhibited, the dreadful depravity of fallen man; the abomination of intrigue and deceit; the horrid cruelty, of which man is capable; the hardness of the way of transgressors; the simplicity of the christian temper; the safety of confiding in God in the darkest scenes; his protection of the innocent; the supports afforded by the christian faith when outward means fail; and the wisdom of God in turning headlong the devices of the crafty. These things are presented in a detail of events, and unexaggerated facts, which arrest the attention; and which are singularly calculated to exhibit the detestable nature and consequences of licentiousness and vice.

The reader will excuse the circumstantial details, in the course of the events narrated, of various smaller incidents. For in such incidents the feelings of piety are often beautifully illustrated. That God, who numbers our hairs, and shews the wonders of his providence in the most minute things, often exhibits his care for his people, and excites their confidence in him, in numerous small incidents of life. And the rehearsal of such incidents, interspersed in such a narrative as the following, relieves the mind from a fatiguing pursuit of more interesting objects; and instructs with a pleasing variety.

In transcribing these memoirs, I have taken liberty to abridge some pages,—to shorten some sentences,—and to adopt a better word, where the sense designed would evidently be more perspicuous, and more forcibly expressed. But I have taken care to preserve *entire* the sentiment of the manuscripts. I have been careful to give no stronger expressions of the wickedness, or cruelties of Major Bailey, than those found in the manuscripts. But in various instances, expressions of

1*

his wickedness and cruelty, found in the manuscripts, are here omitted; not from the least apprehension of their incorrectness; but to spare the feelings of the reader.

INTRODUCTION.

Mrs. Abigail Bailey, the writer of the following memoirs, was a daughter of Deacon James, and Mrs. Sarah Abbot, who died some years since in Newbury, Vermont. She was born in Concord, New Hampshire, Feb. 2, 1746, where she lived in her father's family, upwards of seventeen years. Her father moved, not long before her birth, from Andover, Mass. and was a kindred of the noted Abbot family in that place. Her mother was a daughter of Samuel Bancroft, Esq. of Reading, Mass. In the eighteenth year of her age, being of a serious turn of mind, and of an unblemished moral character, she applied to the Rev. Mr. Walker to join herself to his church, and was received Sept. 4, 1763. In the November following, her father's family, with herself, moved to Newbury, Coos. Her diary furnishes an account, that soon after her arrival at Newbury, hearing the pungent preaching of Rev. Peter Powers, she became convinced that she had no true religion at heart, and was thrown into great distress of mind. She says, "I saw myself to be a guilty and a very filthy creature. My heart appeared to me to be of all things the most corrupt and abominable. By searching the Bible, and trying myself by it, I found my heart to be full of all manner of evil. I was almost plunged into despair. I was full of unbelief. I thought that God was unable, or if able, surely unwilling, to save so great a sinner, as I saw myself to be."

After remaining some time in this distress, she was brought out of darkness into God's marvellous light. She gives a most rational and satisfactory account of her repentance and faith; and adds; "Now I saw that I had nothing to do, but to believe in Christ. I saw what great safety there was in this way of salvation. Oh glorious Saviour, (my soul exclaimed!) O wonderful salvation, which God has provided for poor sinners; and for me, the chief of sinners."

She was now prepared to unite in the first formation of the church of Christ in Newbury; (of which the Rev. P. Powers took the pastoral charge;) and was one of the fifteen members, who at first composed that church, including their Pastor and his lady.

Something of Mrs. Bailey's turn, and state of mind, in those days, may be learned from the following extract from her diary.

"*June* 29, 1766. This Sabbath I thought I might say, I was in the Spirit on the Lord's day. It was indeed a very precious season to my soul. My desires and affections did not mingle with the world; but were set on things above. I think I had as sweet and full enjoyment in God my Saviour, as my capacities were able to receive. The Lord did graciously smile upon me, and mercifully meet me in every part of duty and worship;—in the closet, in the family, and in public worship, through the day. I think

I may truly say, that from the time I arose, early in the morning, on this holy Sabbath, till I retired to rest, the latter part of the ensuing night, I was in such a frame of mind, the whole time, that I neither saw nor heard any thing, which at all diverted my attention from heavenly and divine things. Jesus Christ was very precious to me; and he took the full possession of my heart. I beheld such beauty, such fulness in Christ, such safety in trusting in him; and such excellency in his service, that I longed to have all people come and enjoy him, and to have christians live near to him. I longed to have his kingdom built up on earth. The preaching of Rev. Mr. Powers this day, upon the symbolic woman, Rev. xii, and upon dying the death of the righteous, was to me instructive and delightful. I had sweet satisfaction in thinking on death and eternity. In the views of the latter I was for a time so absorbed, that I seemed to lose all view of the things of time, and hardly to know that I was in the body. So wonderfully did God favor me this day, that my heart was kept from vanity; and if I heard any idle word, it only excited my compassionate desires that every heart might be filled with true piety.

"Blessed are the pure in heart; for they shall see God." "We shall be like him; for we shall see him as he is." Oh, to see God, and be like him, is bliss indeed. God is the same glorious, immutable Being forever. If I could always be sensible of this, and be submissive to his will, as I ought, I could never feel uncomfortable, let my outward circumstances be, in their nature, ever so grievous."

Again Mrs. Bailey wrote as follows; "How amiable are thy tabernacles, O Lord of hosts! My soul longeth, yea even fainteth for the courts of the Lord. My heart and my flesh cry out for the living God. Sanctuary privileges are very precious to christians. For they do desire the sincere milk of the word, that they may grow thereby. When the children of God can meet, and worship, and commune together, such seasons furnish the richest pastures. Here christians go from strength to strength."

Thus none can doubt the early and fervent piety of the person, whose memoirs follow.

Relative to her person, she was tall and slender. She had a black, piercing, but pleasant eye. She had very comely, but grave features. Her mind was sedate, and very unusually contemplative. Her heart was tender, affectionate and kind; and her speech grave and impressive.

I have no recollection of ever hearing of her piety and goodness being called in question. It was indeed difficult to be an enemy to Mrs. Bailey. Vile characters felt constrained to revere, and to shrink from her presence. She lived highly respected and loved by christians; and died deeply lamented. As she lived in the Lord, so she died in the Lord, triumphing over death and the grave; not with a rapturous, but an unshaken, soul-purifying faith. "The memory of the just is blessed."

THE EDITOR.

Hopkinton, Aug. 28, 1815.

MEMOIRS.

I ABIGAIL BAILEY (daughter of Deacon James Abbot of Newbury, Coos, who moved thither from Concord, N. H. A. D. 1763) do now undertake to record some of the dealings of the all-wise God with me, in events, which I am sure I ought solemnly to remember, as long as I live.

I shall first, in few words, record the merciful dealings of my heavenly Father, in casting my lot, not only under the gospel, but in a family, where I was ever treated with the greatest kindness by my tender parents; and particularly with the most religious attention from my very pious mother; and where I was ever treated with the greatest tenderness by my brothers and sisters. I can truly say, it was seldom that an angry word was ever spoken in my father's family—by parents, brothers, or sisters —against me, from my infancy, and during my continuance in my father's house. So that I passed the morning of my days in peace and contentment.

April 15, 1767. I was married to Asa Bailey, just after having entered the 22nd year of my age. I now left my dear parents;—hoping to find in my husband a true hearted and constant friend. My desires and hopes were, that we might live together in peace and friendship; seeking each other's true happiness till death. I did earnestly look to God for his blessing upon this solemn undertaking;— sensible, that "Except the Lord build the house, they labor in vain that build it." As, while I lived with my parents, I esteemed it my happiness to be in subjection to them; so now I thought it must be a still greater benefit to be under the aid of a judicious companion, who would rule well his own house.

It had been my hope to find a companion of a meek, peaceable temper; a lover of truth; discreet and pleasant. I thought one of the opposite character, would be my greatest disappointment and trial.

But the allwise God, who has made all things for himself, has a right, and knows how, to govern all things for his own glory; and often to disappoint the purposes of his creatures. God often suffers mankind sorely to afflict and oppress one another; and not only those who appear as open enemies;—but sometimes those who pretend to be our best friends, cruelly oppress. Cain slew his brother. And the brethren of Joseph hated him, and sold him into Egypt.

It is happy when cruel treatment is overruled to promote a greater good. Job's afflictions did thus. The trials of Joseph but prepared the way for his greater exaltation. David, by being hunted and distressed by Saul, was prepared for the crown of Israel. Daniel in the lions' den, and the three children of God in the raging furnace, were prepared for deliverance, honor and salvation.

Relative to my new companion, though I had found no evidence that he was a subject of true religion; yet I did hope and expect, from my acquaintance with him, that he would wish for good regulations in his family, and would have its external order accord with the word of God. But I met with sore disappointment.—I soon found that my new friend was naturally of a hard, uneven, rash temper; and was capable of being very unreasonable. My conviction of this was indeed grievous, and caused me many a sorrowful hour. For such were my feelings and habits, that I knew not how to endure a hard word, or a frowning look from any one; much less from a companion. I now began to learn, with trembling, that it was the sovereign pleasure of the allwise God to try me with afflictions in that relation, from which I had hoped to receive the greatest of my earthly comforts. I had placed my highest worldly happiness in the love, tenderness, and peace of relatives and friends. But before one month, from my marriage day, had passed, I learned that I must expect hard and cruel treatment in my new habitation, and from my new friend.

My complaint was not to man, I had learned to go, with my trials, to a better Helper than an arm of flesh. I poured out my soul to God in earnest prayer, that he would graciously afford me wisdom and patience to glorify him by a suitable behaviour, on all occasions. This sacred passage opened to my view, with some light, power and comfort; "Be ye therefore wise as serpents, and harmless as doves." I longed and hoped to be able to obey this direction. I felt that of myself I could do nothing. But I rejoiced that through Christ I could do all things; and that the same God, who commands the doing of duty, is able to work powerfully in the hearts of his people, both to *will* and to *do* of his good pleasure.

I think God gave me a heart to resolve never to be obstinate, or disobedient to my husband; but to be always kind, obedient, and obliging in all things not contrary to the word of God. I thought if Mr. B. were sometimes unreasonable, I would be reasonable, and would rather suffer wrong than do wrong. And as I hoped Mr. B. would kindly overlook my infirmities and failings, with which I was conscious I should abound; so I felt a forgiving spirit towards him. Many times his treatment would grieve my heart. But I never was suffered to my knowledge, to return any wickedness in my conduct towards him; nor ever to indulge a revengeful feeling or ill will. For some years I thought his repeated instances of hard treatment of me arose,—not from any settled ill will, or real want of kind affection toward me;—but from the usual depravity of the human heart; and from a want of self-government. I still confided in him, as my real friend, and loved him with increasing affection.

After about three years—alas what shall I say? My heart was torn with grief, and my eyes flowed with tears, while I learned, from time to time, the *inconstancy* of a husband! In September, 1770, we hired a young woman to live with us. She had been a stranger to me, I found her rude, and full of vanity. Her ways were to me disagreeable. But to my grief I saw they were pleasing to Mr. B. Their whole attention seemed to be toward each other; and their impertinent conduct very aggravating to me, and (I was sensible) provoking to God. I learned to my full satisfaction, that there was very improper conduct between them.

Now I felt as though my earthly joys were fled. I laid my new troubles deeply to heart. I grieved and wept from day to day. I mourned the loss of my husband, not only on my own account, and on account of our tender offspring, but especially on account of his precious soul, which I viewed in the swift way to ruin.

I kept my troubles to myself as much as I could. But I most earnestly pleaded with Mr. B. from time to time to consider the evil of his ways; and to forsake the foolish and live. But he turned a deaf ear to all my entreaties, and he regarded neither my sorrows, nor the ruin of his family, and of himself, for time and eternity.

In my distress, my only refuge was in God my Saviour, the Hope of Israel, the Saviour thereof in time of trouble. I thought it most prudent not to make my troubles known to the world, and thus to load my husband with public disgrace. But I felt obligated to bear my faithful testimony to him against his wickedness; which I repeatedly did.

Some vent to my private grief I found in writing it; but in such language, as none but myself, or a

guilty companion, could understand. I gave vent to
the feelings of my broken heart, as follows; Alas,
how is man's nature depraved! so that nothing is
too vile for his wicked heart to do! Those, who
should be friends, become the worst of enemies. O
my soul put not thy trust in man; nor take the present world for thy portion. Its enjoyments appear
to me vanity and dust. I behold emptiness and
vanity in all things below the sun. Even the very
sun beams seem dark to me. Great is my sorrow.
My heart is full of grief, and my eyes of tears, because of the cruelty of enemies. They, who are
mine enemies wrongfully exalt themselves. They
vainly dream they shall never be moved; even
while they live in scandalous sin, and take pleasure
in unrighteousness. They know not, nor will they
consider, that their folly will cause bitterness in the
end. Unexpected evils have overtaken me. My
sorrow is great. Relative to my present trouble, I
am as those who have but little hope. I mourn also
in spiritual desertion. My prayer seems to be shut
out from God, as though he regarded not my
mourning. From the commencement of this trial
my mind has been dark in relation to it. I feel unable to form much expectation that I shall be delivered from it in the reformation of the guilty par-
ty. But I must say in the language of Jacob, in
another case, "If I am bereaved, I am bereaved."

At another time I consoled my tortured heart as
follows;—Now I pray God to make me truly humble to feel my unworthiness of the least mercy, and
to see that every good gift is from God's free grace.
May I give glory and praise to him for the many
mercies I do enjoy, and for faith in Jesus Christ,
though some deep affliction be laid upon me. I
think I can truly say, "In my distress I sought the
Lord;" and "I found him whom my soul loveth."
"In the time of my affliction, I cried unto God, and
he heard my groaning." My complaint came be-

fore his throne. Oh, that I may ever have right thoughts of God, and adore him for his goodness, and his wonderful condescension to regard so vile a worm, as I feel myself to be. May I ever feel as nothing before him. Thou, O Lord, art a shield for me; my glory, and the lifter up of mine head. Why then should I be afraid of ten thousand that should set themselves against me round about! I can do all things through Christ, who strengtheneth me. I will not fear, though the earth be removed. God will, in his own time and way, afford me the best kind of relief. Thy will, O merciful God is the best, and thy time the most fit. Wait patiently, therefore, O my soul, wait I say on the Lord. Remember thy word, O Lord, on which thou hast caused me to hope. May God, for Christ's sake, pluck him, who troubles me, as a brand from the fire. And, O merciful God, arise and have mercy upon Zion; the time to favor her, yea the set time, may it soon come.

Soon after this, through the mercy of God, I prevailed to send away the vile young woman from our family. After this Mr. B. became again more regular, and seemed friendly. But alas, my confidence in him was destroyed in a great measure. But this I kept to myself. I labored to put these evils from my mind as much as possible; still keeping a due remembrance of the wormwood and the gall of divine chastisement, that my soul might be humbled within me. I considered that my Saviour, who had given so many rich, precious promises of good things, has also declared, "In the world ye shall have tribulations." Trials and persecutions await his people. But Christ says, "In me ye shall have peace." And "all things shall work together for good to them who love God." The fruit of all their affliction is the taking away of sin.

July, 1773. Alas, I must again resume my lonely pen, and write grievous things against the husband of my youth! Another young woman was living with us. And I was grieved and astonished to learn that the conduct of Mr. B. with her was unseemly. After my return home from an absence of several days visiting my friends, I was convinced that all had not been right at home. Mr. B. perceived my trouble upon the subject. In the afternoon (the young woman being then absent) he fell into a passion with me. He was so overcome with anger, that he was unable to set up. He took his bed, and remained there till night. Just before evening he said to me, "I never saw such a woman as you. You can be so calm; while I feel so disturbed." My mind was not in a state of insensibility. But I was blessed with a sweet composure. I felt a patient resignation to the will of God. I thought I enjoyed a serene peace, which the world can neither give nor take away. I conversed with Mr. B. as I thought was most suitable. At evening I went out to milk. I spent some time in secret prayer for my poor husband. I endeavoured to intercede with God that he would bring him to repentance, and save him from sin and ruin, through the merits of Christ. I think that God at this time gave me a spirit of prayer. And I interceded with God that my husband might not be suffered to add to his other crimes that of murder. For I really feared this was in his heart. But I trusted in the Lord to deliver me. When I came into the house, I found Mr. B. still on the bed. He groaned bitterly. I asked him if he was sick? or what was the matter? He then took hold of my hand, and said, I am not angry with you now; nor had I ever any reason to be angry with you, since you lived with me. He added, I never knew till now what a sinner I have been. I have broken all God's holy laws, and my life has been one continued course of rebellion against God. I deserve his eternal wrath; and wonder I am out of hell. Mr. B. soon after told me, that as soon as

2*

I went out to milk, he rose from his bed, and looked
out at a window after me; and thought that he would
put an end to my life, before I should come into the
house again. But he said that when he thought of
committing such a crime, his own thoughts affright-
ed him, and his soul was filled with terror. Nor
did he dare to stand and look out after me; but fell
back again upon his bed. Then he said he had a
most frightful view of himself. All his sins stared
him in the face. All his wickedness, from his childhood to that hour, was presented to his mind, and
appeared inexpressibly dreadful. All the terrors
of the law, he said, pressed upon his soul. The
threatenings and curses denounced against the
wicked, in the whole Bible, seemed to thunder
against him. And these things, he said, came with
such power, that he thought he should immediately
sink into eternal woe. In this distress, he said he
cried to God for mercy. Upon which, the invitations and promises of the Gospel came wonderfully
into his mind; and the way of salvation by Christ
appeared plain and beautiful. He was now, he said,
overcome with love. His soul was drawn out after
Christ. And he hoped he never more should desire any thing, but to glorify God. After this Mr.
B. pretended to great peace of mind; and to be full
of joy. The night following we conversed much
upon religion. He confessed some of his sins; particularly his vile conduct while I was gone; that in
heart and attempt he was indeed guilty of the sin I
had charged upon him. But he gave me to understand that he was unable to accomplish his wicked designs.

Such was his appearance, that I felt some encouragement, and hoped he might prove a child of
God. At least this seemed to me a special interposition of Providence thus to restrain and reform him.
But I much doubted whether Mr. B. had experienced a work of grace. For some time he did indeed

appear to live a new life, and to be a very different man from what he had been. He told me one day of his hearing a man swear, and take God's name in vain; and he seemed much affected with it. He said he now knew how I used to feel, when I heard him use such wicked language. He now often conversed in a way not only pleasing, but instructive to me. He expressed many correct and good ideas in religion. If I knew any thing of true religion, my heart was warmed with love and gratitude to God, and my faith strengthened, by Mr. B.'s instructive conversation. For years I had been possessed of strong desires for the conversion of my dear husband. Much time I had spent upon my knees, in my closet, pleading with God for him. I longed and wept for him in secret places. I had long been impressed with an idea, that Mr. B, would not lead a common life;—that he would be uncommonly *bad;* or uncommonly *good.* And now when so great an alteration appeared, I hoped, though with much fear, that God had plucked him as a brand from the burning, and made him a vessel of mercy. I now lived in peace and comfort with my husband; —willing to forgive all that was past, if he might but behave well in future.

In 1774 I again experienced a scene of mortification and trial. The young woman, of whom I last spake, who had lived with us, was induced to go before a grand jury, and to declare under oath that while she lived at our house, and while I was absent, as I before noted, Mr. B. in the night went to her apartment; and after flatteries used in vain, made violent attempts upon her; but was repulsed. All but the violence used, Mr. B. acknowledged. This he denied. So that there was a contradiction between them. Thus my surprise and grief were renewed. But I could do nothing but carry my cause to God, who searches all hearts, and knows the truth.

May 26, 1774. I endeavored to console my afflicted heart with my pen, by writing as follows; "Why art thou cast down O my soul? and why art thou disquieted within me? Hope thou in God; for I shall yet praise him, who is the health of my countenance, and my God." Why should an enemy be viewed as strong; or a child of God fear an arm of flesh? Arise, O my soul, meditate with joy and comfort upon the divine strength, wisdom and goodness. The great and wise God is never at a loss how to accomplish his own purposes. Remember God's care over his people from the beginning of the world. Wonderfully has he preserved the church, and all his children, in their greatest dangers. When to the eye of sense there was no hope, no way of escape. God ever knew how to open the most unexpected ways for the salvation of his people. He made a path through the sea. There his chosen Israel escaped their enemies, and marched toward their promised land. God can abate the force of the most raging furnace, when any of his dear children are in it. He can shut the mouths of lions, while a Daniel of his is lodged in their den. God mercifully prepared a great fish to swallow Jonah, when cast into the mighty deep. God knew how to preserve his very imperfect prophet in the belly of that sea monster, even under the foundation of mountains, with the weeds wrapped about his head. God knew how and when to cause him to be disgorged upon the dry land. Wonderful, marvellous is the deep providence of the Most High! Unbelief despairs. But faith comes in and ensures deliverance.

> "Just in the last distressing hour,
> The Lord displays deliv'ring power,
> The mount of danger is the place,
> Where we shall see surprising grace."

Cast thy burden upon the Lord then, O my soul; for hitherto hath he helped thee. God has been with me in six troubles, and in seven.

June 8, 1774. "Great peace have they, who love thy law, and nothing shall offend them." If Shimei insult, David eyes and submits to the hand of God in it. "Let him alone; for God hath bidden him. God hath said to him, Curse David. It may be God will look upon my affliction, and deliver me out of the hands of mine enemies."

Aug. 7, 1774. Now I believe the Lord hath heard my prayer; not for any merit or worthiness in me; but for his own name's sake; for Christ's sake; for his own honor and glory. God knows who it is that suffers wrong from another. And sooner or later, he will make the truth to appear. Let the just lot be cast; and let him be taken, whom God shall please. Let the guilty be taken. No earthly object is so dear to me, as that I desire to withhold it from justice. I have no choice. Let the will of the Lord be done.

Now for a while I will turn from those painful scenes, and survey things more agreeable; before trials, far more distressing than all the preceding, must be recorded.

The smiles of God attended us in kind providences, of which I would take a grateful notice. Though Mr. B. had done so much to blot his name, and to injure his family; and though his character for some time was low; yet he seemed, after a while, strangely to surmount all those difficulties. In a few years he seemed to be generally and highly esteemed. He was indeed a man of abilities. And as he grew in years, he seemed to advance in prospects of usefulness in society. He became a leading man in the town. No one had more influence in public concerns. In matters of difficulty among men, which must be settled by arbitration, he was abundantly

applied to, both in town, and from other towns.
He was honored with a major's commission. For
a course of years he served in this office; and was
celebrated as an active and good officer at the head
of his regiment. I perceived the hand of God in
trying Mr. B. with prosperity, to see if he would
become and remain a regular and good man. "For
promotion cometh neither from the east, nor from
the west; but God putteth down one, and setteth up
another."

As to our property, after we moved into Landaff,
we were highly prospered. Mr. B. owned land in
plenty. The farm on which we lived, contained
two hundred acres of excellent land, so delightfully
situated, that we might stand at our chamber window, and see a calf or sheep in any part of fifty or
sixty acres. This farm was sufficient to summer
and winter forty or fifty head of cattle; beside a
proportionable number of horses and sheep. Thus
God, in his great mercy, tried us with prosperity.
We seemed to be able to live as well as we could
wish. Our family were, at the same time, blessed
with remarkable health. All our children came
daily around the table to partake of the full bounties of Providence, except our oldest daughter. She
was comfortably settled in family state within call
of our door. Such mercies, alas, too commonly are
ungratefully overlooked!

A. D. 1788. This year God granted me some
special blessings in the things of religion. I had opportunity to hear preaching more than before. For
I may say I had suffered a long famine of hearing
the word, and of the ordinances of the gospel;
there being no regular preacher settled in Landaff.
The Rev. Mr. Powers, my old beloved Pastor,
came and preached at our house, and baptized
some of our children. My faith was now strengthened, and my joy in God abounded. I found he is
indeed a God, who hears prayer; and who will, in

the best time and way, accomplish the holy desires of his people.

Mr. B. went a journey to the westward, and was absent several weeks. In this time, I had some signal trials of mind, occasioned by strange dreams. I have no idea that dreams are generally much to be noticed. But when I reflect upon what I then experienced of this nature, and compare it with trains of subsequent facts, I am constrained to believe, that God did see fit to afford me some solemn premonitions in sleep; and thus gradually to prepare me for scenes of trial, under which, had they come suddenly and unexpectedly, it seems as though I must have been destroyed. One night I dreamed Mr. B. came home and told me he had sold our farm, on which we lived, and intended to move to a great distance to the westward, and to take some of the sons to help him away with his interest. I thought he then took three of our oldest sons, and went away, as he proposed. After a while I again saw him, as I thought, but our second son Asa was missing; and I could not find what had become of him; or whether he was dead or alive. My husband would only reply to my earnest inquiries, *He is gone!* This loss of my son, and the strange conduct of his father, I thought, filled my heart with great distress; so that I groaned; and awoke from my sleep. I threw it from my mind, and again went to sleep. And again I dreamed the same thing in the same order; and waked myself by groaning, as before. I felt a degree of anxiety now excited;—I set up in my bed;—and thought on the matter. But I again thought I would dismiss the painful subject as a dream. I lay down again, in hopes of quiet sleep, and that I should think of those things no more. The third time I dreamed the same things, without any variation; and waked myself again by groaning. Upon this I confess I felt a

gloomy and solemn apprehension that new and signal trials would rise in my family.

Further dreams, in such a case, (or when the
mind becomes impressed with a subject,) may seem
to be easily accounted for. But when I compare
some of my after dreams with subsequent distressing events, which will be related, I am truly constrained to view them as of an admonitory nature;
and that a merciful God took this way to prepare me
to endure scenes of most unusual afiliction. I afterward dreamed that Mr. B. came home, but did not
appear to be at home, nor conduct as usual; but was
in great haste in making preparation to go away
again. Then he would be gone, but I knew not
where. Again for several times I should see him;
but we never any more lived together; but only now
and then fell in together, to manage some of our affairs of mutual interest. I thought I was oppressed
with gloom, both when we were together, and
when apart; being sensible that our separation
was forever. The cause of the separation, I thought,
I could not learn. I dreamed that I myself went a
long and doleful journey with Mr. B. and left my
family in a strange manner; that I had much distress about them, during my absence, not knowing
what would become of them, or how they could live.
Yet so it was I could not help going this journey.
All this trouble, I thought, was occasioned by that
strange unaccountable something, which had parted
Mr. B. from me.

After a while my husband returned from his journey. I rejoiced in his return; and hoped that our
peace and happiness would continue. Within half
an hour, he said, What would you say, if I should
sell our farm, and move over to the westward
where I have been? I replied, O my dear, I pray
you do not talk of any such thing. Upon this he
turned the conversation to things more agreeable.

My fearful apprehensions, or something, contin-

ued occasionally to disturb my imagination in my
sleep. One night I dreamed of seeing Mr B. in the
horrid act of murdering his children in cool blood.
I thought I screeched, and begged of him to forbear.
He said he knew what he was doing. He knew that
every body in these parts had become his enemy;
that those who used to be his friends, who respected
and honoured him, were now turned against him.
And he was determined to leave the country, and
go to a great distance. And as he could not carry
his small children, so he would not leave them
among his enemies.

I thought my horror and grief were unutterable;
and yet that I was under some kind of necessity of
keeping all to myself. But that having lost all confidence in my husband, I thought I was planning
how I might make my escape from him. I feared he
would perceive my design, and prevent it. I thought
we retired to rest. And as soon as I found he was
sound asleep, I crept from the bed, and fled with
the utmost haste. I scarcely touched the ground; but
seemed to fly upon the wings of the wind, till I came
where I found my friends. I began to relate to
them my troubles; but was so overcome with the
rehearsal, that I awoke:—And behold it was a
dream! I was safe by the side of the man, whom I
loved, and who I hoped and prayed might ever
more treat me well. I wondered why my thoughts
should wander at such a wild distance from every
thing that was real. I had been living in much
peace with my companion. Though in years past
I had seen troubles on his account, as has been noted; yet of late I had discovered nothing of the kind.
All those difficulties had been buried, and I had
hoped for peace. Though Mr. B. was of an unhappy
temper; yet with prudent management with him, he
would often remain in a pleasant mode for weeks
together. I had much comfort in him, and hoped
I could now confide in his friendship. It is true I

3

had given up all thoughts of his being a real christian. For though he had made so high pretences
to religion many years before, as has been
mentioned, yet he had evidently turned back to
the world; and he daily shewed himself to be destitute of saving grace. But he had a good knowledge
of the sacred scriptures; and I took great satisfaction in conversing with him upon them. I felt the
tenderest affection for him as my head and husband. I ever rejoiced when he returned from
abroad. Nor did I see him come in from his daily
business, without sensible delight. Much pleasure
I took in waiting upon him, and in doing all in my
power to make him happy. And I pleased myself
that I was now favored with a happy return of his
kind affection. He appeared to place in me the most
entire confidence; delivering into my hands his money, keys, notes, deeds, papers of every description,
and all such kind of concerns. Most sincere delight I took in taking the best care of them.

Now, I thought, why are my sleeping imagina-
tions roving on such foreign, unaccountable objects?
Most gladly would I have banished them all from
my mind, and have been released from all the fore-
bodings of evil, which had by them been deeply
impressed on my soul. But I could not but rest under a melancholy apprehension, that God had noti-
fied me of some signal calamities to be by me and
my family endured. Those things I kept all to
myself; excepting that I poured them out before
God, in seeking a preparation for whatever he
might see fit to bring upon me.

One day I thought it probable that some part at
least of my afflictions was coming. Two of our sons,
Asa and Caleb, were sent into two different towns,
to do some business. As they went to distances
about equal, we thought they might return about
the same time. They had each to go through considerable of woods. A terrible storm of wind arose,

which tore the forests. This much endangered
their lives by the falling of trees and limbs. Some
time before night Caleb returned, and said he had
narrowly escaped with his life. Asa did not return,
and I could not well send after him. Night came
on; it was very dark and rainy, and the wind continuing to blow violently, I had great apprehensions
for my son. I feared he was crushed under some
tree, or limb, and either dead, or dying; perhaps
calling for help, but in vain. Some time in the night,
however, he returned unhurt, though he had been
in danger. I felt that the mercy of God did indeed
attend us. I endeavored to examine myself, whether I was always prepared to give up worldly comforts, when God should call? And I must truly say,
I felt myself to be guilty before God. I found my
affections were too closely tied to my friends, and
my earthly blessings. I found I loved my family
with too much creature fondness. And I did earnestly look to God that he would enable me to dedicate all my comforts to him; and that I might not
be content with saying in words only, "Thy will be
done," but that my will might be sweetly bowed to
God's will. I endeavored earnestly to beseech the
Father of mercies to keep me always in such a
frame of soul, as that whenever he should see fit to
take from me my dearest worldly comforts, I might
humbly submit, and say, "it is the Lord; let him
do what seemeth him good." Those things appeared to me the most solemn, and I longed for grace
to be prepared for all that was before me; and that
my family might be prepared for all God's sovereign will. I looked on my family comforts, one by
one, beginning with my husband, down to the youngest babe, carefully watching my heart, to see if it
was reconciled to God, and prepared to meet him
in any such afflictions as I dreaded. I feared I was
not prepared; and I had much concern on this account. I hence did earnestly attempt to look to

God for strength, and to cast my burden on him; till I was brought to be able to say, not as I will, but as thou wilt. Thy will, O Lord, be done. These things were strongly impressed on my mind for months together.

About this time a godly minister preached a lecture at our house. He had for a text, Luke xxii, 28, 29, 30; "Ye are they, who have continued with me in my temptation: And I appoint unto you a Kingdom, as my Father hath appointed me; that ye may eat, and drink at my table, in my Kingdom, and sit on thrones, judging the twelve tribes of Israel." He treated, in a clear and wonderful manner, upon the trials and sufferings of the followers of Christ. I truly thought God had prepared this sermon peculiarly for me; and sent his servant, the present preacher, to teach and strengthen me, relative to whatever trials he might be preparing for me, that I might not faint in the day of adversity, but learn patiently to endure affliction. After this servant of God departed, I endeavored to impress these things on the minds of my husband, and children, with an ardent desire that they might feel their need of the Saviour, secure his salvation, and be prepared for all the will of God concerning them.

An event occurred about this time, which gave me uneasiness. The town of Landaff was settled under two charters; some of the inhabitants under what was then called the old charter; and some under a charter granted to Dartmouth College. My husband held his land under the latter. And the government of that college reposed much confidence in him, that he would befriend them, relative to their interests and claims in the town. The president had made a confident of Mr. B. and desired his assistance in those matters. He had spent much time with Mr. B. and had often written to him, upon this subject. And I had ever supposed Mr. B. very friendly to the interests of the college. But after a while, to my surprise, he turned about, deserted those interests, put himself under the old charter, and induced many others to do the same. And I conceived him to have been the means of turning almost all in town, who had been in favor of the college claims, to renounce them. This was to me a sore grievance: for I thought he did wickedly in betraying trust reposed in him.

. On a certain day I mentioned to Mr. B. something, which he did the day before; and tenderly wished, (without any view of offending him,) for some explanation. He was much displeased. I immediately tried to pacify him; but it was out of my power. In great rage he uttered very vile and abusive language, and soon left the room; leaving me to reflect on what I had witnessed. I reexamined what I had said, and the manner of my saying it: and I could not see that I had given any just cause of offence. Whether his mind had been riled by treatment from some other person, or why he conducted as he did, was unknown to me. I was much grieved to see him in so wicked a frame; and the more, as I had been (though without design) the cause of it. I mourned, and longed for his return, and for his friendship, as a hungry child longs for the breast. I soon recollected, that in all my troubles, Christ was my hiding place; my refuge was in God. Hither I betook myself in prayer: and I endeavored to fly to God's word, that I might learn my duty, find consolation, and have my faith, patience, and submission strengthened. I opened my Bible, and my eyes fastened on 1 Sam. xvi, 1, "And the Lord said unto Samuel, how long wilt thou mourn for Saul, seeing I have rejected him? &c." I was struck with the passage, which seemed to open powerfully on my mind. Oh, I hoped God was not about thus to reject my poor husband! The thought looked to me dreadful: but I felt that I must leave this all with God.

3*

Now, alas! I must begin the sad detail of events, the most distressing; and which awfully verified my most fearful apprehensions; and convinced me, that all my trials of life hitherto, were as nothing.

December, 1788. Mr. B. began to behave in a very uncommon manner: he would rise in the morning, and after being dressed, would seat himself in his great chair, by the fire, and would scarcely go out all day. He would not speak, unless spoken to; and not always then. He seemed like one in the deepest study. If a child came to him, and asked him to go to breakfast, or dinner, he seemed not to hear: then I would go to him, and must take hold of him, and speak very loudly, before he would attend; and then he would seem like one waking from sleep. Often when he was eating, he would drop his knife and fork, or whatever he had in his hand, and seemed not to know what he was doing. Nor could he be induced to give any explanation of his strange appearance and conduct. He did not appear like one senseless, or as though he could not hear, or speak. His eyes would sparkle with the keen emotions of his mind.

I had a great desire to learn the cause of this strange appearance and conduct. I at first hoped it might be concern for his soul; but I was led to believe this was not the case. He continued thus several days and nights, and seemed to sleep but little.

One night, soon after we had retired to bed; he began to talk very familiarly, and seemed pleasant. He said, now I will tell you what I have been studying upon all this while: I have been planning to sell our farm, and to take our family and interest, and move to the westward, over toward the Ohio country, five or six hundred miles; I think that is a much better country than this; and I have planned out the whole matter. Now I want to learn your mind concerning it; for I am unwilling to do any

thing contrary to your wishes in things so important
as this. He said he wished to gain my consent, and
then he would consult the children, and get their
consent also. I was troubled at his proposal; I saw
many difficulties in the way. But he seemed much
engaged, and said he could easily remove all my objections. I told him it would be uncertain what
kind of people we should find there; and how we
should be situated relative to gospel privileges. He
said he had considered all those things; that he well
knew what kind of minister, and what people would
suit me; and he would make it his care to settle
where those things would be agreeable to me; and
that in all things he would seek as much to please
me, as himself. His manner was now tender and
obliging: and though his subject was most disagreeable to me, yet I deemed it not prudent to be hasty
in discovering too much opposition to his plans. I
believe I remarked, that I must submit the matter
to him. If he was confident it would be for the interest of the family, I could not say it would not be
thus; but really I could not at present confide in it.

He proceeded to say, that he would take one of
our sons, and one daughter, to go first with him on
this tour, to wait on him; and that he probably
should not return to take the rest of the family under a year from the time he should set out. He
said he would put his affairs in order, so that it
should be as easy and comfortable for me as possible, during his absence.

Soon after, Mr. B. laid this his pretended plan
before the children; and after a while he obtained
their consent to move to the westward. They were
not pleased with the idea, but wished to be obedient, and to honor their father. Thus we all consented, at last, to follow our head and guide, wherever he should think best; for our family had ever
been in the habit of obedience: and perhaps never
were more pains taken to please the head of a family, than had ever been taken in our domestic circle.

But alas! words fail to set forth the things which followed! All this pretended *plan* was but a specious cover to infernal designs. Here I might pause, and wonder, and be silent, humble, and astonished, as long as I live! A family, which God had committed to my head and husband, as well as to me, to protect and train up for God, must now have their peace and honor sacrificed by an inhuman parent, under the most subtle and vile intrigues, to gratify a most contemptible passion! I had before endured sorrowful days and years, on account of the follies, cruelties, and the base incontinency of him who vowed to be my faithful husband. But all past afflictions vanish before those which follow. But how can I relate them? Oh tell it not in Gath! Must I record such grievousness against the husband of my youth?

> Oft as I try to tell the doleful tale,
> My quivering lips and faltering tongue do fail;
> Nor can my trembling hand, or feeble pen,
> Equal the follies of this worst of men!

I have already related that Mr. B. said he would take one of our sons, and one daughter, to wait on him in his distant tour, before he would take all the family. After he had talked of this for a few days, he said he had altered his plan; he would leave his son, and take only his daughter: he could hire what men's help he needed: his daughter must go and cook for him. He now commenced a new series of conduct in relation to this daughter, whom he selected to go with him, in order (as he pretended) to render himself pleasing and familiar to her; so that she might be willing to go with him, and feel happy: for though, as a father, he had a right to command her to go, yet (he said) he would so conduct toward her, as to make her cheerful and well pleased to go with him. A great part of the time he now spent in the room where she was spinning; and seemed shy of me, and of the rest of the family. He seemed to have forgotten his age, his honor, and all decency,. as well as all virtue. He would spend his time with this daughter, in telling idle stories, and foolish riddles, and singing songs to her, and sometimes before the small children, when they were in that room. He thus pursued a course of conduct, which had the most direct tendency to corrupt young and tender-minds, and lead them the greatest distance from every serious subject. He would try to make his daughter tell stories with him; wishing to make her free and sociable, and to erase from her mind all that fear and reserve, which he had ever taught his children to feel toward him. He had ever been sovereign, severe and hard with his children, and they stood in the greatest fear of him. His whole conduct, toward this daughter especially, was now changed, and became most disagreeable.

For a considerable time I was wholly at a loss what to think of his conduct, or what his wish or intentions could be. Had such conduct appeared toward any young woman beside his own young daughter, I should have had no question what he intended: but as it now was, I was loth to indulge the least suspicion of base design. His daily conduct forced a conviction upon my alarmed and tortured mind, that his designs were the most vile. All his tender affections were withdrawn from the wife of his youth, the mother of his children. My room was deserted, and left lonely. His care for the rest of his family seemed abandoned, as well as all his attention to his large circle of worldly business. Every thing must lie neglected, while this one daughter engrossed all his attention.

Though all the conduct of Mr. B. from day to day, seemed to demonstrate to my apprehension, that he was determined, and was continually plotting, to ruin this poor young daughter, yet it was so intolerably crossing to every feeling of my soul to admit such a thought, that I strove with all my might to banish it from my mind, and to disbelieve

the possibility of such a thing. I felt terrified at
my own thoughts upon the subject; and shocked
that such a thing should enter my mind. But the
more I labored to banish those things from my mind,
the more I found it impossible to annihilate evident
facts. Now my grief was dreadful. No words can
express the agitations of my soul: From day to day
they tortured me, and seemed to roll on with a re-
sistless power. I was constrained to expect that he
would accomplish his wickedness: And such were
my infirmities, weakness and fears, (my circumstances being very difficult) that I did not dare to
hint any thing of my fears to him, or to any creature. This may to some appear strange; but with
me it was then a reality. I labored to divert his
mind from his follies, and to turn his attention to
things of the greatest importance. But I had the
mortification to find that my endeavors were unsuc-
cessful.

I soon perceived that his strange conduct toward
this daughter was to her very disagreeable. And
she shewed as much unwillingness to be in the room
with him, as she dared. I often saw her cheeks
bedewed with tears, on account of his new and astonishing behaviour. But as his will had ever been
the law of the family, she saw no way to deliver
herself from her cruel father. Such were her fears
of him, that she did not dare to talk with me, or
any other person, upon her situation: for he was
exceedingly jealous of my conversing with her,
and cautioning her. If I ever dropped words,
which I hoped would put her upon her guard, or
inquired the cause of her troubles, or what business
her father had so much with her? if I was ever so
cautious, he would find it out, and be very angry.
He watched her and me most narrowly; and by
his subtle questions with her, he would find out
what I had said, during his absence. He would
make her think I had informed him what I had

said, and then would be very angry with me: so that at times I feared for my life. I queried with myself which way I could turn. How could I caution a young daughter in such a case? My thoughts flew to God for relief, that the Father of mercies would protect a poor helpless creature marked out for a prey; and turn the heart of a cruel father from every wicked purpose.

After a while Mr. B's conduct toward this daughter was strangely altered. Instead of idle songs, fawning and flattery, he grew very angry with her; and would wish her dead, and buried: and he would correct her very severely. It seems, that when he found his first line of conduct ineffectual, he changed his behaviour, felt his vile indignation moved, and was determined to see what he could effect by tyranny and cruelty. He most cautiously guarded her against having any free conversation with me, or any of the family, at any time; lest she should expose him. He would forbid any of the children going with her to milking. If, at any time, any went with her, it must be a number; so that nothing could be said concerning him. He would not suffer her to go from home: I might not send her abroad on any occasion. Never before had Mr. B. thus confined her, or any of his children. None but an eye witness can conceive of the strangeness of his conduct from day to day, and of his plans to conceal his wickedness, and to secure himself from the light of evidence.*

* The discreet reader will repeatedly wonder that this pious sufferer did not look abroad for help against so vile a son of Beliel, and avail herself of the law of the land, by swearing the peace against him. Her forbearance does indeed seem to have been carried to excess. But when we consider her delicate situation at this time; her peaceable habits from youth; her native tenderness of mind; her long fears of a tyrannical cruel husband; her having, at no time of her sufferings, seen all that we now see of his abominable

From the commencement of this new series of
wickedness, I did all that I thought proper to frus-
trate those abominable designs. But I had the mortification to find how unavailing my endeavors were
to reform so vile a man.

No language could now express the sorrow and
grief of my soul. I gave myself up to weeping and
mourning. In these I seemed to find a kind of solitary pleasure. I now thought I could truly say, in
the language of the prophet, "Behold and see; if
there be any sorrow like unto my sorrow."—"O
Lord, behold my affliction; for the enemy hath
magnified himself against me.—Mine eyes fail with
tears. What thing shall I liken to thee, O daughter of Jerusalem? For thy breach is great like the
sea. He hath made me desolate. I forgot prosperity. Remember, O Lord, what is come upon us.
We are fatherless; our mothers are widows. The
joy of our heart is ceased, and turned into mourning."

But O, I thought to myself, who is this cruel oppressor? this grievous rod in the hands of the High
and Lofty One, by whom I am thus sorely chastised?
It was not an enemy; then I could have borne it.
Neither was it he that hated me in days past; for
then I would have hid myself from him. But it was
the man mine equal, my guide, my friend, my husband! He has put forth his hand against such as
were at peace with him. He has broken his cove-

character, as a reason why he should have been brought to
justice; her wishes and hopes that he might be brought to
reformation; her desires not to have the family honor sacrificed; and the difficulty of exhibiting sufficient evidence a-
gainst a popular, subtle man, to prove such horrid crimes;—
these things plead much in her behalf. After all, it will be
difficult to resist the conviction, which will be excited in
the course of these memoirs, that Mrs. B. did truly err, in
not having her husband brought to justice. The law is made
for the lawless and disobedient.

nant. The words of his mouth had often been smoother than oil, while yet they were drawn swords, and war was in his heart.

What then is man? What are all our dearest connexions, and creature comforts? How fading and uncertain! How unwise and unsafe it must be to set our hearts on such enjoyments! God has set me an important lesson upon the emptiness of the creature. This he has taught me, both in his word, providences, and in the school of adversity. But I, a feeble worm, can benefit by divine lessons, only in the strength of Christ. But, praised be the God of grace, I think I can say by happy experience, "I can do all things through Christ, who strengtheneth me." I desire to bless God that he prepared me for the trials which have commenced; that he prepared me in some measure, to meet them with resignation of soul to the divine will, and with confidence in God, that he will order all things for his own glory. I was led earnestly to pray that when any signal trials should commence, I might be blessed with strength and grace according to my day: and I think I did not pray in vain. God has remarkably sustained me.

But I must confess that when this series of trials came on, it was so different from any thing I had expected, and so very distressing, that before I was aware, I gave myself up to grief and mourning, and seemed overwhelmed with anguish of soul. For a season, I was indeed tempted to feel as though I did well to abandon myself to grief. I said, with Job, "My stroke is heavier than my groaning. O that my grief were thoroughly weighed; for now would it be heavier than the sand of the sea. He breaketh me with breach upon breach; my face is foul with weeping; the days of affliction have taken hold on me; my harp is turned to mourning, and my organ into the voice of them that weep." I now sometimes thought my distress must soon finish my days, and bring me down with sorrow to the grave.

4

In my distress I cried unto the Lord, and poured out my complaint before the most high God: though for some time it seemed as if I was forced to say with Jeremiah, "Yea, when I cry and shout, he shutteth out my prayer." For some time I could not obtain a comforting view that those unusual afflictions were in mercy, and not in judgment; for the rod seemed so severe, that I was tempted to say in the words of Jacob, "All these things are against me." I was left for a season to mourn in darkness, and could not obtain those comforting views of the light of God's countenance, which at other times God had graciously afforded for my support.

I think I may say, that by the grace of God I had been in the habit of flying to God in trouble, and feeling my need of his aid, as much as I felt my need of the air for breath. But I now at first found it difficult to have my will fully conformed to the will of God. I thought my troubles were greater than to be called to lay one of the best of husbands in the grave, or even ten, had it been possible. I thought if all, who were mourning the loss of dear companions, or parents, and children, could come and mingle their sorrows with mine, their little drops of grief would soon be lost in the more extensive flood of sorrow, in which I was overwhelmed. But I saw no way to put a stop to the evil, under which I was oppressed. And I seemed unable to open my difficulties to any one: I must bear them all alone.

I strove to suppress, as far as possible, the anguish under which my heart was tortured and broken. I felt that I ought to obey the voice of the Most High, "Be still, and know that I am God." I now felt that it was not for me to say what trouble God should send, or that mine was greater than any other might be. God knows best what I need, and what will be for his own glory. He will make the wrath of man to praise him; and the remainder he will restrain.

I saw that it was as much my duty to submit to God under one trial, as under another; and to say, with a holy filial heart, "If I am bereaved, I am bereaved." "Shall we receive good at the hand of the Lord, and shall we not receive evil?" The Lord gives comforts, and the Lord takes them away, and blessed be his name.

Thus I quieted myself as a weaned child. Casting my burdens on the Lord, I was by him sustained. Plead my cause, O Lord. They have rewarded me evil for good. Mine eyes are unto thee. When wilt thou pluck my feet out of the net? Cause me to escape. My times are in thine hands. Be it unto me according to thy word.

I now thought God dealt mercifully with me, in sustaining and comforting me under my affliction. As the flood of iniquity increased, so my faith and trust in God increased. In piercing trials, I felt myself, and all that was dear to me, in the hands of Him, who is my covenant God in Christ; and hence could say, "It is the Lord, let him do what seemeth him good." I now felt that I had more reason to be astonished at the tenderness in which God dealt with me, than to complain of this, or of any trial, which I ever endured. God now "shewed himself marvellous unto me." It appeared to be wonderful kindness in him, that he had prepared me for affliction, by giving me some premonitions of it, and enabling me to seek and obtain a preparation. For I thought, had not this been the case, my nature must have sunk under the violence of the shock. So much divine goodness appeared in this, toward a vile worm, that I could say, "The Lord is good, and his mercy endureth forever." "He stayeth his rough wind in the day of his east wind."

The black cloud, rising like a storm of hail, had rolled on, and had gathered over my head. I clearly saw that Mr. B. entertained the most vile intentions relative to his own daughter. Whatever difficulty attended the obtaining of legal proof, yet no remaining doubt existed in my mind, relative to the existence of his wickedness: and I had no doubt remaining of the violence, which he had used; and that hence arose his rage against her. It must have drawn tears of anguish from the eyes of the hardest mortals, to see the barbarous corrections, which he, from time to time, inflicted on this poor young creature; and for no just cause. Sometimes he corrected her with a rod; and sometimes with a beach stick, large enough for the driving of a team; and with such sternness and anger sparkling in his eyes, that his visage seemed to resemble an infernal; declaring, that if she attempted to run from him again, she should never want but one correction more; for he would whip her to death! This his conduct could be for no common disobedience; for she had ever been most obedient to him in all lawful commands. It seemed as though the poor girl must now be destroyed under his furious hand. She was abashed, and could look no one in the face.

Among the many instances of his wickedly correcting her, I shall mention one. One morning Mr. B. rose from bed, while it was yet dark. He immediately called this daughter, and told her to get up. She obeyed. And as she knew her daily business, she made up her fire in her room, and sat down to her work. He sat by the fire in the kitchen. As my door was open, I carefully observed his motions. He sat looking into the fire for some time, as though absorbed in his thoughts. It soon grew light. The small children arose, and came round the fire. He looked round like one disappointed and vexed. He sprang from his chair, and called his daughter, whom he first called. She left her work in her room, and came immediately to him. In great rage, and with a voice of terror, he asked why she did not come to him, when he first called her? She respectfully told him that he called her to get up, which she immediately did, and went to her work. But she said she did not hear him call her to come to him. He seized his horse whip, and said, in a rage, he would make her know that when he called her, she should come to him. He then fell to whipping her without mercy. She cried, and begged, and repeated her assertion, that she did not know he called her to come to him. She had done as he told her. She got up, and went to her work. But he was not in the least appeased. He continued to whip her, as though he were dealing with an ungovernable brute; striking over her head, hands, and back; nor did he spare her face and eyes; while the poor girl appeared as though she must die. No proper account could he ever be prevailed on to give of this conduct.

None can describe the anguish of my heart on the beholding of such scenes. How pitiful must be the case of a poor young female, to be subjected to such barbarous treatment by her own father; so that she knew of no way of redress!

It may appear surprising that such wickedness was not checked by legal restraints. But great difficulties attend in such a case. While I was fully convinced of the wickedness, yet I knew not that I could make legal proof. I could not prevail upon this daughter to make known to me her troubles; or to testify against the author of them. Fear, shame, youthful inexperience, and the terrible peculiarities of her case, all conspired to close her mouth against affording me, or any one, proper information. My soul was moved with pity for her wretched case: and yet I cannot say I did not feel a degree of resentment, that she would not, as she ought, expose the wickedness of her father, that she might be relieved from him, and he brought to due punishment. But no doubt his intrigues, insinuations, commands, threats, and parental influence, led her to feel that it was in vain for her to seek redress

4*

My circumstances, and peculiar bodily infirmities, at that time, were such as to entitle a woman to the tenderest affection and sympathies of a companion. On this account, and as Mr. B. was exceeding stern, and angry with me for entertaining hard thoughts of him, I felt unable to do any thing more for the relief of my poor daughter. My hope in God was my only support. And I did abundantly and earnestly commit my cause to him. I felt confident that he would, in his own time, and as his infinite wisdom should determine, grant relief.

Sept. 15, 1789. A son and daughter, twins, were added to our family. The son lived but seventeen days. The distresses of the poor helpless babe were dreadful while he lived. I did hope that his dreadful fits, and his death, might be a means of awakening the conscience of his father. But alas, the father seemed to be given over to a reprobate mind indeed. He seemed wholly unaffected, as if his heart had been made of stone. And he proceeded in his wickedness.

After a while, through the mercy of God, my health was restored. One sabbath morning, Mr. B. talked of going to meeting. He seemed in good health, and in earnest to attend, that day, on public worship. I was glad, and told him I wished to go with him. But before meeting time he said he had a head ache, and could not accompany me to meeting that day.

He told an older daughter (beside his favorite one,) that she might have his horse, and ride to meeting. I was sorry for his concluding not to go. For I wished to go; and the riding was bad; we had a bad river to ford; and I wanted his company and aid. But he pretended to be unable to go.

The next morning I took an opportunity with Mr. B. alone to have solemn conversation. My health being now restored, I thought it high time, and had determined, to adopt a new mode of treatment with Mr. B. I calmly introduced the subject, and told him, plainly and solemnly, all my views of his wicked conduct, in which he had long lived with his daughter. He flew into a passion, was high, and seemed to imagine, he could at once frighten me out of my object. But I was carried equally above fear, and above temper. Of this I soon convinced him, I let him know, that the business I now had taken in hand, was of too serious a nature, and too interesting, to be thus disposed of, or dismissed with a few angry words. I told him I should no longer be turned off in this manner; but should pursue my object with firmness, and with whatever wisdom and ability God might give me; and that God would plead my cause, and prosper my present undertaking, as he should see best. I reminded Mr. B. of my long and unusually distressing illness; how he had treated me in it; how wicked and cruel he had been to the wife of his youth; how unable I had been to check him in that awful wickedness, which I knew he had pursued; that all my inexpressible griefs and solemn entreaties had been by him trampled under foot.

I therefore had not known what to do better than to wait on God as I had done, to afford me strength and opportunity to introduce the means of his effectual control. This time I told him had arrived. And now, if God spared my life, (I told Mr. B.) he should find a new leaf turned over;—and that I would not suffer him to go on any longer as he had done. I would now soon adopt measures to put a stop to his abominable wickedness and cruelties. For this could and ought to be done. And if I did it not, I should be a partaker of his sins, and should aid in bringing down the curse of God upon our family.

By this time Mr. B. had become silent. He appeared struck with some degree of fear. He, by and by, asked me what I intended or expected to do, to bring about such a revolution as I had intimated? whether I knew what an awful crime I had laid to his charge? which he said could not be proved. He wished to know whether I had considered how difficult it would be for me to do any such thing against him? as I was under his legal control; and he could overrule all my plans as he pleased. I told him, I well knew I had been placed under his lawful government and authority, and likewise under his care and protection. And most delightful would it have been to me, to have been able quietly and safely to remain there as long as I lived. Gladly would I have remained a kind, faithful, obedient wife to him, as I had ever been. But I told Mr. B. he *knew* he had violated his marriage covenant; and hence had forfeited all legal and just right and authority over me; and I should convince him that I well knew it. I told him I was not in any passion. I acted on principle, and from long and mature consideration. And though it had ever been my greatest care and pleasure (among my earthly comforts) to obey and please him; yet by his most wicked and cruel conduct, he had compelled me to undertake this most undesirable business—of stopping him in his mad career; and that I now felt strength, courage and zeal to pursue my resolution. And if my life was spared, he would find that I should bring something to pass, and probably more than he now apprehended.

As to what I could prove against him, I told Mr. B. he knew not how much evidence I had of his unnatural crimes, of which I had accused him, and of which *he knew he was guilty.* I asked him why he should not expect that I should institute a process against him, for that most horrid conduct, which he had long allowed himself to pursue, and with the most indecent and astonishing boldness?

I told him I well knew that he was naturally a man of sense; and that his conscience now fully approved of my conduct.

Mr. B. seeing me thus bold and determinate, soon changed his countenance and conduct. He appeared panic-struck; and he soon became mild, sociable and pleasant. He now made an attempt, with all his usual subtlety, and flatteries, to induce me to relinquish my design. He pretended to deny the charge of incest. But I told him I had no confidence in his denial of it; it was therefore in vain! Upon this he said, he really did not blame, or think hard of me, for believing him guilty of this sin. He said, he knew he had behaved foolishly; and had given me full reason to be jealous of him; and he repeated that he did not at all think hard of me for entertaining the views which I had of him. He then took the Bible, and said, he would lay his hand on it, and swear that he was not guilty of the crime laid to his charge. Knowing what I did, I was surprised and disgusted at this impious attempt. I stepped towards him, and in a resolute and solemn manner begged of him to forbear! assuring him, that such an oath could not undo or alter real facts, of which he was conscious. And this proceeding, I assured him, would be so far from giving me any satisfaction, that it would greatly increase the distress of my soul for him in his wickedness. Upon this he forbore, and laid his Bible aside.

Mr. B. now said, he was very sorry he had given me so much reason to think such things of him; and that he had so far destroyed my confidence in him as a man of truth. He then begged of me to forgive all that was past; and he promised that he would ever be kind and faithful to me in future, and never more give me reason to complain of him for any such conduct. I told him, if I had but evidence of his real reformation, I could readily forgive him as a fellow creature, and could plead with God to forgive him. But as to my living with him in the most endearing relation any longer, after such horrid crimes, I did not see that I *could*, or

ought to do it! He then anxiously made some remarks upon the consequences of my refusing to remain his wife, and seeking a separation from him.
These he seemed unable to endure. I remarked,
that I well knew it was no small thing for a husband
and wife to part, and their family of children to be
broken up; that such a separation could not be
rendered expedient or lawful, without great sin indeed: and that I would not be the cause of it, and
of breaking up our family, for *all the world*. But,
said I, you have done all in your power to bring
about such a separation, and to ruin and destroy our
family. And I meet it as my duty now to do all in
my power to save them from further destruction.

Much more was said upon the subject. We
spent the whole day in the most solemn conversation. I abundantly expressed to him my views of
his wickedness and cruelties. I faithfully labored
to affect his mind with them, and with the inexpressible trials he had occasioned me. He said he
did truly pity me; and was very sorry he had occasioned me so much trouble. He repeatedly asked my forgiveness. And as often promised good
behaviour in future. He particularly promised
that he would never think hard of me for my faithful dealings with him this day. He begged of me
to inform him what he could or should do, so that
I could once more try him, and see if he would
not prove as good, in future, as his present promises! He did not feel free to confess the worst crime,
laid to his charge; yet he said he would feel quite
content that I should think I had forgiven him as
great crimes, as those, with which I charged him;
and he would never feel uneasy with me on this
account. He now pretended to feel much tenderness, and said he was very sorry for all his sins.

I was too well acquainted with Mr. B. to suppose
that I now discovered any real evidence of a penitent heart, or to be much deceived by his flatteries.

But I did entertain some hopes that he would now reform from his gross abominations. And as I was sensible of the difficulty of proving, to legal conviction, the crimes I had alleged against him, (the daughter never yet having consented to testify against him,) also the consequences of such a process seemed to me of the most terrible kind; I seemed to feel constrained to let those things rest, for the present, as they were; feeling a confidence in God, that if Mr. B. did not reform, or if it were best I should part from him for his past wickedness, God would render my path of duty plain.

Thus upon the many promises Mr. B. had made, I gave encouragement, that I would suffer him to have one season more of trial; that if he would indeed reform, and take the word of God for the guide of his heart and life, and would treat his family as he ought, I might overlook all that was past; and submit to him again, as my head and husband.

Joy and gladness beamed in his countenance. He said he never should be able to express suitable thanks to me for my condescension, in that I had thus far overlooked his ill and unreasonable treatment of me. Mr. B. then took my right hand in his, and said, I call God and angels to witness, that I, from this time, will be to you a loving, kind, and faithful friend and husband. As to that daughter, I will never more do any thing, that shall grieve or trouble you. Nor will I ever more give you cause of uneasiness with me, on account of any female on earth. And I will henceforth take the holy word of God for my guide, and the rule of my life.

Mr. B. then begged of me to banish from my mind all that was past. I replied, that the manner of his engagements seemed solemn. I earnestly wished that he might feel them binding on his soul. And if he did henceforth live according to these promises, my carriage towards him should be kind and respectful; and I would never upbraid him of

his past evil deeds. But I suggested to Mr. B. that
it would not be possible to banish these things from
my mind, or to feel as though they had never been.
I would try, however, to do it as far as possible.
Thus the day closed.

For several weeks nothing more was said upon
the subject. And Mr. B.'s conduct towards me
and the family was pleasant and agreeable. I really began to hope that I should never again have occasion of any such distressing perplexities.

But God, in his infinite wisdom, did not see fit
that my peculiar trials should end thus. A long
and most insupportable series of afflictions still
awaited me, to be occasioned by this most perfidi-
ous of men.

I again clearly perceived that the same wicked
passions, as before, were in operation in Mr. B.'s
heart. Alas, "Can the Ethiopian change his skin?"
Upon a certain sabbath, I went to meeting. Mr. B.
did not go. Before I reached home at night, I met
with evidence, which convinced me, that the same
horrid conduct had on this holy day been repeated
in my family! I rode up to the door. Mr. B. stood
waiting for me. He seemed very kind, and was
coming to take me tenderly from my horse. I leaped from my saddle, before he had opportunity to
reach me. My heart was disgusted at the proffer
of his deceitful help. I said nothing upon the dreadful subject this day. Some broken stories of the
children corroborated the information I had received. But Mr. B. probably pleased himself with the
idea that all was concealed, and he was safe.

The next day, I took him alone, and told him of
what he had again been guilty, even after all his
vows, and fair promises of fidelity. He started, and
seemed very angry, that I should think such a thing
him. I told him I charged him only with facts; and
hence I was not worthy of his censure! He asked
how I knew any such thing? I replied, that the

thing was true; and he knew it! And I felt myself under no obligations to inform him how I came by the knowledge of it. If that God, who protects the innocent, and upon whom with his angels he (Mr. B.) had lately so solemnly called to witness his vows of fidelity, had sent an angel to inform me of this renewed perfidy, he had no right to object. But the truth of the thing he knew; and a holy Providence had unfolded it to me. I added, that as he was now renewing my most grievous afflictions, by his unnatural wickedness; and violating his most solemn appeals to God; so he had reason to expect that God (who regards the cry of the afflicted, and relieves those who trust in him) would bring to light his abominable deeds, and deliver an injured wife from such cruel hands. I added, your right hand, which so lately renewed the covenant, is a right hand of falsehood. And, though you did wish and hope to hide from me, and from every eye, that conduct, of which you now know not how to endure the mention; yet God, who seeth in secret, was determined to bring your deeds to light, after all your vain dreams of secrecy.

Mr. B. now attempted again to flatter me. He renewed the most solemn promises of amendment. And earnestly begged that I would once more pardon him. He now again seemed cautious as to an acknowledgment of the alleged offence; and yet implicitly acknowledged it; and urged me to bury all that was amiss; and most solemnly engaged that if I would do it, I should find him a true and faithful friend in future. I told him, he had obliged me to view him as one of the worst of husbands; which was much more grievous to my soul, than to cut and mangle my own flesh. I said that I thought it would now be abominable for me ever to live with him any more. For it was impossible for me to feel the least confidence in his word. From this period, said I, I shall want something more than

5

your word, to convince me of the truth of any thing.

Mr. B. said he believed there never before was any man, who was so great a fool as he had been! that after I had so kindly settled with him for his past offences, and upon such low and reasonable terms, that he should again move me to jealousy, and thus destroy all my confidence in him. He said he wished he could be set back on the ground he had left, or had remained on so favorable a footing, as that on which I had placed him, in our settlement. I replied, that I really thought too, that he was one of the most foolish of men; that I had long been constrained to view him not only extremely *wicked*, but extremely *foolish!*

I told him he had truly been a wonder to me. I had looked upon him with astonishment. He was naturally, I added, a man of sense; he was a man of much knowledge;—had acquired property; and had been a man of considerable note. And that he should thus degrade and ruin himself, soul and body; and destroy a large promising family, as he had done, it was indeed most astonishing! I reminded him that he had been much in good company; and many gentlemen had honored him with their friendly attention. I asked, if any sum of money would induce him to be willing that those gentlemen should know that of him, which I knew? And, that though he seemed to be too willing to throw himself away, as though he were of no worth, I assured him, I did yet set something more by myself, than to be viewed as capable of conniving at such detestable conduct.

Mr. B. replied, that if I had made up my mind no longer to live with him, I need not be at any trouble to obtain a legal separation. For he would depart to some distant country, where I should be troubled with him no more. I remarked, that when Abraham's wife was dead, he wished, however well he had loved her, to have her now buried out of his sight. And, though I could by no means compare him to the pious Sarah; yet, if true virtue and friendship in my husband were dead, I did truly wish him to be removed from my sight. And that true virtue and friendship were indeed dead in him, I thought I had the most melancholy and incontestable evidence.

Our unhappy daughter now became eighteen years of age, and thus legally free from her father. She immediately left us, and returned no more. As she was going, I had solemn conversation with her relative to her father's conduct. She gave me to understand that it had been most abominable. But I could not induce her to consent to become an evidence against him. I plead with her the honor and safety of our family; the safety of her young sisters; and her own duty; but she appeared overwhelmed with shame and grief; and nothing effectual could yet be done.

I hence saw, that in relation to commencing a legal process, God's time seemed not yet to have arrived. I must still wait and look to him to open the path of my duty.

I now gave myself up to fasting and prayer, that I might seek of God a right way. I thought it best to be pretty still, till I could avail myself of full legal proof; then I felt determined to bring our difficulties soon to an issue. I lived in daily fear for the safety of my family. For though that daughter was now at a safe distance, yet I thought, as was said of the builders of Babel, "this he has began to do; and now nothing will be restrained from him, which he may imagine to do." But I saw that my strength was to sit still; to hope in the Lord, and wait patiently for him;—trusting also in him, that he might bring it to pass. I comforted myself with God's direction to Israel, "Stand still and see the salvation of the Lord." It was my constant and most earnest prayer, that God would lead me in the right way, and enable me to do what I ought. I felt at the same time that proper means were to be used. My ears and my mind were therefore attentive to instruction. I strove to watch at wisdom's gates, and wait at the posts of her doors. Day and night the word of God was the man of my counsel. And I narrowly watched the providences of God, particularly in relation to my family.

April 20, 1790. I determined to renew my diligence in seeking to God for direction. I set apart seven days, viz. the Wednesday of every week, for seven weeks, for special fasting and prayer, and searching the scriptures. My supplications were, that, under my peculiar trials, God would give me peculiar grace; that he would teach me what I ought to do? that I might learn of the Lord Jesus Christ to be meek and lowly in heart; that I might feel my nothingness, and dependence; and might not dishonor God; but might glorify him. During this period, while I confessed and lamented my sins and leanness, and prayed for covenant mercies, for the Redeemer's sake, God, in his infinite mercy, did wonderfully cause to shine upon me the light of his countenance. I felt most wonderful spiritual enjoyment, and such movings of his power and grace, that all the faculties of my soul were most sweetly captivated, and drawn out in holy love to my most glorious Lord and Saviour. During these seven weeks, and long after, I constantly felt myself in the presence of the great and holy God. I was enabled to realize, with solemn awe and delight, that my words, actions, and secret thoughts, were all naked and open to the eyes of Him, with whom I have to do. I had such a sense of God's dreadful Majesty, as filled my soul with awe and reverence. And I enjoyed a most refreshing and soul satisfying view of the fulness of divine grace in Christ;—of his faithfulness and tenderness, in all his dealings toward his followers. I found unspeakable delight in contemplating the being, attributes, and works of God.

I could diligently labor with my hands in my family affairs; and have my soul, at the same time, continually lifted up to God, being weaned from the world, and swallowed up in the things which are unseen and eternal. I seemed to be able to derive instruction from every thing, which I saw, heard, or met with. God was in every thing. Every thing led my mind to him. I was filled with a kind of pleasing astonishment at his infinite condescension in taking such notice of a most unworthy worm. I seemed remarkably delivered from the tempter, and the corruptions of my own wicked heart. As I was enabled to keep my heart with all diligence, and to hate vain thoughts; so I was unusually delivered from their defiling power. Through the silent hours of the night, my enjoyments of God were wonderful. I could truly say with the Psalmist, that on my bed my meditation of him was sweet; and when I awoke, I was still with him. "I prevented the dawning of the morning and cried. I hoped in thy word." I delighted in God's law; and in it I meditated day and night. The holy sabbath God blessed to me. I could truly say, it was the Lord's day. I delighted in its return. And every sabbath brought me a sabbath day's blessing. Two sabbaths in a special manner were wonderful days to me, in which God did most marvellously display his grace and glory in Christ. I had felt most ardent longings for the sabbath, that I might appear before God in his sanctuary, and have sweet fellowship with him in his ordinances. On a sabbath in June, as I read the 84th Psalm, my mind was greatly enlarged with a view of the beauty of the church of Christ;—the loveliness of his public worship;—the glories of God there to be enjoyed. No words can express my views of the excellency of these things; and of my utter unworthiness of them. I felt a humble and holy boldness to plead with God, through Jesus Christ, for nearness and conformity

5*

to him. I rejoiced that he knew what was best for me; how to fulfil his own wise decrees, as the sovereign King of the universe, and display his own glory. This afforded me the most solemn and real joy. I could now cast all my cares upon him, even the most distressing trials in my family.

The next sabbath I was blessed with an opportunity of attending public worship in Haverhill, Coos. This seemed a more peculiar blessing, as there was then a blessed work of the Spirit in that place. I went thither on Saturday, and had an agreeable opportunity with numbers, who were engaged in religion. Some were inquiring, what they should do to be saved? Others were rejoicing and praising God. I had a delightful opportunity with a minister of Christ there. Without letting him know my particular trials, I asked him many questions, which had a relation to them. My desire was, that God would direct him to give answers suitable to my case, which I think he was led to do. He remarked upon the trials of Joseph; and of various of the ancient people of God, and he was led to give me a most lively view of the duty of casting my burdens on the Lord, and waiting patiently for him. I felt great consolation in my soul. For I was conscious that I had been thus waiting on the Lord, and trusting in him. On the sabbath, the minister preached three sermons. This was a joyful day to me. God did truly meet me, in the assembly of his saints; and I could say, "It is good to be here." God shewed me a token for good; and I was convinced of his special notice and tender care for a most unworthy creature. My desire was, that God might have all the glory. For a considerable time after this, my delight in God continued in a great degree uninterrupted. My soul seemed to be emptied of the creature; and filled with the Creator. I sweetly felt the truth of those words of Christ; "In that day ye shall know that I am in the Father, and you in me, and I in you." "Abide in me, and I in you." "If a man love me, he will keep my words; and my Father will love him; and we will come unto him, and will make our abode with him." "The Comforter, whom the Father will send in my name, shall abide in you." For sometime, I was so swallowed up in God, that I seemed to lose a view of all creatures. I do not know that I had a thought of myself. I seemed hid from a sight of the world in an ocean of bliss. Truly I found that the peace of God passeth understanding. The 33d, and 34th chapters of Exodus, where Moses prayed God to show him his glory, and God made all his goodness to pass before him, were to me most delightful passages. I thought I could unite in the prayer, that God would show me his glory. And truly I think I was blessed with the greatest view of the glorious goodness of God which I ever had, and as my frail state was well capable of sustaining.

On a sabbath day, not long after, God again met me with the abundant refreshings of his grace,—with the most delightful communion with Jesus Christ. I was detained from the house of God. But being unable to wait on God at his house, I found him a delightful sanctuary in my own. Reading the 74th Psalm, it was a wonderful passage to me. The prophet complains of the desolations of the sanctuary. "O God, why hast thou cast us off forever? Thine enemies roar in the midst of thy congregations. They said in their heart, Let us destroy them together. We see not our signs; neither is there any among us that knoweth how long. O Lord, how long shall the adversary reproach? Why withdrawest thou thy hand?—For God is my King of old, working salvation.—Thou didst divide the sea by thy strength. Thou breakest the heads of the dragons.—The day is thine; the night also is thine. Remember this, O Lord, that the enemy hath reproached and blasphemed thy name. O deliver not

the soul of thy turtle dove unto the multitude of the
wicked.—Have respect unto the covenant.—O let
not the oppressed return ashamed. Let the poor
and needy praise thy name. Arise, O Lord, plead
thine own cause.

In such words I poured out my soul to God. I
longed for the overthrow of Satan's kingdom; and
that the kingdom of Christ may be built up in glory.
This cause was most dear to my soul. Sin, and the
conduct of the enemies of God, appeared to me inexpressibly hateful. I loathed my own sins; and
thought I had a sense of the feelings of Daniel, when
he bewailed the sins of his people, and made inter-
cession for the cause of his God. While I pleaded
God's gracious promises, and felt the most piercing
sense of my own unworthiness, I felt a solid peace
and heavenly calmness, and intense love to God the
Father, Son and Holy Ghost. I was struck with
wonder at the union between Christ and believers.
This union, I felt a humble confidence that I did enjoy. But to inform how forcibly divine promises
were now applied to my soul, and what delight I
felt in the word of God, words seem inadequate.
My desires, ever to lie at the feet of Christ, and receive the impressions of grace as the wax before the
seal, that I might be like Christ, and imitate him in
all his imitable glories, were ardent beyond expression. I can only say, "Eye hath not seen, nor
ear heard, nor can the heart conceive the things
that God hath prepared for them that love him."
Be astonished, O my soul, that while these things are
hid from the wise and prudent, they are revealed to
such a babe as I, the least of all the saints. Oh,
what shall I render to God for such goodness. I
will take the cup of salvation, and call upon the
name of the Lord. May I praise him while I have
a being. May I serve the Lord with fear, and rejoice with trembling.

Thus the Lord dealt most mercifully with me,

relative to the state of my soul; while he seemed greatly to frown, relative to my most important earthly comforts. And thus graciously did God meet me, when I set myself, by special fasting and prayer, to seek him. And truly I can say, that his spiritual blessings conferred, far more than over-balanced all my outward calamities. So that I could say with Paul, relative to afflictions, tribulations, or the greatest trials of life, "Nay in all these things we are more than conquerers through him that loved us."

One result of all my examinations and prayers was, a settled conviction, that I ought to seek a separation from my wicked husband, and never to set-tle with him any more for his most vile conduct. But as sufficient evidence, for his legal conviction, had not yet offered itself, (though I as much believed his guilt, as I believed my own existence,) I thought God's time to bring Mr. B.'s conduct to public view had not yet arrived. But I was confident that such a time would arrive; that God would bring his crimes to light; and afford me opportunity to be freed from him.

Several months had passed, after Mr. B's last wicked conduct before mentioned, and nothing spe-cial took place. The following events then occur-red. One of our young daughters, (too young to be a legal witness, but old enough to tell the truth,) in-formed one of her sisters, older than herself, what she saw and heard, more than a year before, on a certain sabbath. This sister being filled with grief and astonishment at what she had heard, informed her oldest sister. When this oldest sister had heard the account, and was prepared to believe it, (after all the strange things which she herself had seen and heard,) she was so *shocked*, that she faint-ed. She was then at our house, I administered camphire, and such things as were suitable in her case. She soon revived. She then informed me of

the occasion of her fainting. I had long before had
full evidence to my mind of Mr. B's great wickedness in this matter; and I thought I was prepared
to hear the worst. But verily the worst was dreadful! The last great day will unfold it. I truly at
this time had a new lesson added, to all that ever I
before heard, or conceived, of human depravity.

I was now determined to go and see the daughter, who had suffered such things. Mr. B. perceiving my design to go where she was, set himself
to prevent it. But kind Providence soon afforded
me an opportunity to go. She was living at the
house of her uncle, a very amiable man, and one
whom Mr. B. in his better days, esteemed most
highly; but of whom he became very shy, after he
abandoned himself to wickedness. Mr. B. now
could not endure the thought of my going to his
house. No doubt his guilty conscience feared what
information I might there obtain, and filled him
with terror.

With much difficulty, and by the help of her
aunt, I obtained ample information. I now found
that none of my dreadful apprehensions concerning
Mr. B's conduct had been too high. And I thought
the case of this daughter was the most to be pitied
of any person I ever knew. I wondered how the
author of her calamities could tarry in this part of
the world. I thought that his guilty conscience
must make him *flee;* and that shame must give him
wings, to fly with the utmost speed.

My query now was, what I ought to do? I had no
doubt relative to my living any longer with the author of our family miseries. This point was fully
settled. But whether it would be consistent with
faithfulness to suffer him to flee, and not be made a
monument of civil justice, was my query. The latter looked to me inexpressibly painful. And I persuaded myself, that if he would do what was right,
relative to our property, and would go to some dis-

tant place, where we should be afflicted with him no more, it might be sufficient; and I might be spared the dreadful scene of prosecuting my husband.

I returned home, I told Mr. B. I had heard an *awful account* relative to *some man.* I mentioned some particulars, without intimating who the man was; or what family was affected by it. I immediately perceived he was deeply troubled! He turned pale, and trembled, as if he had been struck with death. It was with difficulty he could speak. He asked nothing, who the man was, that had done this great wickedness; but after a while said, I know you believe it to be true; and that all our children believe it; but it is *not* true! Much more he said in way of denying. But he said he did not blame me for thinking as I did.

He asked me, what I intended to do? I replied, that one thing was settled: I would *never live with him any more!* He soon appeared in great *anguish;* and asked what I could advise him to do? Such was his appearance, that the pity of my heart was greatly moved. He had been my dear husband; and had destroyed himself. And now he felt something of his wretchedness. I now felt my need of christian fortitude, to be firm in pursuing my duty. I was determined to put on firmness, and go through with the most interesting and undesirable business, to which God, in his providence, had called me, and which I had undertaken. I told him his case to me looked truly dreadful and desperate. That though I had long and greatly labored for his reformation and good, yet he had rejected all my advice. He had felt sufficient to be his own counsellor; and now he felt something of the result of his own counsels.

Relative to his question, what he now should do? I told Mr. B. he knew something of my mind, from an interview upon the subject sometime since, when he proposed retiring to some distant region, and forever leaving me and his family. I informed

him, I now could see no better way for him than
this; that I had rather see him gone forever, than
to see him brought to trial, and have the law exe-
cuted upon him, to the torture of myself and family;
as it would be, unless he prevented it by flight. He
was then full of his consultations, relative to the
mode of his going;—whether to ride, or go on foot?
what property to take? and similar queries. I let
him know that I was willing he should ride, and
not only take a horse, but take property enough to
make him comfortable. I proposed he should turn
a one hundred acre lot, which we could well spare,
and take the avails of it.

I earnestly entreated him to break off his sins by
unfeigned repentance, and make it his immediate
care to become reconciled to God through Jesus
Christ, who died for lost man, and even for the
greatest of sinners. I suggested to Mr. B. that if he
would reform, and would never injure his family relative to the interest, I could truly wish him well,
and so much peace as was consistent with the holy
and wise purposes of God. But that if he should
undertake any farther to afflict our family, or any of
his dear children, he might expect punishment in
this life, and that the judgments of God would follow
him. I begged of him to treat his family well, in relation to our property, and to treat all mankind,
henceforth, well.

I then brought him his clothes, and laid them before him, that he might take all, or as many of them
as he pleased; for he had an abundance of them,
and some of the best kind. We had very large
saddlebags; and he packed up as many clothes and
things as he wished. I now saw that the time had
arrived, which I had long painfully anticipated,
and of which God had given me solemn premonitions.
Though I had *improved* tne opportunities afforded,
to labor with Mr. B. upon the things, which had so
much tortured my heart; yet he discovered no tok-

ens of true penitence for his wickedness, and the most distressing trials he had brought upon me. I had therefore, (in a painful anticipation of being, at some period, obliged to experience such a parting scene as this,) prepared *writings*, to put up secretly in Mr. B's clothes; which I hoped might be of service to him in his flight, and lonely retreats. The writings were as follows:

Mr. B. as your conduct for a long time has been such, as to force a conviction on my mind, that your remaining in your family could not probably be of long continuance; but I was constrained to expect that the day would soon come, when you must flee to some distant region, and leave your family forever; as I know not how soon this solemn event shall arrive; or whether I shall have much opportunity at that period to tell you my views of your conduct;—under these distressing apprehensions I think I must invent some method to speak to you, and try to do something for the benefit of your *soul*, after you are finally gone from us, and have opportunity for serious reflection. To accomplish this my desire, I have written a few lines, with a view to place them among your things, where you may find them some time after having left us. When I wrote this, I still had some hopes you had not accomplished your most infamous designs. Or if you had, I knew not that I could obtain legal evidence of it. But my apprehensions then, relative to your conduct and intentions, and the result of them, were dreadful.

I have thought, in times past, that I had sore trials indeed, on account of your unfaithfulness to your marriage covenant. Yet you know, notwithstanding those distressing trials, which you occasioned me, I overlooked those offences, and repeatedly forgave you. Not because I thought lightly of your crimes; or viewed such wickedness small in the eyes of God; or that it might be viewed small by man. But I hoped you did, in some small de-. gree at least, see the error of your ways; and would henceforth relinquish such transgressions. And the thought of being separated from you, and of the breaking up of our family, and under such disgrace, was to me dreadful. From those thoughts, I hoped it would not be sin in me so far to pass over your transgressions, as I did, in hopes of your better conduct in future. You know that I lived most kindly and peacefully with you. I labored to win you with kindness. I was most cautious never to reflect upon you; or needlessly to injure your feelings. And now, how have you rewarded me? Most ungrateful of men! Is this your kindness to your best friend? I well know, and you know, that you have ever had confidence in me as a true hearted and faithful friend. How often have you said, you had one of the kindest and best of wives? and that you had desirable and promising children? Oh then, were they not worthy of parental protection and regard? But what, alas, have you done? What shall I say? Words fail! No poet, in his highest strains, can reach the horrid subject, or depict the sorrow, grief and mourning, which have tortured my throbbing breast. Under the cruel horrors of your conduct, and when my situation was most delicate, I felt my flesh wasting, my strength failing, and I could say with the Psalmist, " *I am afflicted and ready to die.*—O Lord God of my salvation, I cry day and night before thee. Thou hast afflicted me with all thy waves.—Lover and friend hast thou put far from me."—You were no more a friend to me, no more a comfort to your kind and faithful wife. You have withdrawn from me all your kind and tender affection:—Nor for any injustice, or want of kindness in me, as your conscience testifies. Your dear children, who have always treated you with the most obedient respect, you have unnaturally sacrificed. All your tender love, fondness, and care.

for them, have vanished. So well have you been acquainted with the feelings of my heart, and my great fondness for friendship and peace, that you well knew your conduct was most cutting to my soul! Oh your unnatural conduct toward a daughter! What cruelty! what wickedness! What an ample cause for our final separation! Particulars —— alas, you know them! No tongue can express the tortures of my soul, while I saw you pursuing your wickedness. I had joyless days, and sorrowful nights, while I sighed and mourned like a lonely dove. All my past sorrows sunk to nothing before this. I knew, to my grief, that you had often been very unreasonable, cruel, and unfaithful; and that you was very guilty in the sight of God; yet all this was small, compared with your final abominations and cruelties.

Could I have believed, when you told me, at the close of your strange conduct for several days, that you had been planning to sell our farm, and move to the westward; expressing a most kind attention to the best interest and future good of our family, seeking my consent, and that of your children, to such a measure, and we all finally obediently submitted to your proposals;—could I have thought it possible, O false hearted lover! that under the cover of such pretences, you was then planning the ensuing scenes of infamy, the ruin of a daughter! and the disgrace of your own family! It was most distressing to my heart to entertain a jealous thought of your intentions, when you was pursuing your foolish conduct with that poor child, under pretence of making her willing to go with you. But your conduct forced a series of dreadful convictions on my distracted mind, which cannot be named.

But whom am I addressing? What enemy has been capable of such things as these? Ah, let your conscience reply! Is this the man, who chose me

for the wife of his youth? promising before God,
angels and men, to be to me a kind and faithful husband, till death should part us? Is this the man
whom I took in my youth, to be my kind head
and husband, my guide, my bosom friend, the
partner of my joys and sorrows? Am I dream-
ing? Or are these things realities? I am left alone.
You have deserted me. You have chained me
down to sorrow and grief. And though I sigh and
groan, under my present load, yet I foresee that
this is but the beginning of my sorrows. For such
conduct must bring on a separation! yes, probably
an *eternal* separation! And such is the nature of my
troubles, that I cannot open them to neighbors and
fellow-creatures, and thus have some to bear the
burden with me. I must bear it alone. It is but in
silence that I can say, "Behold and see, all ye that
pass by; is there any sorrow like unto my sorrow!"
Say, then, O treacherous friend, are you only without feeling, without pity? You have hardened your
heart against all kindness. While for some time I
did not dare to tell you the worst that I thought of
your conduct; yet you did know my dreadful suspi-
cions; and that I labored to dissuade you from your
wicked intentions; and labored to win you, and save
you from that destruction, into which I saw you was
precipitating yourself. But to all my entreaties you
ever turned a deaf ear. You was angry at my
tears. You frowned at my groans. I therefore expect no more pity or comfort from you.

But though you have thus hardened yourself, and
deserted me, I cannot forget the dear connexion,
which has been, and which ought faithfully to have
been maintained, between you and me.

Alas, the tortures of my wretched case!
Just as we see the feeble vine, that needs
Support, intwining with the pricking thorn.

She feels the smart; her need she also feels,
Both of support, and healing for the wound.
Nor will her hold let go, till forced and torn.
So I, confiding in a faithless friend,
By you am torn and wounded to the soul!
With sorrow, pain, and hopeless grief I sigh,
And mourn the friendship of a husband lost!

At the time when you read these lines, I shall
expect no more aid or friendship from you. But my
wish is, that there may be excited in your heart
some feeling sense of the miseries and tortures you
have occasioned me; and may return to God with
a humble penitent soul. Where you may be when
these lines shall be by you found and perused, God
only knows. But I beg of you to read and solemnly
to consider the cause of these complaints and moans
of your injured wife. I cry out of wrong. And had
not God sustained me, I had fainted and sunk under
burdens long ere this day!

I pray you further to consider, as you have, without cause, torn yourself from the earthly enjoyments
in which you have taken delight, where can you
expect to find such happy days, as once shone upon
you?—when you rejoiced with the wife of your
youth; and your tender offspring, as olive branches,
were round about your table! Then your fruitful
fields brought forth in plenty such riches as you
needed. Your stores were filled with the finest
wheat; your barns with hay, and agricultural treas-
ures. Your rich pastures were covered with flocks;
your herds fed and skipped in your enclosures; and
you was respected by multitudes. Again therefore
I ask, when, and where, can you expect that you
shall ever again find such blessings as you have
abandoned? Believe me, you never will! Poor
wretched man!—From my heart I truly pity you,
most unwise and wretched! Truly, "the way of
transgressors is hard." I pray you, think on your

6*

ways. Where are you? What are you pursuing?
Oh, where shall you land, when you end your mortal race? You cannot plead ignorance of these things! You do know your accountability to God for all the deeds done in the body.

Your afflicted and forever deserted wife,

A. B.

The following letter I also put up with the preceding.

Mr. B. I once more assume my most sorrowful pen, to speak a few things to you, when you shall forever have gone from my sight; in hopes that you may yet become alarmed at the terrors of your case, and turn and be reconciled to God. You will now peruse what I wrote while you was, with the heart of a tiger, pursuing your intrigues and cruelties in our family; and I was unable to control your wickedness.

O false hearted, and unnatural friend! Times and circumstances have obliged me to keep a long silence. And now attempting, in this way, to speak, where, O where shall I find suitable expressions to open my mind to you? Can language be found, suitable to address you on such an occasion? Who can express the blackness of your crimes? Who can paint the melancholy and distress, which your conduct has produced in my mind? The pains occasioned by your perverse conduct, incessantly torture my broken heart.

It is indeed painful in the extreme to have occasion thus to deal with one, who ought to be my nearest and dearest friend on earth. To be obliged to write such grievousness to such an one, is indeed a task! Your strange conduct has destroyed all my confidence in you, as a friend, either to me, or to your children. My affections therefore have been constrained to withdraw from such a husband. I could not view myself as acting a rational part, had it been otherwise, or had I continued to regard you, as in times past. I reflect on past years and domestic scenes; I look back to happier days, and compare them with the present; and alas, it adds fresh anguish to my wounded heart! You have gone on from one degree of wickedness to another, hardening yourself in sin, till God only knows what enormities you may next be induced to undertake. Think, O think on the deeds you have done! What could have exceeded them? I have been so worn out with your unnatural conduct, that I have daily watched the lingering sun, in his circle round the skies, with ardent desire that he would bring the expected day, when God, in his holy providence, would bring some relief, or some change of times in our distressed family. What the change will be, I know not; nor can I much fear that it can be for the worse; even though it should separate you from us forever. A few months ago, when I first thought of being deprived of the head of our family, it seemed too much for me to bear. But now it is my only hope, that so great a judgment and terror as you have become, may soon be removed. Think not therefore, when you shall read these writings, in your distant and lonely retreats, that I am wishing for your return. No, I wish you might return to God. I mourn for the cause of our separation; and am grieved for your sins and miseries. But I never desire your return to me. This point is decided!

Our children, who had come to the age of ten or twelve years, and older, have been so grieved and troubled at your strange unnatural conduct, that your separation and absence would be a far greater relief to them, than a trouble. This I have learned from them. You may be assured you are one of them, who trouble their own house; and hence I shall inherit the wind: Oh, for a father thus to trouble his own children! That children should have cause to lament, that they must be numbered in such an afflicted and miserable family! Yes, may I not say, your dear little infant, when but seventeen days old, as though ashamed to show his face, and own himself a son of so unnatural a father, closed his eyes in death, and hid himself in the cold grave!

Now let me ask you, are you not a terror to yourself? Does not your vile conduct haunt you from day to day, and from place to place? Are you not in continual expectation, that God will meet you in some surprising judgment? Have you not already seen the hand of God, remarkably blasting your interest? Can you not behold that every part of it has been smitten with a consumption? I have seen this with amazement. And I thought you too had perceived it. For when I have tried to converse with you on the unprosperous state of our affairs of late, you ever have fallen into a passion, as though conscious and angry, that the hand of God was upon you; and as though you thought me taking sides with divine justice against you;—though I said no such thing; and I spake only in the most tender and prudent manner. Surely if whoredom shall bring a man to a piece of bread, what must you expect will be the consequence of your aggravated crimes? And will not your deranged affairs be a swift witness in the judgment against you? Most unhappy man! Consider at what a dear rate you have sinned. You have had great light and knowledge. You have enjoyed rich religious privileges. You once professed great love to God, and great attachment to the cause of Christ. You are the father of a great family; and have some grand children. Now, after all these things, (you being under such advantages, and such obligations to glorify God, and to give your children good advantages, to set before them good examples, and to guard them from all vice,) that you should most barbarously conduct as you have done, and seek to destroy your own family;—it is in every view most astonishing! This solemn testimony against your wickedness, and this last call to repentance, I leave with you. Let me be clear from the blood of your soul. A. B.

These writings, for some time prepared, I put up with the things of Mr. B. so that he might, at some time after his departure, come across them.

Sept. 8, 1790, just at break of day, Mr. B. bid us farewell, and rode away. He did not tell, nor did I ask, where he designed to go. I thought, as things were, I could not expect, nor did I desire, ever again on earth, to see his face. The scene was to me truly solemn.

I took my Bible, and read for divine worship in my poor fatherless family. I was reading in course. I had arrived at this time, to Psalm 125. I read this, and several following Psalms. And truly I think God did now meet me in his word. I saw the passages contained a word in season; which I read with great satisfaction and confidence in God. I felt the propriety and safety of trusting in the Lord at all times as here directed. "They that trust in the Lord, shall be as mount Zion, which cannot be removed, but abideth forever.—The Lord is round about his people from henceforth, even forever. For the rod of the wicked shall not rest on the lot of the righteous.—As for such as turn aside unto their crooked ways, the Lord shall lead them forth with the workers of iniquity; but peace shall be upon Israel.—Many a time have they afflicted me from my youth up, may Israel now say. Many a time have they afflicted me, yet have they not prevailed against me.—The Lord is righteous; he hath cut asunder the cords of the wicked,"

After Mr. B.'s departure, I was in some hopes that the cause of his going might be kept concealed. I found it necessary to make it known to some intimate friends. But infinite wisdom did not see fit that such wickedness should be any longer concealed. The birds of the air seemed to carry the news. It flew every way with great rapidity. And when I found that all had become acquainted with it, I found a melancholy relief in conversing with others upon the subject, which had so long been confined in my sorrowful breast. I felt a great desire that all my children might make a humble and sanctified improvement of the great public scandal, which lay upon us. I labored to instruct them and impress their minds relative to this duty. I was cautious of speaking to them of their father's conduct. Much of it they well knew. And I informed them that probably he would never again return; that the whole care of them had now devolved upon me; and they must be tender, kind, obedient and faithful. I endeavored to lead them, as much as possible, to consider that it was now a most critical time with them; that each was now forming a character for eternity; that they must remember, fear, and obey God; and, as to their fellow creatures, they must be "wise as serpents, and harmless as doves." I informed my children, that they must no longer expect to derive the least advantage from being known as the children of Major Bailey. They must gain the good will of people by their own good behaviour and merit. I longed and labored with them that they might be wise for time and for eternity. I thought I might truly say to them, as Naomi to her daughters, "For it grieveth me much for your sakes, that the hand of the Lord is gone out against me."

I took advice of the most wise and judicious men I could find, especially col. J. of H. a most judicious and godly man, relative to my children, and worldly interest; and I received much support and satisfaction in the advice I received. It was hard to think of putting out any of my children. But I was determined to consult their good, and not my own fond feelings. And I comforted myself, that as God had remarkably sustained me hitherto, so he would not forsake me in such a day as this; but would impart to me wisdom to guide my affairs with discretion. I most sensibly felt that without much divine aid, I was very insufficient to manage the many and great concerns, which had now devolved upon me. My young sons went on finely with our farming business; and things seemed to begin to look smiling.

But alas, my troubles from Mr. B. were not yet at an end. Grievous things were yet in store for me. I heard nothing from Mr. B. after he went away, for almost five weeks. Nor did I learn any thing which way he had gone. But late one evening he surprised me with his return. I feared him as an enemy. I was soon disgusted to learn that he had returned with hopes of being able to persuade me that he was yet my friend. I knew not what to do with him; but was peremptorily determined not to be deceived or traduced by all his wiles. I had some advantage here, for I had long known him. He found a very cold reception.

In as melting and moving language as he was capable of, he said that he most humbly begged for some opportunity to talk once more with me. After conversing a little with me and the children, who had not retired to rest, I took up our little son, under three years of age, who was in a very sound sleep. I sat down with him in my arms near his father. He waked. I said nothing to him of his father. But as soon as he saw him, he brightened up, and with fixed eyes, and solemn countenance said, in the most earnest manner, "My Pa, what have you done? Where have you been? How could you go away and leave Ma'am and me so long? Do you love me?" This child (as all may well think) had no knowledge of the cause of his father's going away. It appeared to me wonderful to hear him speak as he did. Both his words, and the pathetic manner, in which he uttered them, seemed to me strikingly providential, as a reproof of most aggravated wickedness. Mr. B. could make no reply. He seemed as though he would sink, and give up the ghost.

Mr. B. afterward conversed with me. He said he had been several hundred miles distance; and that he might have been in a comfortable way to live, if he had never returned. But he said, he could have no peace of mind:—He could not live, but must surely die, and that very soon, if he could not confess his sins to me and have my forgiveness. He told me he found those papers, which I had put in his bundle, and had attentively perused them. Oh he said, no tongue could express the dreadfulness of his tortures, on reading them! He said he never before had any sense of the distresses he had occasioned me. Now he said he had felt them most truly and keenly; and that there was no comparison between his troubles and mine. For he had been his own tormentor. He had been the wicked cause of all his own troubles; and of mine likewise; and hence he must bear his own; and in a sense mine also. Whereas (he said) it was quite otherwise with me. I was entirely blameless; and had only innocently to mourn the wrongs done to me, and to the family. He assured me, I had never thought half so bad of him, as he now thought of himself. He added, when he went away, he felt unwilling to confess to me any thing of that awful wickedness, of which he *had indeed been guilty*, respecting his daughter. He hence denied it. For he had thought the sin was only against God, and not against me; and hence he was under no obligations to confess to me, or to own the fact. But he said, he now viewed the matter in a very different light; and had found that he could have no peace in those views of the subject. For he found that though he had most awfully sinned against God; he had in the most shameful manner sinned also against me.

Mr. B. went on to state his troubles. He said, while he was absent, wherever he put up at night, and saw men at home, with their wives and children, he was tormented; he could not endure the sight, but was obliged to get away to bed as soon as possible, that he might hide from the face of mortals, and gnaw his own tongue for anguish of soul. And wherever he was, he could find nothing that afforded him the least comfort. And he felt that if he were possessed of the whole world, he should be equally incapable of peace, or comfort. Therefore all the hope, which he had (he assured me) was, that he might return, confess to me his wickedness, and hence obtain some comfort. For whether I forgave him, or not, or whether I could shew him any favour, or not; yet he felt this to be the only way in which he could get relief to his distressed soul from that insupportable load of guilt and misery, under which he could not live.

Mr. B. proceeded and said, that he had attended public worship on several Lord's days, while he was gone; and that it seemed as if every text and sermon he heard was on purpose for him. All pointed directly against him. One text was, "lie not one to another." This and other texts, and faithful sermons, he said gave pain to his soul, which was beyond description. He went on exclaiming against himself, as most filthy and abominable; as self-condemned, and without the least excuse. He condemned all his cruel treatment of me since we had lived together; and he repeated it, that he hated himself, in that he had made himself to appear so vile in my eyes. Oh, he said, he could almost pluck the hair from his head, and tear the flesh from his bones.

This strain Mr. B. continued. Sometimes he would fall upon his knees before me, and in the most humble and self-abasing terms would renew his confessions of all the wrongs he had done me. All

this he pursued, with tears flowing down his
cheeks, with trembling limbs and quivering voice;
adding in the most humble expressions possible,
that he well knew he did not deserve the least possible favor from me. Yet he would, in the most moving and affecting language, and the greatest earn-
estness, beg of me to forgive all the injuries he had
done me. Sometimes he would fall down upon his
face before me, and beg of me to tread upon him;
pretending it would be a gratification to him, if
I would tread him into the dirt. But Oh, if I could
only pardon his cruel treatment!

These things were truly cutting to my heart. To
see my former head and husband, the father of all
my children, the companion of my youth, in such a
situation, and for such reasons. Oh judge if you can
what must have been the feelings of my soul! His
conduct had truly been so abominable, that I could
not conceive it to be consistent with duty to live
with him again. I felt that I never could again
feel that complacency in him that I ought toward
a husband. Nor could I again ever place confidence in him. And yet I pitied him! Oh, I pitied
him from my inmost soul! I felt the greatest compassion for his wretched case. I never had felt the
least desire to be avenged on him, or to see him injured. I informed him that I could readily forgive
him so far as to *wish him well,* and to feel for him
in the most tender pity and concern; that I wished
he might obtain the mercy of God, and future salvation. And I should delight in his being as happy in this world, as it is possible for him to be, after
such crimes. But I told Mr. B. I could see no
cause for altering my mind, as to ever again living
with him. He answered, that he could not desire
me to receive him again, unless I had real evidence that he was a better man. For if he was not
better, he was worse, and should be likely to grow
worse, and be more vile than before. And he said he
had so much love to me, that unless I could believe

that he would do much better by me, than he had ever before done, he could not wish me again to live with him. But he did sincerely long, he said, for an opportunity to convince me, that if it were possible for him to make amends for some of his past miscarriage, he would most gladly do it, by the greatest possible tenderness and kindness in future. Nothing in this world would render him so happy as to be in my company, and to be doing something for my comfort. I replied, that if he did now, after all, truly wish for my comfort, I begged of him not to disturb my lonely peace, and destroy the comfort, which I might have in my desolate and melancholy situation, by urging me to that, which I could not think would be proper, but would be sinful.

The more Mr. B. perceived my determination to reject his proposals, and to place no further confidence in him, so much the more distressed and urgent he became. Sometimes he would try to work upon my tender feelings, and move my pity, by pleading his own wretched case in the most moving language. Then he would attack my fear, by setting forth in the most striking manner, the difficulties I must unavoidably encounter, in taking the whole charge of so great a family, and mostly young children, and of all our numerous affairs, without any head or helper. Then he would add, that he knew his conduct had been so abominable, that he did not ask the honor of his usual place in the family; but I should have the preeminence, and he would willingly take the place of an assistant. He would do all he could for the honor and benefit of the family, and every thing should be under my direction. For he said I was indeed worthy of it; and to me it did most properly belong, as things were. He then would take the strain of flattery and tell me of the love and solid respect he had for me; that he had by long acquaintance known my great worth; and he could not speak of it in strains too exalted. He said it seemed to him he had just now come to see things as they truly were; and that he had never before known how to prize what was truly lovely. He said he always knew he had found a good wife, and had thus obtained favor of the Lord. But he had never suitably considered till lately, how highly he ought to prize her virtues. Lately he had been made most sensible how great a blessing a good wife is; and how happy he should have been, if he had followed the good examples, and the wise and kind counsels and warnings from me, with which he had often been favored. He said he did now see the worth of these things, and did feel his great need of them, notwithstanding that he had so wickedly rejected them in times past. For him now to think of being forever deprived of these great blessings, by being separated from so kind, good and faithful a friend and companion, was to him dreadful beyond expression.

In confessions, entreaties, arguments and pleadings, like these, Mr. B. spent his time for several days. He truly had a talent at this kind of business. And I have no doubt but he had been led to feel his present wretchedness, to a great degree.

None can conceive of the trial, which these things occasioned to my mind. It was indeed something different from my past trials. But it seemed as though nothing could be more severe. I had felt, when Mr. B. was gone, as though, in the language of one in another case, "the bitterness of death was past." But here I found it had pangs still left. I had, with long consideration and prayer, made up my mind never again to live with Mr. B. and in this I was not to be shaken. The point with me was conscientiously settled. This therefore was out of the question. But Oh, to behold the distress and hear the cries and entreaties of him, whom I once loved as my own soul, as my dearest companion.

Judge, ye tender partners in life, what must have been my scenes of woe.

Had the way been prepared, by the due adjustment of our property, to be sure it would have been best to have decided the point at once with a firm tone, and told him he must immediately flee and be gone! But no proper settlement was as yet made. And I was sensible he had it in the power of his hands to injure and distress us. And truly, I may say, I pitied him from my very heart. I conversed freely with him. I told him that in point of deep, long and thorough consideration upon the nature and distressing consequences of our separation, I had got far the start of him. For while he was, in most heedless cruelty, preparing the way to bring it about, my melancholy foreboding had outstripped his abominable deeds, and had often and most familiarly taken a sorrowful view of myself and my large family of children, as forever deserted by our head, and brought into the state, upon which we had now actually entered. The doleful scene had hence long been familiar to me.

I labored to impress on Mr. B.'s mind, from a view of his own most doleful case, the awful danger of being under a spirit of opposition to God, and of giving way to the abominable wickedness of the heart. For this conduct had blinded the eyes of his reason; had plunged him into the way of destruction; and procured his ruin. This ruin, I told him, I had long foreseen; and I had labored to save him from it; but in vain. He had refused to foresee the evil, and avoid it. He had pressed heedlessly on toward it; and now must be punished. His wound was now incurable, as to my healing it, or helping him in the way he wished. For I ought to fear God rather than regard man, to God's dishonor.

As to myself and poor unhappy children, I remarked to Mr. B. I most sensibly did feel our need

of a head, a kind friend, a comforter, a guide, to
protect us from the thousand evils, to which we
were exposed. But I hoped God would provide for
us; and that he would enable me to take heed to
choose suffering rather than sin; and to cast my
burden on the Lord, and trust in him, who has ever
shewn the most tender care for the widow, the
fatherless, and such as have no helper. I added,
that Israel was solemnly warned against returning
back to Egypt; or leaning on an arm of flesh. And
when they took due heed to such warnings, God
marvellously delivered them. I told Mr. B. that
he himself had said, he did not wish me again to
live with him, unless I could really believe that he
had become a better man. And I thought I ought
to deal so faithfully with him, as to tell him, I did
not think I had evidence of any real change in him,
whereby he would be likely, on the whole, to lead
a better life, than he had before done. So that
there appeared to me no certainty, if there did the
least probability, that my case would be made better by again admitting him. I informed him, that
I was constrained to think the direction to the
Corinthians now applicable to me, relative to him,
"Wherefore come ye out, and be ye separate, saith
the Lord, and I will receive you, and will be a
Father unto you." And they were commanded to
put from among them the incestuous person. As
to my excellencies and faithfulness, of which he
had spoken, I told Mr. B. I felt myself a poor unworthy creature. I hoped I had been in some degree faithful to my fellow creatures, and to him.
But he had refused to profit by it, or by all my
labors of love. And I thought the cause of Christ
now required me to treat him as I did. And I
ought to prefer this Jerusalem to my chief joy.

Mr. B. strangely persevered in laboring to carry
his point. He wished, the short time longer that he
should tarry, that I would improve every opportu-

'nity to talk with him upon the dreadfulness of his conduct, and continually to remind him of it; that he might be kept humble. Oh, I thought, how distressing must be his situation! For a man of such a temper, such a disposition, who had ever felt so important, so wilful, and haughty, and so unwilling to acknowledge any wrong;—for him now to be upon his knees, upon his face, and begging of me to put my feet upon his neck; appeared like a strange turn of things. But I felt, that I had every reason to believe him destitute of true penitence; that his object was only to work upon my weakness, and to better his own wretched situation. He was forced to feel some of the consequences of his extraordinary wickedness; and that he had reduced himself to such a pit of wretchedness, that he had no way but as it were to crawl out upon his face and knees: —and that however distressing this was to his haughty feelings, he now thought that his own interest demanded it. I was unable to view his humiliation in any better light than this. I discovered no evidence of grief that he had disobeyed and dishonored God. Though he attempted to make me believe this was the case; and spake of his having spent days in fasting and prayer.

Mr. B. again prepared to depart. This he said he should do, whether I ever consented to live with him, or not. For he would never live in these parts. He chose the covert of night for his retreat; and he departed. He could not endure to be seen in this town, or in these parts, where he was known. It was indeed most distressing to think of his situation. He once was not afraid to be seen; was fond of home, and of quiet nights. But now the scene was changed. His iniquities had found him out, and were hateful. "The wicked flee when no man pursueth."

Inured to crimes and deeds of night,
And by the powers of darkness led;—
Those crimes now caused a wretched flight,
And tore his pillow from his head.

Ah, poor man! He had refused to be taught, but
with briers and thorns of the wilderness! Now he
felt their smart. One instance of his feeling it, before this departure, I will mention. The selectmen
of Landaff, and some other gentlemen, came one
day to see and converse with him. Mr. B. saw
them coming, and shyly made his escape. They
came in, and respectfully wished to see and converse with him. I went to the place to which I supposed he had retreated; but he was not there.
Pains were taken to find where he was. I then went
to him, with the promise of these gentlemen, that if
he would come and converse with them, they would
not take any advantage of it to injure him. He then,
with much mortification, came in. Not so did he
use to meet his neighbors! He used to be glad to see
them at his house; and they were glad to see him
at their houses. Nor in doing town business, was
he the least among them. He had been one of the
first. But now the scene was changed. Who, that
had, in times past, seen him riding in front of his
regiment, would have thought of ever seeing him
skulking from his neighbors coming in at his door?
Mr. B. confessed to these gentlemen that his conduct had been *very bad;* and that he had destroyed
himself, and ruined his family. He said he looked
more filthy and abominable to himself, than it was
possible he could to them.

I thought to myself, Oh the deceitfulness of sin;
that, with all its enchanting flatteries, it yields such
bitter fruits as these! How astonishing, that too
many of mankind, even the most cunning in other
things, will so effectually work out their own ruin.
Who can deny man, utter moral depravity?

These gentlemen and Mr. B. conversed freely upon the state of his family, and his interest. He gave them clearly to understand, that he well knew the necessities of his family; and that, as he had interest enough, ample provision should be made for them. He said, though he had done so much to wean his family from him, yet he did not intend to leave them in such a situation as to lead them to feel as though he was their enemy. But they should be left under comfortable circumstances. The gentlemen conversed in a way calculated to confirm these his resolutions; and that it *ought*, and *must* be thus.

Mr. B. was now gone; I knew not where. I had not thought it best to inquire of him relative to his intended place of retreat. I comforted myself, and managed our family concerns as well as I could. I very sensibly felt for our relatives, as well as for myself; especially for aged parents, who must have been deeply afflicted with Mr. B.'s conduct.

After several months, late in one stormy winter night, Mr. B. again returned. He informed that he did not mean to tarry many days. He did not now come in any humble posture, as before. He still said, he believed he had a penitent heart, that he did repent of his sins, and was reconciled to God. But he did not, at this time, appear to exhibit much tenderness. He said, after he went away a thought come into his mind relative to a particular person, who he feared would try to injure us as to our property; and he wished to return and make arrangements to prevent this. Also he wanted more of the property to carry away with him. He should not quit so. He appeared hard. His shame for his wickedness seemed almost, if not wholly abated. He appeared even brazen and stout hearted. His conduct convinced me, that I had not erred in declining to make a settlement with him, as a penitent, so as again to live with him.

Mr. B. soon packed up his things to be in readiness; for he said he should be gone again in a few days. But he *tarried*—and *tarried*. He seemed to have his mind much taken up in planning matters, between him and me, as to our property. He said, as we could not live together any more, he was willing to have some proper arrangement made. Sometimes he would propose one plan; and sometimes another; nor did he appear very unwilling to afflict me. Sometimes he would suggest a wish that I would forget all that was past, and go to a distance and live with him. Sometimes he would be angry, and call me stubborn and rebellious. Then he would threaten, that if I did any thing, in seeking help against him, from the selectmen, or from any other authority, he would stand it out, till every farthing of his interest was expended, and till he had spilt the last drop of his blood. Sometimes he would seem to forget all his past acknowledgments of his crimes, and tell me that I was making a great noise about him, as though he had done some mighty crime, which he would defy me to prove. In short his carriage was now most unkind and unreasonable. His treatment of me became exceedingly cruel, and appeared like the insults of an enemy. I felt myself to be placed, by the providence of a holy God, in an iron furnace of affliction. I felt that I needed great wisdom to know how to conduct, so as not to dishonor God's name. This was my greatest fear. I felt great insufficiency in myself to manage my concerns, or to know what was best to be done. My wish was for an equitable adjustment of our affairs of interest; and then for Mr. B. to be gone. But I was perplexed relative to the best way of bringing it about. Many things rendered it very undesirable to commence a legal process against Mr. B. And I hoped he would, by and by, do what was right, and then betake himself to his distant retreat. God had di-

rected and comforted me, in days past. But now I
felt great desertion, and uncertainty, as to the path
of my duty. And I greatly feared I should now be
left to dishonor God. I can truly say I feared this,
more than I felt for my own personal salvation.

The world now appeared to me very trifling and
vain. I attended merely to the daily and most necessary duties of life. And the rest of my time I de-
voted to searching the scriptures, and to fasting and
prayer. And I was led to hope and trust that God
would, in his own time and way, lead me out from
my present embarrassments, and guide me by his
counsel. I rejoiced in the idea that "the meek God
will guide in judgment; the meek he will teach his
way." I could at times rejoice in his power, wisdom, and faithfulness.

Relative to our property, Mr. B. finally agreed,
that he would divide with me. He would have half,
and I half. And he would be at half the expenses
of the family. Of this I felt no disposition to complain. It was concluded the property must be sold;
and we would divide the avails. I thought if he
would abide by this agreement, I would not disturb
him, or ask for more. But if he should undertake
to wrong me; I should take a different course with
him, and secure as much of the estate for the support of myself and children, as I could obtain. I
conversed with Mr. B. freely on this subject. I ad-
jured him to be faithful to his word and promise, and
not wrong his family out of their due proportion of
our living. I told him I did not believe God would
suffer him to do it: and if he attempted it, he had
reason to believe not only that he would be defeated
in his plans, but that his wicked attempts would
prove only as a moth, and as a fire to consume
what he had obtained. The judgments of God, I
did believe, would overtake him, if he should undertake to wrong his poor family out of their living.
And he would but make himself more wretched

than at present. This seemed to have some effect upon him. For he appeared to fear my warnings of evil, and my prayers. One day as I came out of my retired room, he asked what time of day I thought it was? I told him, about noon. He asked whether I did not think that if a person had neglected secret prayer in the morning, it was more suitable to omit it till evening, than to attend to it at this time of day? I replied, that I esteemed it a great privilege to seek to God by prayer at any time, and at all times. That we were commanded to pray always;—to pray without ceasing. That we find in the word of God instances of noon being taken, as a proper time for set prayer, as well as morning and evening. And it is an astonishing mercy that such needy vile creatures may come with boldness to the throne of grace, through a glorious Mediator, to obtain mercy, and find grace to help in every time of need. God's ear is ever open to the cry of the humble. As Mr. B. seemed first to take it for granted that I had been retired only to make up a neglected morning devotion; I informed him, that I had not, that morning, nor had I any other morning that winter, afforded any person opportunity to speak to me, before I had presented my supplication before the Lord. And as I did esteem it both a duty, and great privilege, first, and above all things, to dedicate myself anew to God every morning; so I hoped I should not set my hand to any secular employment, nor have my heart taken up with the cares of the world, before I had given thanks to the great Preserver of men, and Father of mercies, for his renewed goodness; and prayed for the continuance of his favors, and for needed blessings. Mr. B. asked me, how I prayed? whether I felt a forgiving temper? For if I did not, God would not hear my prayers. He wished also to know whether I prayed against him? I replied, that if I made wicked or hypocritical prayers, he need not *fear them.* It was only the effectual fervent prayers of the righteous, that would avail much. I told him I had no fear of *his* prayers. For if he prayed with the spirit of God, they could never injure a child of God. And if he prayed with a wicked or selfish spirit, such prayers (he might depend) would be very ineffectual, either to injure others, or benefit himself. I told him, it was the desire of my soul, when I prayed, that God's will might be done; and that he would make me to know and do what was right in his sight. And that if through the deceitful wickedness of my heart, or through ignorance, I had at any time done otherwise, that God would forgive, and lead me in the right way.

As to my forgiving others, I told Mr. B. I well knew that a forgiving spirit was essential to a spirit of prayer. And I thought it was the desire and delight of my heart to forgive all others, just as I begged of God to forgive me. I never allowed myself to ask God to forgive me in my impenitence, or while I was still disposed to pursue my sins. Such a prayer would be an abomination; as is a similar prayer to us, from men, who still persist in injuring us. As to my praying against him, I told Mr. B. I had employed a great deal of time, for many years, at the throne of grace, in his behalf, interceding for his reformation and salvation. But I had much reason now to fear, that all these prayers, and all his great privileges, would issue in his more dreadful destruction. For, as all things shall work together for good to them, who love God; so they will work together for the ruin of the opposite character. That the wicked are treasuring up wrath against the day of wrath. And I had great reason to fear that he was of that miserable class. And I added, that the prayers of the oppressed (that God will appear for them) do indeed engage the justice and judgment of God against their oppressors.

Thus I replied to Mr. B's inquiries. It was very

8

evident that the greatest fear he had of me was from my prayers, seeking and obtaining help from God. He had discovered evident fear of this.

In these days of suspense, while Mr. B. was at home the second time, I wrote thus to my father's family.—As I conclude you all bear a part with me, in my sorrows and trials, you will be glad to hear something from me. My present opportunity will permit me to write but a few lines. And even in these, I hardly know what to say. I am, like Joseph in the prison, waiting on God to bring my feet out of the stocks, to loose my chains, in his own time. Or like Israel in Egypt, believing in the promised deliverance, and waiting God's time to come forth from bondage. Like David in his distresses, I attempt to encourage myself in the Lord my God. I know not what a day will bring forth. But I hope shortly to see you, and tell you some of the dealings of the allwise God, in his holy providence, toward me; and how his rod and staff comfort me. Be not too anxious on my account. For I believe the great God will overturn, overturn, and overturn, till he has adjusted the concerns of our family, just according to his holy will; and that I shall yet praise him for his delivering mercy.

I ask your prayers for

Your affected daughter, and
sorrowful sister,   A. B.

In some of my scenes of trouble, while laboring to adjust our affairs with Mr. B. I resorted to my consoling pen, and wrote thus: Alas, my perplexities! Surely I think there never was a benighted traveller, who had lost his way, and found himself enveloped in a desolate wilderness, among savages, and beasts of prey, who ever longed more to find his way out, that leads to a habitation of rest and safety, where he may enjoy friends, and the comforts of life,—than I desire, from day to day, that I

may know and do the will of the Lord, in my difficulties! Was ever a situation more pitiable than
mine? But why do I speak of pity? I am unworthy
of it from the least christian. How much more unworthy of pity from the great and holy God!

The preacher says, "Surely oppression maketh
a wise man mad." If so, what must become of me,
a poor simple woman, under distressing oppression?
But O, it is no matter of discouragement, though
much matter of humility, to behold my own weakness, while God enables me by faith to behold at
the same time his allsufficiency, and the fulness of
grace in the Captain of our salvation. It is with
inexpressible delight that I contemplate the power,
wisdom, goodness and faithfulness of God; that he
does regard his people; that he has a tender care
for all his chosen in Christ. Now, "when I am
weak, then am I strong." Even divine corrections
are in love and faithfulness. "All things shall
work together for good to them that love God." I
see such safety in trusting in him, that though the
earth be removed, such as confide in him need not
fear. There is the greatest satisfaction in casting
our burdens on such a God. Unworthy as I am, I
am sure God careth for me. For it has been his
supporting mercy, that has held me up under the
trials I have endured, and has given me a patient
resignation to the divine will, and a confidence in
God of deliverance. So that I think I can, like
Daniel in the den of lions, and Jonah in the belly of
the fish, confidently look to God's holy habitation.
God will cause the wrath of man to praise him;
and restrain the rest. I will say, with David, "Although my house be not so with God, yet he hath
made an everlasting covenant with me, ordered in
all things, and sure. For this is my salvation and
all my desire."

Although Mr. B. tarried, at this time, a considerable
while with us, yet I found he tarried in fear. This

accounted for his preparing his things, when he first came home, as before noted, under pretence of going in a few days, He meant to be in readiness to flee at once, if any difficulty were about to assail him. I found his guilty conscience foreboded that he probably should have a visit on some night, and from those who might not be disposed to treat him very tenderly. He once asked me, if he should receive such a visit, whether I would be for him, or against him? Knowing the peculiarity of my situation, I turned him off as well as I could, without giving any such answer as he sought. I knew some had indeed talked of paying Mr. B. such a nightly visit. I solemnly feared it. And I thought it would place me in the most critical predicament. For my circumstances at this time were such, as ill to become the danger and alarm, which such a visit must have occasioned. Through a kind Providence such an event did not occur. Mr. B. went away again in peace.

A few days before he went away the third time, he changed his manners, and seemed to be very kind in his feelings and carriage toward me. He said he did not love to go away, and leave me just upon the point of being sick; and asked me if I should think hard of him for going away before my confinement? I replied, that as things were I *should not*. For it was impossible, I added, for me to be so happy with him there, as I should be in his absence! For though he had, in years past, ever been kind at such times, and he knew I could not, on such occasions, in times past, endure the thought of his absence; yet now the case was such, that his presence would inconceivably add to my sorrows! He did not now appear offended. But he said he would go immediately; and added, that he should take some of his sons with him. This I had not expected; and the thought of any of the sons' going, was to me very grievous. But I knew no better way

-than to be resigned to the affliction, as from the hand of God.

Mr. B. now made his third departure; and he never returned again to Landaff. He set off on foot, and across lots, to avoid the sight of man. And he ordered our second son, Asa, to meet him, with his horse, on such a day, in such a place in Vermont. Oh, my heart flowed in streams of pity for the poor man! Ten thousand worlds would I have given, had it been in my power, and it had been the will of God, that he might now have been at home, in peace and love, having never forfeited his character. Oh, what miseries has he brought upon himself, and entailed on his poor wife and children! But, as things were, I was glad at his departure.

The next day, Asa, a dear son, and very feeble, must go from us, and follow his father. This was a new trial indeed. It is impossible to express my sorrow and grief on parting with him. But all this I had to suppress, as far as possible, lest he should sink under his sorrows. For he was much attached to me; and he was old enough to know the peculiarities of our affairs. I gave him the best instructions, of which I was capable. I cast my care for him upon the Lord; I committed him to my heavenly Father for protection. I knew not where he was going, nor when he might return, if ever. The Lord supported me. Blessed be his holy name!

Abigail, a daughter, on whom I made much dependence, had gone, a few days before Asa went away, to take care of the family of a man, who had just buried his wife. On the day of the departure of this son, word came that Abigail was very sick, being violently seized; and that it was not expected she would live. She was some miles distant, and my situation was such, that I could not go to see her. You may try to conceive of my distress. I shall not attempt to describe it. But I saw the hand of God in it all. I recollected the sacred injunc-

tion, "Be still and know that I am God." To obey,
I felt, was both my duty, and support. I endeavored renewedly to give my children up to God in the
arms of faith and prayer; and to feel that if he
should see fit to take forever from me one, or both
of these my children, I ought most humbly to say,
"It is the Lord; let him do what seemeth him good."
I considered that I truly had much more reason to
bless God for the mercies still continued to me, than
to complain of the trials, which I then feared.

But God was merciful beyond my fears, relative
to the sick daughter. Her dangerous symptoms,
the next day abated, and great hopes were entertained of her recovery. But the hand of the Lord
seemed to be stretched out still. It was but a few
minutes after hearing of the more favorable symptoms of Abigail, before I heard a sad out-cry at
the door. I hasted to see what it was. And I
met Caleb leading my little daughter Anna, who
was in her fourteenth year, into the house, covered
with a gore of blood. A horse had run over her,
and had trodden directly upon her face. She looked as though her face was broken all to pieces.
And the blood was profusely flowing from her mouth,
nose, and wounds. As she seemed to be struck in a
measure senseless, she could tell nothing where she
was most injured. I feared for her vital parts.
And it seemed that she must bleed to death in a short
time. A messenger went with all speed for a doctor. We greatly feared it was a death wound.

When I first saw the little daughter in her
frightful plight, the first thought I had was, The
Lord has done it. And the more he is pleased to
try me, by varying the distressing scenes, from
day to day, so much the more I ought to be patient, to not open my mouth, but to be deeply humbled before the great Disposer of all things. God,
at that time, blessed me with such a view, not only
of his wisdom, power, and sovereign right to con-

trol but also of his righteousness and goodness, as no words can express. I thought the more I was chastened, the more I longed to live near to God, and could truly say, with Job, "Though he slay me, yet will I trust in him."

Though this daughter was very badly wounded, yet it was not unto death. She after a while recovered. "The mercy of the Lord endureth for ever." "He hath not rewarded us according to our trangressions." "As a father pitieth his children, so the Lord pitieth them that fear him."

Our oldest son, Samuel, was living as a hired man, in Peacham. As Mr. B. went on his journey, he went to him, ordered him home, and directed him to take another horse, and meet him at such a time and place. Samuel came home, and made ready for his journey. And in five days after the departure of his father, he also left us. My trials seemed to "step on the heals of each other." Such passages as this occurred to my mind; "What is man, that thou shouldest visit him every morning, and try him every moment?" I recollected the sad case of Job; and found that I was in some respects far behind him yet, in point of trials. I entreated God for grace that I might truly say, with that godly man, "What, shall we receive good at the hands of the Lord, and shall we not receive evil?" I think, through the mercy of the Lord, I was enabled, in those days of calamity, to feel as great contentment, as I ever did in my greatest prosperity. I well knew my situation was melancholy indeed; and I ought to be deeply humbled under it, and affected with it. Yet this was my support and comfort, that my afflictions were just such as my heavenly Father had seen fit to order.

My husband I had lost, in a way tenfold more aggravating than death. My two oldest sons were gone; and I knew not where their father would lead them; or how he would treat them. A num-

ber of my other children were gone from me.
Though they were gone by my own choice; yet it
was trying, to have the family thus broken up, and
scattered as sheep without a shepherd. All the
children, whom I now had at home, were Caleb
and Anna, (twins, in their fourteenth year,) and
four other children, the oldest of whom was under
seven years of age. I was expecting very soon to
be confined, and was very unwell. And all I had
in my family to depend on, was the help mentioned
above. The daughter in her fourteenth year was
so injured with her wound before noted, that, so
far from helping me, I had daily to wait on her.

I did at this time truly have occasion to feel my
hourly dependence on God. And I constantly looked to him for fortitude of mind, and for strength of
grace according to my day.

Eighteen days after the departure of Mr. B. a
tenth daughter was added to my family. Every
thing relative to this day was ordered in singular
mercy. My neighbours were most attentive, pitiful, and kind. My little daughter I named Patience. On no christian grace had I thought more,
than on the grace of patience. And the word
sounded pleasant to me. This occasioned the
name of my dear babe. I was so favoured in Providence, as to have health restored to my daughter
Abigail; so that she took care of me in my sickness; and I had every thing as comfortable as
could be expected.

Mr. B. before he went away the last time, put
all his worldly interest and concerns into the hands
of a brother of his, who was a capable man. He
was to sell the farm, as soon as he could to advantage. I had the promise of having half the avails,
as noticed before. It seemed probable it would
take four or five months, for the turning of our
property. I sometimes had great fear that wicked
attempts would be made to wrong me and the

children out of our part of it. But I considered that no person would be likely to purchase the property, without my concurrence in the conveyance of it, I felt it my duty to watch, and guard as far as possible against being defrauded. And I felt a joyful confidence, that God would be my guardian.

One day contemplating my sad condition, and the danger there might be, that attempts might be made to injure me in point of property, I took my Bible:—For this was my daily helper. Here I sought relief.

"Had not thy word been my delight,
 When earthly joys were fled;
 My soul, oppress'd with sorrow's weight,
 . Had sunk amongst the dead."

I happened to open to Psalm 68. "Let God arise," &c. Here I found great joy and relief. The faithfulness of God, in such passages as the following was strikingly opened to my view. "Let them also that hate him, flee before him. But let the righteous be glad; let them rejoice before God. A Father of the fatherless, and a Judge of the widow, is God in his holy habitation.—The Lord gave the word—Kings of armies did flee apace; and she that tarried at home divided the spoil.—Blessed be the Lord, who daily loadeth us with his benefits, even the God of our salvation. But God shall wound the head of his enemies, and the hairy scalp of such an one, as goeth on still in his trespasses—The Lord hath commanded thy strength; strengthen, O God, that which thou hast wrought for us.—The God of Israel is he, that giveth strength and power unto his people. Blessed be God." My fears were now all hushed to sleep. For though outward things looked dangerous; yet I had such view of the weakness of man, in accomplishing wicked devices by his own wisdom, and that all things were in the hands of the God of infinite wisdom, power and goodness, that I felt the greatest safety and satisfaction in giving up all to his disposal And I did firmly believe that God would guard me in my rights against any intrigues of enemies. That, in my case, she that tarried at home, should so far divide the spoil, as to obtain my just part of our property. Christ says, "Your heavenly Father knoweth that ye have need of these things. Seek first the kingdom of God and his righteousness, and all these things shall be added unto you." I thought I had done thus; and God would fulfil his grace.

Sometimes I had such a sense of my own utter unworthiness, in the sight of a holy God, that it was with difficulty I could believe God would accomplish any of these things for me. But again my faith in the mercy of God, which triumphs over all the unworthiness of his most imperfect children, would prevail. Also I could not think that a man, who had committed such sins, and had so greatly dishonored God, and provoked him to anger, would be suffered to prevail against his injured wife and children, so as to rob them of their livings. I thought I might pour out my heart to God in this language of the prophet Habakkuk, "Art not thou from everlasting, O Lord my God, mine holy One? We shall not die, O Lord. Thou hast ordained them for judgment; and O mighty God, thou hast established them for correction. Thou art of purer eyes than to behold evil; and canst not look on iniquity. Wherefore lookest thou upon them that deal treacherously, and holdest thy tongue, when the wicked devoureth the man that is more righteous than he?" Enough I found every day, in God's word, to support my hope and trust in God, for all things needed, both for time and eternity.

My friends and relatives talked, at this time, in a way very discouraging to me, and thought I should never see more favorable times. They considered

Mr. B. a cunning, crafty man; and thought that as he had chased himself, by his wickedness, from his family and home, he would be likely so to form his plans, as to take the property to himself, and leave his family destitute. I considered there is a time to speak; and a time to keep silence; and that, at the present time, the latter was my duty. In relation to God, I considered the duty in this passage, as now enjoined on me; "I was dumb, I opened not my mouth, because thou didst it." And in relation to men, our affairs were so situated, that I thought prudence required me to say but little. When any christian friends spake discouraging, I replied, either that "my times were in God's hands;" and my hope was in him alone; or with some such reply I often dismissed the subject. I sometimes said to my friends, when expressing their great fears for me, that I wondered I must have faith all alone relative to the favorable issue of my affairs; and that others could not hope and believe with and for me, as well as I for myself. I for some reason could not greatly fear; but felt constrained to believe God would protect me. And I did believe that this my hope was not groundless, or senseless presumption. I had been blessed with so much experience of God's mercy and faithfulness, that I seemed, much of my time, unable to doubt whether he would make all these trials terminate in my best good; or even whether they should have an issue favorable to me in my life time. I felt a supporting confidence it would be thus.

About eight months rolled off without my hearing any thing from Mr. B. or Asa, our second son. I had been informed that Samuel had been left, by his father, as a hired man with a Mr. Warner, in Hartford, with whom I had had some acquaintance, and of whom I had a good opinion.

At this time a man, by the name of Ludlow, came to our house from the westward. He said, he came directly from Mr. B. that Mr. B. had returned from the westward to Mr. Warner's of Hartford, where he now was. And that he, and our oldest son Samuel, were well. I asked if Asa was not with him? He said he was not; but his father had left him in Whitestown, New York.

Mr. Ludlow informed me, that he was sent by Mr. B. to know whether I would agree to the sale of our home farm to him, for such pay as he could make for it? I replied that I was so troubled that my son Asa was thus left behind, (he being in a very feeble state when he went from home,) that I knew not how to converse upon the subject he had proposed. He asked if I had a greater desire to see Asa, than to see Mr. B.? I waved an answer to his question. He attempted to palliate for Asa's being left behind. But he did not at all mend the matter.

Mr. Ludlow proceeded to propose his pay for our farm in wild land, lying somewhere in the state of New York; but could pay little or no money. I soon informed him I should not consent to trade thus. He urged the matter, and said it would be very agreeable to Mr. B. who yet would not do it without my consent.

As to our family trials, Mr. Ludlow, without my introducing a word upon the subject, gave me to understand he was not ignorant of them. He said, in short, that he knew all about them. From his conversation, I learned that he did know something about them; but that he had been misinformed relative to the real cause of our family afflictions. He spake freely of those slanderous reports, the evil works of some designing persons. And he seemed to think very well of Mr. B. and seemed very desirous that I too should think well of him. Two things thus appeared evident, viz. That one great object of this stranger was to bring about a reconciliation between Mr. B. and me. And that this was not to be done on the ground of Mr. B's confessing his crimes; but on the ground of his concealing them; and my aiding the concealment. Here then, was ample evidence that Mr. B. was not yet a penitent, nor possessed of an honest heart.

I said but very little to Mr. Ludlow upon these things. I had no inclination to undertake to unfold to him my sad detail of family trials. But relative to our interest, I let him know, very firmly, that I should endeavor well to look out for myself and children. Mr. Ludlow replied, that he had studied law, and practised some as an attorney; and he thought if I did not become reconciled to Mr. B. I was in considerable danger of losing my part of the interest. I told him, he could talk very fast, and make things seem smooth, and fair:—But his talk was in vain. I told him I had no necessity of informing him on what I had made up my judgment and determination. But my mind was fixed. And he could neither flatter nor terrify me to alter it. I should not do what I deemed wrong, whatever the consequences might be. And I did not believe, (I informed him,) that God would suffer Mr. B. to take away the part of the property, which justly belonged to me and my children.

He said it was wonderful to find a woman so firm and unmoved, as he found me to be. He said he knew before considerable of me; but he had pleased himself that he should be able to persuade me to think upon these points much as he wished. But his flattery was in vain.

After a few days spent in our family, Mr. Ludlow went abroad among the neighbors, and spent some days among them. After this he appeared to have relinquished his object, both as to buying our farm, and bringing about a reconciliation between Mr. B. and me. For he said, he believed he had been greatly misinformed; that Mr. B. was a very bad man, and had greatly abused me and his family. He added, that he believed I was an honest and good woman; and he now could not advise me to live with Mr. B. any more.

As to the property, he said, Mr. B. ought to take little or nothing more than he had already taken; but leave it all for those whom he had treated so very injuriously. And Mr. Ludlow added, that he himself would not buy the place. For should he do it, and come to live here, it would look like taking sides with so bad a man. He said there was no way, in which Mr. B. could do so much honor to himself, as to give up his property to his family, and distress them no more. Thus, on conversing with the neighbours, Mr. Ludlow turned directly about, and pleaded my cause as earnestly, as he had before that of Mr. B. He said he now saw the truth of the old proverb, that "one story is good, till the other side is told." He soon went away; but not till he had delivered to me a letter from Mr. B. written at Mr. Warner's, where he now was, requesting me to appoint him a time and place for an interview, that we might settle our affairs. For he said he did not like to come to Landaff. I was glad he was not coming there. I returned an answer that I would meet him at brother Brock's, at Newbury, at such a time. Mr. B. wrote to his brother D. with whom he had left the care of his affairs, to meet him at the same time and place. This brother had found out, about this time, that it was a settled point with me never to live with his brother again. This he appeared much to dislike. His countenance and feelings toward me were much altered. I went to Mr. Brock's, at Newbury, at the time appointed. Mr. B's brother also went. Mr. B. was not yet come. His brother set off to meet him, saying that if *God spared his life*, he would see his brother B. before I should see him. This looked to me terrifying. I did not know how much he might be disposed, or be suffered, to do with Mr. B. to prevent his doing justice to me and the family. But I knew all was in the hands of God. This brother had been gone but a little while, (with a view to meet Mr. B.) before his wife sent an express that one of his children was *dying!* The messenger rode on and overtook him, before he met his brother, and he turned back, and set off for home. Thus he did not see Mr. B. before I saw him; though God *spared his life.* But God took the life of his child. And thus his designs, however cruel they might be, were frustrated.

Mr. B. came to the place appointed. But we were not very successful as to making any arrangement. I found it was to me a most fatiguing thing to get any business of this kind done with him. Want of health, on my part, or want of decision on his, kept us parleying for a number of days. I was among my friends. I had chosen this situation, in hopes it would have some favorable effect on Mr. B. and that I might be favored with their advice. After some days of fruitless attempts, Mr. B. proposed to me to go with him to his brother Foster's of Bradford, a few miles below Newbury, and see if we could not there form our settlement. I felt exceedingly afraid to venture myself with him from among my friends. But it seemed necessary. And I set off with him; looking to God for aid and protection. For I had a longing desire to have this business between us brought to a close, that I might be released from him forever. Excited with this desire, I put on all the resolution possible. And I felt as though I could go through fire and water in the path of evident duty. I now felt as though I feared nothing but sin. Every thing else I could stem, in order to bring our matters to a final termination. I thought there never was any person, afflicted with a most painful sore, who longed more intensely to have it come to a head, than I longed to have our difficulties, relative to our property, settled. I longed to be forever delivered from the man, who had so long and so grievously afflicted me. And I viewed my situation most critical. I greatly feared that I should, through ignorance, or weakness, be a means of dishonoring God, wounding his children, and of giving occasion to his enemies to reproach. The saints were to me the excellent of the earth, in whom was all my delight.

In this interview at Bradford we exchanged our farm at Landaff, for Mr. Foster's farm and seat where we now were. This I thought was favorable. For Mr. Foster's was a saleable place; and a number of men were wishing to purchase it, and would make good and ready payment. I hoped the sale of it could be made immediately; and every thing settled while I was now with Mr. B. With this thought I for some time pleased myself. But Mr. B. seemed in no haste to accomplish our matters. He said, if he seemed indifferent about selling, some person would, by and by, appear and give more. But my thought was, that we should never have so good an offer again. For several men were wishing to obtain the place; and I thought they offered a good price. One of the men offered four hundred pounds; which in those days, and in that part of the country, was a great price for a farm. He would pay five hundred dollars down, and the remainder soon. Mr. B. declined selling to him, under pretence that he could get more. I was very sorry for his delay. But I saw that I must submit to the providence of God, and that his time for my deliverance had not yet come.

I returned to Landaff, and left Mr. B. at Bradford. I hoped and trusted that he would soon sell our place there. And I did not believe he would fail of improving so good an opportunity as he now had. Mr. Foster's family were soon coming on to Landaff. My affairs there must soon be set in order, to leave the house.

I, not long after, received a letter from Mr. B. informing that he had seen a man, who would give five hundred pounds for our farm in Bradford. And he wished to have me come down, as soon as convenient, in order that the bargain might be completed, and I take my half of the avails. It was very painful to me to be called there again. But I saw no way to avoid it. Interest and duty called.

As I knew I must very soon move my family from the place where we now lived, (Mr. Foster's family being soon to come on,) and as I had determined to move either into Bradford, or its vicinity, in order to enjoy greater religious privileges, than I had enjoyed in Landaff;—so I took my family, and moved on, having with me at that time but eight of our children. As our place in Bradford was not yet sold, and as I knew not yet where I should be able to find a place of residence for myself and children, I therefore took my children with me to our house in Bradford, Feb. 21, 1792.

Mr. B. now informed me, that the man, who would give five hundred pounds for our farm in Bradford, was a Capt. Gould, of Granville, New-York. I feared some evil; and tried to persuade Mr. B. to trade with one of the men nigh home, who wished to purchase, as before stated. Mr. B. said it would be very foolish to sell the place for four hundred pounds, when he was offered five hundred. The latter offer would make fifty pounds more for me. And all that was now wanting was for me to agree, and aid in the business. Capt. Gould, he said, would pay the greatest part of the five hundred pounds in cash; and the rest in such articles, as would accommodate Mr. B. as well as the money, so that I might take my half in cash. This I thought was very favorable, if it were true. I could find no evidence of the truth of it, but Mr. B's word, and some corroborating circumstances; such as, that I thought he *must*, and *did*,

9*

wish to sell the place. He could take four hundred pounds for it in Bradford. But this he declined, alleging that Capt. Gould would give five
hundred. This I thought amounted to considerable
evidence, that what Mr. B. said might be true.
And I was sure he wished to go from these parts.
He was afraid even in Bradford of being visited in
the night by such a company, as would handle
him roughly. From a consideration of those things.
I was led to give much credit to his assertions, relative to Capt. Gould's wishing to purchase the
place.

Mr. B. said he had agreed with Capt. Gould to
go to his house in Granville, to accomplish this business, and take his pay; and that he was to go by
sleighing, or before spring opened; otherwise the
proposed bargain was to be relinquished. And he
said, I must go with him to Capt. Gould's, to aid
in the completion of the bargain; and to take my
half of the money. To this I objected. I could by
no means consent to take a journey with him. The
business must be some other way accomplished.
This matter lay along for some time. Mr. B. urged the matter. He said he would not go without
me. For if he did, he could not complete the business without my concurrent aid. Capt. Gould
would not leave his business to come over to Bradford. And Mr. B. said he had agreed to go to his
house. The business, Mr. B. said, belonged to me,
as well as to him. If I would go, we could arrive
there in three days; finish the business at once; I
should return with my two hundred and fifty
pounds; and should very soon be home again with
my children. I labored to dissuade Mr. B. from
his object. I told him I had much rather take my
two hundred pounds here, than to go this journey
for the additional fifty pounds. But my exertions
were in vain. He made the most solemn and abundant promises, that if I would go, and thus aid in

the accomplishment of our mutual concerns, he would use me tenderly and well in every thing. He now appeared very pleasant and kind; and did all that could be done, by words, to convince me of his truth and sincerity in this matter, and to remove all my fears.

I now felt myself in great trial. I knew not how to consent to go. And I knew not how to refuse. The thought of taking a journey with him seemed very sorrowful and gloomy. And I feared that notwithstanding all I could say to others to evince the apparent necessity of it, it would seem a matter of blame; and I should wound the cause of Christ.

I considered the selling of our place, as the first step toward bringing my affairs with Mr. B. to a close; and that I must agree with him in some plan, in order to bring it to pass. And as I had failed of being able to dispose of our property in the way that I thought best; so I saw no way but I must conform to his plan. And I had some confidence in this, that his self interest must induce him to sell the place, and to the best advantage.

In short, it seemed to me Providence was pointing out the way that I must take this journey; that God was laying this additional burden upon me; and I must submit. I finally made up my mind to go with Mr. B. to Granville.

Upon my conclusion to undertake this journey, Mr. B. seemed greatly pleased. He well understood that I was much afraid to undertake such a journey with him, and was perplexed upon the subject. And he appeared not at all offended at this. He talked kindly, and seemed to wish to relieve and comfort my mind. He frankly said, he did not at all blame me, but he truly pitied me, for the fear I had of him; for he said he well knew he had given me great reason to be afraid of him. He now promised, and labored to make me believe, that he would be true and kind, in every thing, in this journey.

For some time, while we were preparing for this tour, Mr. B. took it upon him to labor to gain my confidence, that he had no evil intent in this journey, but was true and faithful in all his pretences. He seemed unable to endure the thought that I should feel jealous that he would farther injure me. He renewed his promise and assertions, that he had no ill intentions; that he would treat me well; and I should have half the property. Sometimes he would say that he now bound himself by a solemn oath, that he would do every thing according to his agreement with me. He said he wished it was in his power to do any thing, that should remove from me my fear, and cause me to feel a confidence in him, that he would do every thing for my comfort, and according to my mind, as far as possible, during the little time that we were to be together; that so I might feel cheerful and enjoy myself. He added, that he well knew he had so broken his promises to me, in times past, that he had no wonder I could not now confide in him. But he said he did not use, in days past, to have such a sense of the nature and weight of an oath, as he now had. For he had of late, thought much upon this subject; and to swear falsely did now appear to him a most heinous crime indeed. One day, renewing his conversation upon this subject, he took my right hand, and pressing it to his breast, said, If you knew what is in my heart, you would not be so afraid of me as you now are. He said, bad as he was, he would not take a false oath for all the world. He asked what he could say, or do, to induce me to confide in him. My reply was, that words could no further do it. It must be deeds, which could evince to me the rectitude of his intentions. He said, he certainly did feel himself as firmly bound by the oaths he had taken, as he could be, had they been made before all the justices in the state. Mr. B. then renewed his query, whether I could not put confi-

dence in him? I allowed that it seemed as though
there must be some confidence placed in solemn
oaths. And as he had voluntarily bound himself
by so many oaths, I did believe that God would
hold him to his word, so that he should not be suffered essentially to injure me, whatever might be
his private intentions; and that however much I
might be called to suffer by his treachery, yet God
would so order it, that I should come off victorious.

One day, before we were prepared to set out for
Granville, Mr. B. took his Bible to read to me. He
providentially opened to Isa. 33, and began to read,
(little thinking, I presume, of the nature of the passage he had hit upon.) "Woe to thee, that spoil-
est, and thou wast not spoiled; and dealest treacherously, and they dealt not treacherously with
thee! When thou shalt cease to spoil, thou shalt be
spoiled; and when thou shalt make an end to deal
treacherously, they shall deal treacherously with
thee! O Lord, be gracious unto us; we have waited
for thee; be thou our arm every morning, our salvation also in the time of trouble, &c." After he
had paused, I remarked to him, that I wished I
could always see the path of my duty in every case,
as plainly as I could see *his* in *some things*, and as
I could see *him* marked out in the passage just
read! I asked him to take particular notice of the
first verse,—the woe against the spoiler, and treacherous dealer, who had commenced this cruelty and
wickedness, without any just cause; none had treated him in this manner. I tenderly reminded Mr.
B. that he did begin to spoil and to ruin our family,
when they were at peace with him, and none were
molesting him. And I added, that if he should
still continue to afflict or deal treacherously with
them, he might expect, according to the passage
read, that God, in his providence, would prepare
some spoiler for him, and would defeat him in
whatever wicked purpose he might think of pros-

ecuting against his family. I was cautious, in this conversation, to be most tender and friendly, and to keep at a great distance from any thing that might appear like railing, or bitterness. But I really thought the circumstance, of his dropping upon such a passage, when he undertook to please me by reading to me, was a clear call for me to deal faithfully with him.

Through all the scenes of these interviews with Mr. B. he never dropped a word as though he wished me to go to Whitestown, or to any other place, to live with him. Nor did I have a thought of his having any such expectation, after all that he had learned of my full determination relative to a final separation from him.

I consented to go this journey to Granville, under the full apprehension that Samuel, our oldest son, was to accompany us. His father desired he should go and live with him, or be at his direction, so long as he was under age. Mr. B. now sent him on, a few days before we were ready to set out, that he might go as far as Mr. Warner's of Hartford, and wait for us.

The thoughts of leaving my family of small children, even for so short a time, was very grievous to me. They were eight in all, who were now with me;—Caleb and Anna, twins, in the 15th year of their age; Chloe, in her 10th year; Amos, in his 8th; Olive, in her 6th; Phinehas, in his 5th; Judith, in her 3d year; and the babe not over a year old. I did every thing I could to render them comfortable during my absence, which I designed, and fully presumed, would be less than two weeks. I accustomed my babe, before I left them, to sleep with some of the other children; which she did very quietly. I wished for one of my older daughters to have been left now with the children. But this was out of my power. A son of Mr. Foster lived now in the other part of our house. I engaged him to pay some attention to my children, and afford help if they needed; which he engaged to do. I directed and charged the two *oldest*, (both together, and separately,) relative to themselves, and their little brothers and sisters, whether in health or sickness.

Having thus done all in my power, I committed my children and myself to God, hoping in his mercy, that he would preserve and bless us while apart, and return me soon and safely to them again.

Tuesday, March 13, 1792, I parted with my dear little lambs, and set off from Bradford, with a *heavy heart;* but comforting them and myself with the idea, that I should soon be with them again.

The sobbings and tears of the poor little creatures, left among strangers, were enough to rend the heart of a tender parent! We were to get to Mr. Warner's of Hartford, the first night. But we moved on very slowly, and came far short of it. Night came on, and we reached only to Norwich, the third town from home. Our moving on so slowly increased my melancholy, which was now distressing.

Wednesday, March 14, we proceeded on our journey. My heart was heavy and sad. I meditated on the scriptures; particularly on Isa. 5, 9, and 10 chapters, where the sins of Israel, and the consequent judgments of God, are set forth. This text, there recorded, dwelt much upon my mind; "For all this his anger is not turned away; but his hand is stretched out still." It truly seemed to me, these words were applicable to my case. God had seen fit to make use of Mr. B. as a rod for my awful chastisement. He had seen fit to suffer him to go on from one act of singular cruelty to another And it was now impressed on my mind that God's anger was not yet turned away, but his hand was stretched out still. But I thought I could truly say,

The Lord is righteous. I have sinned. I deserve
all this, and infinitely more from God. Yea, I need
it for my good. "Though he slay me, yet will I
trust in him." These words gave some refreshment to my heart. "Nevertheless he left not himself without witness, in that he did good." I felt
that I was daily a witness for God, that he was
good. His supporting goodness to me, under my
signal trials, seemed most marvellous.

After another slow day's movement, we came,
just at night, to Mr. Warner's; where we were to
have reached the first day. Here we tarried over
night. Here we found Samuel, our oldest son. I
supposed he was going on with us. But something
was now exhibited as a reason why he could not go.
This struck me with perplexity and distress. I
could not endure the thought of going this journey
with Mr. B. alone. What could I now do? As Mr.
Warner's family knew little or nothing of our difficulties, I could not say much upon the subject. My
entreaties that Samuel might accompany us, were
overruled. He could not go. I must submit.

Thursday, March 15, we proceeded on our way,
and came only to Woodstock.

Friday, March 16, we moved forward. We ascended the Green mountains;—were 8 or 10 miles
rising. The snow was deep. We creeped on but
slowly. On the mountain night overtook us. We
found a house, and put up. The days seemed to
me distressingly long. And after four tedious days,
we had got but little ways ahead. I began to be
distressed with the thought that my absence from
home would probably be considerable longer than I
had expected. But I tried to keep up as good courage as possible, hoping in God that he would order
all things mercifully for me and my children.

Saturday, March 19, we descended the Green
mountains on the west. I asked Mr. B. how soon
he expected to reach the place, for which we set

out? He answered within another day's ride, after the present. He said we had got along much slower than he expected: but said he was not discouraged; we should yet make out well. He begged of me not to think much of it, if I should be gone from the family a few days longer than I had expected. But he surely would do all in his power to accommodate me. He now renewed his most solemn protestations that he would be true and faithful in the business, on which we had set out; and would be good and kind to me in every thing. These promises he did, indeed, renew daily, in the most solemn manner, which words could express.

I had every day moved on with a heavy heart; yet had been supported with the hope, that all would end well by and by; and I should soon be with my family again, and all my difficulties settled. But on this day new and fearful apprehensions arrested me. It seemed to me I had much reason to fear the motives of the man, who was conveying me off. I was going every day farther and farther from my dear little children, who were twined about my heart; and also from all my friends. I had been supported hitherto with the thought that I was in the way of my duty, going on necessary business; and therefore I could leave my children for a short time. But it began now to be powerfully impressed on my mind, that no such business, as had been held up, was to be done; and that it was all a mere plan, to carry me away, and to afflict me! This overwhelming fear, which I could no longer banish from my mind, did not arise from any apparent unkindness in Mr. B. I was determined, therefore, to keep it to myself; and to reason myself out of it, if possible. I thought if it was reasonable for me to set out this journey with Mr. B. as I did make up my mind before I set out, that it was, then I was unreasonable to indulge these present jealousies. But I could not, by such reasonings, control my fears, which had now become almost insupportable. Whether Mr. B. perceived the workings of my tortured mind, or not, so it was, he went on renewing his promises. He said he would go directly to Capt. Gould's, and do every thing according to his agreement with me. And he discovered no resentment at my having been fearful of his word.

This day as I passed by a house, I observed a child sitting out at the door, crying, and the tears running down his little cheeks. It led me to recollect my dear, dear babes at home, fatherless, and now motherless! My heart could no longer contain. It burst in streams of grief from my eyes! I thought probably my children had much more occasion to sit abroad weeping, than had this little one! Thus I went on through this gloomy day sorrowing. We arrived at Wallingsford, and put up for the night.

Sabbath, March 18. I could not induce Mr. B. to rest and sanctify this holy day. He asked the landlord whether people were there permitted to travel on the Sabbath? He replied that none hindered it. My spirits were deeply depressed. I read in my Bible, or psalm book, all the opportunities I could get. And I found great satisfaction in casting my whole burden on the Lord in prayer. In retirement I had great freedom and enlargement of soul. I think God did now enable me to come to him by faith in Jesus Christ, and most familiarly to plead my particular case, and that of my family, before him. It seemed a great support to me to stretch my thoughts (if I may so express it) upon the unlimited knowledge of the Most High. And to think, that he perfectly knew all my circumstances, the distresses of my mind, and every desire of my heart; and that he is possessed of almighty power, infinite wisdom, and unbounded goodness, for the salvation of his kingdom and people;—the view was glorious indeed.

I could now rejoice in the belief that God could and would, in his own time and way, overrule all my trying affairs for his own glory. I felt such confidence in God, that I felt myself to be perfectly safe in his hands. And, though, as to his dealings with me, I saw that clouds and darkness were indeed round about God; yet I could adore him, as knowing that holiness and righteousness were the habitation of his throne.

I not only had a firm and most supporting faith in what the Bible does expressly warrant, that the Judge of all the earth will do right in every thing; but I had a particular and supporting confidence relative to my own case, and my worldly circumstances, that God would eventually deliver me from every present snare.

As we rode along this day, Mr. B. asked me, how I felt now? It seems he was sensible I was much troubled the day before. And possibly he now discovered some alteration in my countenance. I replied that I felt more calm in the state of my mind, than I had the day before. He wished to know the reason of it. I told him, that, as my greater agitations of mind yesterday had not been excited by any words of his, or any new external appearances; but from a consideration of the painful dangerous state of myself and family, presented to my mind in more vivid colours than before; so now, it was not that outward circumstances appeared any more favorable, that I had more comfort than before. But it was that God (whose I am, and whom I serve) had been pleased of his free grace, mercifully to strengthen me in my soul, by giving clear and most supporting views of his glorious character. That I now see such safety in God for all his true friends, that it was most satisfying to my soul to feel that I was now and ever in his holy hands. That I could and did cast my cares wholly upon him, with a full belief that he would overrule my trying affairs for his own glory; and also with a consoling persuasion, that God would eventually deliver me from those evils in this journey, which I had feared; either that they should not take place; or I should come off conqueror in the end.

Mr. B. now renewed his promises, that he would do all in his power that this journey should turn to my advantage. But he now, for the first time, added, that if he had been so crafty as to lead me from home, as he had done, to answer his own worldly purposes, he could not be to blame for so doing. He affirmed this was not the case. Things were in fact as he had told me. But even should it prove otherwise, as things were with him, he should be justified. And he began to talk considerable in this strain. The hint was sufficient. I had but very little doubt left, whether the whole plausible reason of this journey was a most wicked and cruel farce. I labored to persuade him to let me return back. I told him, I would take one of the horses, and the saddle we had in the sleigh, and I would trouble him no farther. He labored to allay my fears by renewed protestations. And he said we had got almost to our journey's end; and I was very foolish now to be discouraged. I therefore concluded in my mind I would quietly proceed, till fact should decide the truth relative to this business. We put up that night in Rupert. Six days had now passed, and had not brought me to the place, where the third day was to bring me, before we set out from Bradford, according to Mr. B's encouragement.

My apprehensions now relative to Mr. B's real object in this journey were very dark and perplexing. I thought I should have reason to recollect these two preceding days, Saturday, and Sabbathday, as long as I lived. Terrors, and divine consolations, had been most singularly intermixed. The one seemingly enough to sink me into the grave, The other most rich and glorious.

I kept all my trials to myself. I scarcely spake a word to any person in this tavern. The landlady asked some questions, and seemed to wish to know something of the cause of what she probably perceived. But I found it convenient to evade her queries. Here Mr. B. behaved more rudely and arbitrarily toward me, than he had presumed to do before. This alteration in his carriage toward me, and also his hints before noted, relative to his having a right to deceive and allure me from home, left me but little reason to hope relative to his motives in leading me to undertake this journey. But I would proceed on in silence, till the point was made certain.

Monday, March 19, we again moved forward upon my gloomy and sorrowful journey. After a while a man fell in company with us, travelling on foot. Mr. B. had been some acquainted with him. They fell into conversation. After a while the man remarked, that he had walked that day 10 or 12 miles, from Capt. Gould's of Granville. This struck my mind as a strange thing, that we were going to this very place, (Capt. Gould's;) that this man had come from there; had come 10 or 12 miles; and was now going on the same way with us! I asked Mr. B. how this was? Oh, he said, we must go to Granville through Rupert, and come in at the lower end of the town, because of a great mountain, which we could not pass with a sleigh. But this man came over across on foot. Mr. B. added, that we should be there by noon, or a little after.

After we had proceeded several miles, Mr. B. threw off the mask at once, and kept me no longer in the dark, at least relative to what was *not* the object of his journey, that it was not what he had ever said. He told me, we are now in the State of New York, and now you must be governed by the laws of this State, which are far more suitable to govern such women as you, than are the laws of

10*

New Hampshire. He added, that he was not going to Granville; nor had he ever intended to go thither, or to trade with Capt. Gould. But all this plan, he said, he had laid, to lead me off from home, that he might get me away from the circle of the Abbots, and Brocks, and my connexions; and then see if he could not bring me to terms, that would better suit himself. And now, if I would drop all that was past, and concerning which I had made so much noise; and would promise never to make any more rout about any of those things; and to be a kind and obedient wife to him, without any more ado; it was well! If not, he would proceed accordingly. He said, unless I would thus engage, he would drive on among strangers, till that sleigh, and those horses were worn out! He went on conversing in this way. Sometimes he would speak of carrying me to the Ohio; sometimes of taking me among the Dutch people, where, he said, I could not understand a word of their language. And then he would talk of taking me to Albany, or where he could sell me on board a ship. He assured me that I should never return home again. He said he had been cunning enough to get me away from home; and now he believed he should be crafty enough to keep me away. I might *cry*, he added, as much as I pleased; but I could not help myself. If I should try to escape from him, he said, he was as long headed as I was; and I might well expect that he could outwit me. Mr. B. said that his brothers, D. and F. and also E. F. were all confederate with him in this plan. And if I should by any means escape from him, and get home, he had empowered his brother D. to keep all the interest out of my hands, and to advertise me in his name, forbidding all persons harboring or trusting me.

Thus, Mr. B. said, he had not been idle; but had been planning to take care of himself. And he thought he had got things in a very good way!

I now, for once, had full confidence in the truth
of what Mr. B. had said. I believed he had, at last,
told me the truth. I could now place some dependence on his words. But Oh, the terrors of such
truth as this! My mind was astonished! My heart
was broken! My thoughts immediately flew to my
poor forsaken children. My grief for them was
truly inexpressible. I can only say, my sorrow was
complete. My grief arose to the highest pitch that
I thought my nature could endure. Every thing in
the whole scene appeared to me calculated to over-
whelm the soul with horror, grief and distress.

As to my own person, I thought little or nothing
of any tortures, or miseries, that Mr. B. might inflict
on my mortal part. If he should kill the body, he
could do no more. But I had other things on my
mind, which were far more dreadful to me than
bodily tortures, or even death. 1. The miseries of
my dear children. 2. The infinite dishonor my
leaving them, and going off with Mr. B. would do
to religion, in the view of those, who knew not the
circumstances, which had led me away. The latter, as well as the former, appeared to me insupportable. And the situation of my family—Oh my
children, my dear, unhappy, forsaken children!—
The thought of their case would rend my heart
with the keenest distress.

I had in seasons past, after the commencement
of my peculiar troubles, been greatly tried, for fear
I should not exercise suitable wisdom and discretion, under my difficulties, so as to do honor to the
cause of virtue and religion. And now I thought
that I had exceedingly erred in judgment, and had
been very unwise indeed, in thus far hearkening
to Mr. B's stories, and being led off by him, from
all my friends.

I had, after all my knowledge of Mr. B's falsehood and wickedness, been in the habit of placing
some dependence on his most solemn assertions.

He had promised so fair and so much to me relative to my having half the interest; and I had been
so much in the habit of fearing him; and such too
was the delicate nature of our difficulties; that I
had been very cautious and sparing, as to conversing freely with any, even my familiar connexions, upon my difficulties. I ever meant to let all
my friends, and the public, by and by, know the
uttermost of my trials. But I was led to think it
would be well to get my concerns with Mr. B. (as
to the property) first settled. I meant they should
understand, (and I supposed they did understand,)
that I never designed to live with Mr. B. any more.
But I had not been very explicit with them relative
to this thing.

I now felt that I had greatly erred, in not having
opened my mind more fully to them, and sought
their advice in every thing; and particularly relative to this journey. They would now see, that I
was gone off with Mr. B. and did not return, as I
promised my family. They would not know where
I had gone with him; nor the true reason. And
now I thought that people, and even my friends
among the rest, must think that I had not only been
very unwise in going off with such a man; but that
I had been deceitful. I well knew that appearances against me, (if I did not soon return) must be
exceedingly dark. And as I had professed religion,
and had been a great advocate for experimental
and practical piety, I thought this appearance of
absconding with Mr. B. and leaving my family,
would bring a great wound on the cause of Christ.
This I knew not how to endure. I thought people
would be led to apply to me what is said of the Ostrich, that "she leaveth her eggs in the earth, and
forgetteth that the foot may crush them, or the
wild beasts devour them; that she hardeneth herself against her young ones, as though they were
not hers." "Even the sea monsters draw out their

breasts to give suck to their young ones; but the daughter of my people is become cruel." "Can a mother forget her sucking child, that she should not have compassion on the son of her womb? Yea, they may forget." Those and similar texts, run in my mind. It seemed as though people, my friends, and even my children too, must be led to think that I had thus become cruel as the Ostrich, and hardened against my own dear offspring, now like tender helpless orphans, exposed to a thousand evils. If they could see what was in my heart, they would see that those children were dearer to me than my life. But the appearance was altogether against me. Oh, what a monster of a mother must I appear to them, when they find that I do not return! How would the friends of religion mourn, that I had given such occasion to the enemy to reproach! And how would the enemies of religion triumph, and say, Ah, so we would have it! I now thought, how little have I done for Christ in my day! How little has God been glorified by me! And now so worthless a creature has suffered herself to be so strangely deceived, and led off from her young helpless family, under circumstances so dubious, in appearance, so inexpressibly mortifying, and so calculated to wound that cause, which I have earnestly longed to see built up; Oh, every thought of these things cut my soul to the quick, and filled me with unutterable pain.

The following sacred passage run in my mind; "Died Abner as a fool dieth. Thy hands were not bound, nor thy feet put in fetters. As a man falleth before wicked men, so fellest thou." It seemed to me wonderful, that I had been so deluded by Mr. B. I was astonished to think I had suffered myself to be so deceived and fooled by such a man, and led off thus from my family and home! It seemed as though I could not have conceived that he could have got me away, unless he had bound me, and taken me by force. David, when

lamenting over Abner, said, "The Lord shall reward the doer of evil according to his wickedness."
And so in the present case, I did believe that God
would reward the man, who had thus injured and
imposed on innocence and credulity; who had exercised such monstrous falsehood and cruelty
against me and our poor young children, in taking
me from them in such treachery. This act of Mr.
B. I truly thought (inasmuch as it was in such wan-
ton violation of so many promises, and oaths voluntarily made) exceeded all his antecedent barbari-
ties toward his children or me. I had once in a
dream; (as formerly hinted,) beheld this man delib-
erately murdering the younger part of his family;
because by his crimes he was forced to flee to a
great distance, and could not take them with him!
Yes, and had seen myself pursuing, with him, a
strange and doleful journey, for an unaccountable
something, having left my family, and not knowing
how they could live, or what would become of them!
Ah, too late is the recollection of the premonition!
I am caught in the toils. Might but the sequel be
verified also, that I escaped from him, and flew
upon the wings of the wind, till I reached my friends!
The God of salvation can effect this also.

Having thus, in silent astonishment, and for a
considerable time, revolved such things in my mind,
I began to fill my mouth with arguments, and to
try what I could effect, in exciting the feelings,
pity and compassion of Mr. B, toward our own dear
offspring, our young, helpless, deserted children
and babes. For it seemed to me impossible that
he should be wholly destitute of any feeling toward
them. I now adopted every tender consideration
and expression, that I could use; (and surely these
flowed with great ease from my wounded and bleed-
ing heart!) to excite some parental feeling in him.
I attempted to address his natural good sense, and
that he must know that our poor little family, left

as they were, must greatly suffer, in body and mind, if not die, unless I returned to them.—Their hearts broken—their cries and sobs continuing;—till their ruin might close the wretched scene! I thus pleaded their lamentable case, in the most melting manner, of which I was capable. But all my expressions and arguments fell as far short of exciting the least apparent feeling in his heart, as they did of equalling the anguish of mine! He appeared to me to have become totally destitute of natural affection, and even for his youngest children.

When I found that this argument was utterly in vain, I adopted another. I began once more to labor to move his compassion toward himself, I most solemnly entreated him to have mercy on himself, and no longer to carry on a cruel warfare against his own interests, temporal and eternal. I told him he was certainly operating against himself; and if he had any regard to his own honor, peace and happiness, he ought immediately to discover it by helping me home again to our poor children, and by afflicting them and me no more. As for my own life, I told Mr. B. that I did now regard it for my children's sakes, much more than for my own. I told him he could do nothing more to me than to kill my body, even should God suffer him to do his worst. But to himself he was doing an infinitely greater injury. For he was taking the most direct way, not only to destroy his honor and peace in time, but to bring himself, body and soul, into everlasting destruction.

Thus I reasoned and expostulated with the father of my children in the most rational, tender, pathetic manner I was possibly able. But alas, I had the distressing mortification to find, that all was in vain. He appeared totally destitute of all feeling upon these subjects.

Although I had lost all affection for Mr. B. as a husband, or a friend; yet I had much feeling for him as a fellow creature. When he exulted in the thought of his being "long headed," and of his having so completely outwitted me; I saw that he felt very strong in himself. He seemed to imagine that he had done all those feats by his own mighty wisdom: —That he now had me in his power, and could do in all things according to his own will. I pitied the poor man; and felt a desire that he might see his own weakness, and nothingness; and that all these things were overruled by God in infinite wisdom, to effect his own purposes. Hearing the boastings of self importance, I groaned, and said, O poor creature, I wonder you can feel so strong in yourself! I told him it appeared so clear to me, that God governed every thing, even his present wickedness, and that he could do no more than God would overrule for his own glory; that he now appeared no more than a moth, or a worm. And I longed to have him know that he was no more in the hands of God, than the least insect. And unless he repented and turned, he would ere long find that the arm of the Lord, whom he was contemning, was infinitely strong; and that it is a fearful thing to fall into the hands of the living God! And as he was now pursuing so cruel and wicked a course, and seemed so disposed to boast and exult in his own wit and power to bring wicked devices to pass, fearless of the indignation of righteous Heaven, so it seemed to me his case was but little short of desperate.

I had, at that time, such a sense of the wretched state and condition of this poor miserable man, who was thus rushing on to his own disgrace and eternal ruin, as words cannot express. I viewed him in the hands of an incensed God; and yet stout-hearted and stupidly unconcerned; glorying in his shame and cruelty. I can truly say: that for sometime my thoughts were carried away from my own momentary affliction, (though it was now so severe,) and absorbed in the view of *his* infinitely more dreadful wretchedness. I realized his accountability to God; and eternity looked near. His awful case made my soul to tremble for him.

But waving the farther consideration of the guilt and spiritual wretchedness of him who had thus betrayed me, I told Mr. B. that if his two brothers, whom he had named, and Mr. E. F. had indeed conspired with him against me, as he had said, I thought I might say with Job, "My brethren have dealt deceitfully as a brook," and that with Job I might add, "God hath delivered me to the ungodly, and turned me over into the hands of the wicked." But I further remarked to him, if it were indeed the case, that four cunning men had, by putting their heads together, planned the ruin of one poor feeble woman, half distracted with cares and troubles, which his wickedness had brought upon her;—if I had really been deceived by his horrid lies and false oaths, I thought he had no great, of which to boast! If he had laid any plan (I told him) which would have been called fair dealing or manly, I should not so much have blamed him. But as the case was, his conduct was most criminal, horrid and insufferable; and that he was still persisting in it in carrying me further from home, and refusing to let me return. On this I told him, he might depend, that should the merciful God ever again deliver me out of his cruel hands, and set my feet on the ground of liberty, he would want four times four as cunning men as himself, again to decoy me away. But as the case now was with me, I told him, I knew no better way than to submit to him as a *captive*. But though he had brought me to such a distance "from all the Abbots, and Brocks, and my other friends," as he was pleased to call them, yet one thing he might depend on;— he had not yet deprived me of an *honest* and *firm heart.* I was yet, as much as ever, disposed to

11

avoid wrong, and do right. And hence I could not, and would not, ever submit to his proposals, to bury past matters, and live with him as his wife, in future. He might carry me, if he was able, to the ends of the earth, or sell me as a slave, as he had proposed, on board a ship. But this should never alter my mind in relation to living with him, the rest of our days, as he wished. I would make no such agreement, let come what would. But I would yield as a captive to his violent hands, till the Lord should see fit to deliver me. I told Mr. B. I could, through Christ's strengthening me, endure sufferings. But the thought of wickedly yielding to his proposals, was to me insupportable. And that I did earnestly pray to God for grace never to comply with this or any wicked proposal; and that God would hold up my goings in his ways, that my footsteps slip not.

As I was in the course of this day mourning for my children, remarking that it seemed as if they could not live without me, Mr. B. replied that I need not be concerned for the children; for they would soon be along after me! intimating that he had agreed with his brother Daniel to bring them on after us; and they were now probably not far behind us! This was a new thought to me. I had never conceived of the possibility of such a thing. And I knew not now whether or not to attach the least credit to the insinuation. I thought, if it were true, Mr. B. had acted a pretty cunning part indeed, in his wicked plans, and had wonderfully succeeded in afflicting me. I thought it might be probable that he had agreed with those, who he said had united with him in planning against me, to sell the farm to the man who was ready to give four hundred pounds for it, and to make out such security among them, as to satisfy him without my signature to the deed; and that either Mr. B.'s brother, or some friend of his, might be coming on after us with the money for Mr. B. and perhaps with the small children, as he said; and were to fall in with us at some place appointed. But in such a case, I could not conjecture what he would think of doing with me and the small children. The thought of such an event was so far from lessening my trials, it added greatly to them. For to be at such a distance from all my friends, with my little children, to be sufferers with me in the hands of a subtle enemy, it seemed, would render my situation comfortless and hopeless.

I told Mr. B. the children I left at Bradford were most of them too young to come such a journey; and utterly unprepared for it, as to clothing and other conveniences. That if they were taken off thus, in this cold season, and among strangers, it seemed as though they must perish; and especially the babe, under a year old, without any mother; it must most certainly destroy her. I begged of Mr. B. that if they were thus coming on, we might immediately turn back and meet them. But he would pay no regard to my entreaties; but said he was not concerned for the children! And as to the babe, he said I need not fear for her. For I never should see her there. He had made other arrangements for her; but would not inform me what they were.

Thus I was carried on. Sometimes I tried to converse on these affairs, and obtain further information. Sometimes I mused in silence, and sometimes I poured out my heart to God. Sometimes I would sit in silent astonishment, and think thus with myself; Is this a reality, that I am here in such a doleful condition, in a part of the world to me unknown; decoyed away from my family; and they deserted by both parents, and in so helpless a situation? Can it be thus? Is not all this a long and melancholy dream of the night? Or has not my trouble driven me to distraction; so that I have, only in a bewildered imagination, come this strange and horrible journey? For I was so overwhelmed with sorrow, and so amazed at myself, that it sometimes seemed difficult to believe that I really was where I was. I was a wonder to myself; and thought I must be to every body else, who might ever know my situation. I sometimes would wonder, why my lot should be so singular. For I thought that in all the stories I ever heard, or the histories or accounts I ever read, I never found any thing so strange as this! or any case similar to mine.

The query struck my mind, like a fiery dart, whether I was not wholly in a delusion in every thing! whether I had ever had right thoughts of God? or had known any thing about myself, or true religion? For I queried, if I were not the worst hypocrite in the world, why would God so give me up into the hands of the wicked? or suffer me to meet with such uncommon trials? If I had ever had that real trust and confidence in God, which I had thought I enjoyed, why would God now be deaf to my cries, and thus suffer my enemy to prevail and rejoice over my affliction? For Mr. B. had indeed asked me, what I now thought of my former hope and confidence in God? He seemed thus to say with Joseph's brethren, "And we will see what will become of his dreams?" and with the impious, of whom we read, "Where is their God?" And truly at first, and under the force of temptation, I hardly knew what to say to him; or what to think of these things for myself!

But this, under my darkest and most severe conflicts, I was soon enabled to say, and feel, that I had as much confidence in the goodness and faithfulness of God, as I ever had. I doubted only relative to my own heart. I felt as though I knew the Judge of all the earth will do right. This consideration, and that I was in God's hands, was my only support. And I thought, "though he should slay me, yet would I trust in him." I felt that it was not a vain thing to pray to God; or to trust in him.

Repeatedly I thought, in the course of this day, *This is Monday, March 19! And never, never, so long as I have my senses on earth, can it be by me forgotten.*

This day we moved on very slowly. But this was no trouble to me. I thought, the slower the better! For I knew not where I was going. Only I knew I was going from home. Hence I had no desire to get forward. Night at last arrived; and we put up. Seven days were now gone since I saw my *dear, dear* children! Oh, it was a comfort to me that God knew how it was with them; and could take care of them!

This evening there was a young gentleman in the tavern, where we put up, who fell into conversation with Mr. B. He argued that there was no certainty that the Bible was the word of God. And that it was of no consequence to attend to that as a rule of life, any more than to any other book. Mr. B. argued against him; and in an able manner proved, that the Bible is the word of God. And that it is a most perfect system of instruction, and its morality the most excellent, even if we had no regard to any thing future of this life:—That all the men in the world, could not form such a system. That if people do not regulate their lives by this holy book, they will have confusion and wretchedness in this world; and in the world to come, eternal misery. But that the rules of God's word, for the government of man on earth, led to peace and happiness here; and they secured for the future world eternal bliss.

I said nothing to all this; but thought Mr. B. very well pleaded the cause of truth. The first opportunity I had to converse with him, I told him, it was very evident he was condemned out of his own mouth. He really appeared well to know his Lord and Master's will. How happy if he were but disposed to do it! I told him, as he knew I had heard his conversation with the young man, it

11*

seemed to me impossible that he should persist in his cruel treatment of me, and carry me any further from my family, my dear, forsaken young children. But alas, I found him as inflexible as ever!

In this house I saw a woman take a child, and dress a very bad bile under its arm. It was about the age of my youngest child. This circumstance seemed to present my own children, especially my babe, before me. I thought, O what would become of that dear little daughter, if she should have such a sore, and no mother to take care of her? My grief I shall not attempt to express!

I queried with myself whether any thing could be done by me to better my situation? whether I could get a letter to my friends; or could find any body to afford me assistance? And truly it seemed that in those respects I was shut up, and could do nothing. Mr. B. was continually watching me; and was cunning and deceitful. Should it be possible for me to write, I had no way to convey a letter. There were no post-offices; and little or no travelling at that time back to the way we came. And should my friends know of my wretched case, I could inform them nothing where they might find me. Nor should I stand any chance in making friends among strangers, who could be led into the knowledge of my case, or afford them any assistance, I must wait,—I must wait a captive in the cruel hands of my oppressor, till God in his mercy should see fit to open some door of escape.

Tuesday, March 20. Again I was moved forward, not knowing whither I went. The weather was now warm for the season, and the snow was almost gone. We dragged along at a miserable rate. Just before night we came to the North river. There had been a road over upon the ice. But it was now very bad at the shores, getting on and off. And the water on the ice over the whole of the river, almost ran into the sleigh. It appeared to me that crossing must now be very dangerous. But we must go over. Mr. B. pressed forward. I thought it probable we should go under the ice. But I had but little fear of death. The Lord carried us safely over. After we had reached the other shore, Mr. B. exultingly said, "Now you are on the west side of the North river, in the state of New York!" Thus he seemed to triumph, in gaining daily advantage against me. The eighth day of our journey soon closed.

Wednesday, March 21. I again went on;—going still further from home, where my broken heart was with my dear lonely children. The consideration of the badness of crossing the North river, that the sleighing was now nearly gone; and every day it was growing worse; and yet Mr. B. was moving on to the westward, led me to conclude it was very improbable our children were coming on after us, as Mr. B. had suggested. I thought I might pretty safely conjecture, that this was all a farce of Mr. B. to torture me. This was to me some relief to think they were not suffering on the road, motherless and among strangers. This day, (the ninth on our journey,) we came to the springs at Saratoga. Here we put up at a tavern near the rock.

In this house a small incident occurred, which presented my family and my troubles fresh to my mind. Here was a little girl about the age, and much of the appearance, of my youngest daughter but one. The woman of the house was gone out to one of her neighbors. The child appeared pleasant and very affectionate to her ma'am. She often repeated, "I wish my ma'am would come home. I want to see my ma'am." Oh, I thought, how often had this got to be repeated in my family, among my dear little forsaken babes. I recollected how my child of the age of this, (and who appeared much like her,) used to be grieved when I was gone; would rejoice when I came home; would run and set me a chair; and would add, she was glad to see me come home? And now to think of leaving her, and the others, in their lonely helpless situation;—that I was going further and further from them daily; and knew not when, how, or whether ever, I should return to them; and they might mourn, and wish ma'am would come, but in vain! the thought of those things seemed too much for my nature. My heart bled in streams of anguish; and it seemed as though I must die! I seemed to myself to hear the moans, and see the tears and distresses of my little children, when they found that their ma'am was no more coming! But I recollected that I and they were in the hands of God, the Almighty; and he could sustain and provide. I knew he could support my feeble frame under these piercing sorrows, and could give a favorable issue to all my distresses.

Thursday, March 22. This morning, before I set out again on my sorrowful pilgrimage, I went to the rock, and well, whence issued those notable springs of such wonderful medicinal qualities. Here I was pleased with the marvellous works of God.

I went on my journey. The many new objects, and new faces, which I beheld, looked to me strange and gloomy. It almost seemed as though every body and thing was my enemy. I thought, that had I been a captive to some foreign enemy, and torn away from home by force, my state would have been preferable to what it now was. But bad as my state was, I could see no way of escape from the hands of my oppressor. And I must move on, as his captive, till God should take pity on me, and open some door of deliverance. I could not but feel a strong confidence that this in due time would take place.

Mr. B. now began to talk of going to Whitestown; and asked if I should not be glad to go there, and see our son Asa? I told him I had indeed a great

desire to see this son. But I had a much greater
desire to return, and see the dear young children
whom I had left. He replied, that I needed to say
no more upon that subject; for I should not return
at present. But he said, if I would promise to go
peacefully to Whitestown, and never to say any
thing more about these foolish affairs, which had
made so much noise at Coos; he would engage that
Asa should come, and bring me over to see my
friends at Coos, the first convenient opportunity.
And if I would not thus engage, he would not carry
me to Whitestown; but would convey me wherever
he saw fit. For he said he would never have any
of that clamor at Whitestown. He meant to live
there; and to live in peace and honor. And when I
got back again to Coos, (he added) I might make
as much noise as I pleased; he cared nothing how
much.

I now thought that as my son Asa was at Whitestown, I had rather go thither, than to any other part of the country, excepting home. I told
Mr. B. I should probably have no inducement to
make known, at Whitestown, the doleful detail of
our family affairs. I had never been so fond of pro-
claiming them, as he very well knew. And perhaps, if I had erred in these things, it had been on
the opposite extreme. He had long and well
known my wish for peace in relation to these, and
all other things; and was fully conscious that he
had no reason for his cruel implications against
me. It was evident Mr. B. could not endure the
thought of his wicked character's following him to
Whitestown, where I now perceived he meant to
live. And if he could extort a word from me, that
I would not expose him there, he would feel safe.
Such a promise I would not make. But I thought
it probable, that if he would treat me well there,
and let me return home, I should not wish to expose his wickedness.

As we passed on, I reasoned with Mr. B. upon his cruel treatment of me, I told him it must be impossible for me ever more to have the least confidence in him. That I must henceforth look out, and take care of myself. I remarked that he was as likely to be sick as others. And should this be the case, I asked, how he could confide in me, or expect that I should be willing to spend my strength, day and night, as in years past, to wait upon him? He replied, he was not at all afraid of me; nor should he fear in sickness, to trust himself in my hands. For he had more confidence in my goodness, than to think I should ever hurt him. I answered that he had no reason truly to think that I should ever injure him by laying any violent hands on him. But if no other way should appear for me to be delivered out of his cruel hands, and God should see fit to cut him off by death, my goodness, (of which he spake,) if I had any, would lead me to view such an event as a merciful interposition of Providence in my behalf. And I added, that I should cheerfully acquiesce in whatever God should see fit to inflict upon him for his most uncommon sins. I thought it suitable to deal thus faithfully with him. We arrived at Ballstown. And the tenth day of our journey closed.

Friday, March 23. We again moved on; but almost without snow. We had, for several days, dragged chiefly on bare ground; and our sleigh was now nearly worn out. We creeped along as far as New Galloway. Here Mr. B. found he must leave the sleigh, and we must take to our saddles. Our clothing and articles we packed up in saddlebags, and sacks, as well as we could. Here for the first time I learned, to my grief and disgust, that Mr. B. before we left home, had taken quantities of my best clothing, and some clothing of the children's which I had just before procured for them;—and had crowded these things into bags, among his sleigh-furniture! He calmly told me, that he had taken these things, not knowing how great efforts I should make to get away from him. And he thought it best to have as much in his hands as he could! He added, that he should have taken more; but he feared he could not, without my knowing it! And this would have defeated his whole plan. Relative to my own clothing, I cared but little. But I was grieved to the heart for my dear children. For now their father had not only taken me in such a manner from them; but had also robbed them of those articles of clothing, which they really needed; and with which they were well pleased. But alas, this was as good as could be expected from this hardened abandoned man.

One more piece of his cruelty, which had taken place on the road, not long before, I will here relate; which was most grievous to me at the time; but which I now conclude was all a sheer falsehood, to effect his own purposes. As I was pleading with Mr. B. to let me return back, he said, it would no more do for me to live in my own country, than it would for him. I must leave my own kindred and acquaintance, as well as he. This he said he had learned, while he was in those parts. And that a gentleman had assured him, before we came from Bradford, that it was best for me to go off, and leave those parts. I asked on what account? or what crime I had committed? He replied that he understood my fault was, in being too favorable to him, after it was believed he had committed such abominable crimes. And as the case now was, he thought I should do much better to go off among strangers, than to think of residing among those who had formerly been my friends.

I told Mr. B. that if what he had said was true, I was disgusted at his hard-heartedness, that he could bear to me the grievous tidings; when he well knew that he, by his most uncommon wicked-

ness and cruelty, had occasioned my past overwhelming sorrows. And that now he could gravely
tell me, that as he had been the guilty cause of all my
friends withdrawing their tender affection from
me, so I had better flee my country. But, I further
replied, if all he had said was true; or my friends
felt toward me, as he stated; I would never run
from them. And this I told him, furnished an additional motive for me speedily to return. For if I
had done any thing worthy of death, or of bonds, I
refused not to submit to them. If I had done any
thing wounding to my christian brethren, I desired to return and be dealt with according to the
laws of Christ. And the more I had failed, in
times past of living according to the rules of God's
word, so much the sooner would I fly to my christian friends for aid; and would the more closely ad-
here to them, instead of running from them.

Our sleigh we left with a Mr. Ephraim Smith,
in New Galloway. Mr. B. set me upon one horse.
He piled as many of our effects as he could on the
other. And he himself set off on foot, by my side.
We appeared like travellers indeed! I can hardly
say the object of my journey seemed to me adequate
to all this appearance.

The sleighing had been so bad, that journeying
in the sleigh had been very wearisome to me. But
I found it worse and far more dangerous, going on
horseback. For the road was very bad; and my
conveniences for riding were not by any means
pleasant. Mr. B's base treatment and cruelties
had increased. I felt myself in the hands of a cruel tyrannical enemy. The eleventh day of our
journey at last closed.

Saturday, March 24, we moved on toward
Whitestown, as far as Stonerobby; and put up at
a Dutch tavern.

Sabbath, March 25. Mr. B. must go on; though
was the Lord's day. This was very different

from the manner, in which I had been accustomed
to keep this holy day of God, in seasons past. Two
young men, who fell in with us, the day before,
accompanied us. One of them was very kind and
attentive to me, as the riding was very bad. He
would stop and see how I got over bad places; often remarking, that he feared I should be thrown
from my horse, and injured. And truly I much
feared for myself. We came to what is called
Canada-creek. The ice was chiefly broken up and
jammed together. It seemed impossible to cross it.
These young men helped Mr. B. get the horses
over; wading and plunging as they could. Then
one of them took me upon his back, and waded
over with me. It seemed as though we must have
plunged together into the water. But kind Providence prevented. I thought I had great reason for
thankfulness for God's protecting mercy in so many dangers.

In a tavern, this day, I had much satisfaction in
reading in a book, which I found there, upon *God's
tender and constant care for his own chosen friends,
and his delivering mercy in times of trouble.* I found
it was directly to my case. God here furnished me
with rich consolation. I tried to obtain the book to
carry on with me; but could not. How happy if
tavern-keepers would always keep such books
within the reach of travellers. In this way they
might often refresh some of the weary pilgrims of
Zion.

Where we put up on Sabbath night, the children of the family brought my own dear forsaken
offspring to my mind with pain and anguish. I
saw here a little brother and sister, from eight to
twelve years of age. I soon perceived, by the par-
tialities which appeared from the mother, between
them and the other children, that they had a *mother in law.* And I found, by some things dropped
afterward, that it was so indeed. Their own moth-

12

er was dead. My feelings exclaimed, Oh my
children, who have no mother to take care of
them!

Monday, March 26, we came near to Mohawk
river. Being unable to cross the river, we put
up with a Dutch family. There soon came on a
rain, and carried the ice out of the river.

On Wednesday we moved on with a view to
cross the Mohawk. In a house, by the side of the
river, where we were sometime detained, while
preparation was making to cross, some things
among the children of the family brought strikingly
to my view the state of my own dear forsaken children at home. I went abroad to give vent to my
broken heart in a flood of tears. It seemed as
though I must have sunk under my burden, and
have wept my life away. Mr. B. found me; and
was displeased to see me thus overwhelmed in
grief. He inquired for the cause of my sorrows. I
replied, that I wondered he should be so insolent,
as to make such inquiry; when he knew what he
had done in taking me away from my poor children;
in addition to all the other things he had done to
destroy all my comforts in this life. He told me to
wash my face, and go into the house, and appear
cheerful; or the people would wonder what was the
matter. His guilt often made him fear that my
tears and sorrowful looks would betray him,
as being the guilty cause of them. Repeatedly, when we had been coming to a house, where Mr.
B. had been some acquainted, he said he should be
glad to go in, if I would but put on a cheerful countenance, and be sociable. And he would urge me to
lay aside my sorrow, at least for a while; and behave
and appear as though all things were well. These
things brought to my mind the case of the captive
Jews. "By the rivers of Babylon there we sat down;
yea, we wept, when we remembered Zion. We
hanged our harps upon the willows in the midst
thereof. For there they that carried us away cap-

tive, required of us a song; and they that wasted
us, required of us mirth; saying, Sing us one of the
songs of Zion. How shall we sing the Lord's song
in a strange land? If I forget thee, O Jerusalem, let
my right hand forget her cunning. If I do not remember thee, let my tongue cleave to the roof of
my mouth; if I prefer not Jerusalem above my chief
joy." I really felt myself unable to comply with
such requests. They generally enhanced my grief.
So that Mr. B. when he came to the house of his
old acquaintance, instead of going in, he would
usually pull his hat down over his face, and slip by
as fast as he could.

We reached German Flats, and put up for the
night. Here I read in a book an affecting account
of a young lady, who suffered much for her virtue;
but came off victorious at last, and was delivered
from her enemy. Here God gave me a little
strength and courage, to hope for his delivering
mercy. Repeatedly, on this doleful journey, books
seemed providentially dropped into my hands, peculiarly calculated to afford me consolation. But
most of my leisure moments I employed in reading
that book of all books, the word of God. Mornings
and evenings, and sometimes our calls at taverns, in
the course of the day, afforded me opportunities for
reading and retirement. These I esteemed as my
daily and necessary food. Blessed be my God and
Redeemer, that he has purchased and given this
sure word of prophecy; this rich heavenly blessing;—this guide to direct and regulate the hearts
and lives of his chosen and redeemed through this
wilderness state. Blessed be God, the Father, Son,
and Holy Ghost, for this inestimable blessing; and
that he has, from time to time, fed and nourished
my soul by the rich spiritual food therein contained, and made it sweeter to me than the honey.

I often saw something among children which affected me, and led me to recollect my own forsak-

en brood. In this house, their youngest child was about seven years old. He was unwell; and was often asking his mother for something. Her patience seemed exhausted. She said, "You was all day yesterday saying, Mother, mother, mother, about something! And now you have begun the same noise again this morning! I am tired of it; and will not have it!" It cut me to the heart, to see her so wanting as to kind affection to her dear offspring. Oh, I thought, if I could see my children again and hear them calling upon ma'am for aid, I should be so far from being out of patience with them for it, that I would willingly spend and be spent for their good.

Thus I was often meeting with instructive incidents, which sometimes excited my grief and anguish; and sometimes things which animated my hopes, and filled me with consolation in the faithfulness of my Almighty Friend.

Thursday, March 29, I again moved forward, under the control of my enemy, on the western side of the Mohawk. The riding was now bad in the extreme, and very dangerous. In days past, after we left our sleigh, there had been many snow drifts, some two, three, and four feet deep, and so soft, that the horse would plunge in them; and his fore-feet often sink down, so that it seemed as if I must have been thrown over his head. And where the snow was gone, the frost was coming out of the ground, and the horse often broke through. But the Lord watched over me with tender care, so that my life and limbs were kept in much safety. Now we had arrived where the snow was chiefly gone, and the frost mostly out of the ground. But we had mud and mire, and much water. Every stream was much swollen. And the country did not furnish bridges. Eight streams I rode through this day, most of which seemed like rivers for width, and so black with mud and dirt that we could not see their bottom. Repeatedly I was in much fear of drowning. Adored be my gracious Preserver and God, who upheld me. He carried me safely over seven, out of eight, of these streams. And in the last he preserved my life. We came to the eighth stream. It was broad and black with dirt, and looked terrific. I was much afraid to venture in. I had in all these streams to venture on alone; as Mr. B. had sold his other horse; and had to get over these streams as he could. I rode in a number of rods, and came to a bridge just under water, which lay floating. The other side was fast on shore. Here I was stopped. A man appeared at a little distance. I begged of him to come to my assistance. He came, and with a lever crowded away some of the logs that were floating next to me; and attempted to hold the next log with his lever; and told me, he thought my horse would rise upon the bridge. The horse exerted himself with all his might, and brought his fore feet upon the logs of the bridge, which rolled and sank. Upon this he fell upon his side, and plunged me into the water among the rolling and sinking logs, where the horse was flouncing, but could not get out. It seemed as though I must now have been dashed in pieces, by the horse's feet, and the logs. I was bruised, and some injured in one shoulder. The man pulled me out, and helped me to the shore; and then he and Mr. B. got out the horse. God kindly preserved my life, and kept my bones from being broken. I squeezed out a little of the water from my dripping clothes, and went on. We came to a tavern, and put up for the night. Sixteen days had now rolled away since I left my dear children; who before this time had probably begun to wonder at my not having returned. Poor forsaken beings! they must long wonder, and mourn in their orphan state, if God spare their lives!

Friday, March 30. We were now within four miles of Whitestown. We moved forward. I be-

gan to see people broke out with the small pox. I
had never had it. Here was a new occasion of alarm.
I found it was abundant among the people of that
country. Mr. B. saw my trouble on this account,
and tried to persuade me there was no danger. I
resolved to be as cautious to avoid it as possible.

This day we passed by Esq. White's, where Mr.
B. had been acquainted. He pulled his hat over his
eyes, and whipped up my horse, to get by as soon
as possible. No wonder he was ashamed to be
known. Our appearance was truly odd; we having
been, as it were rolled in mud and mire.

Mr. B. said, that we should now soon come to
Mr. Payn's in Whitestown, where our son Asa
was living. Mrs. Payn, he said, was a clever
woman as ever lived; but she knew nothing about
religion. And you, (said he to me) may be as religious in heart, as you please, but it will not be
best to make any shew of it there; but to be
as cheerful and brisk as possible; and you will
please, and fare the better. I groaned in spirit, and
said a few words in favor of the visible fruits of religion; and that those who have the love of God in
their hearts will and ought, on all proper occasions,
to let their light shine before men, to the glory of
God. I now felt a heart to mourn over poor grace-
less sinners, who know not God, and the Saviour;
and know not their lost estate without Christ, nor
the worth of their precious souls. But, while I was
grieved for sinners, and for the wretched state of
my present oppressor in particular; I could find
abundant reason to adore the God of grace, for his
gracious covenant, well ordered in all things and
sure; and for the safety of his dear people in
Christ; that while they have a tempting devil
to resist, their inbred corruptions to subdue, and
the threats, flatteries, and fiery darts of wicked
men to withstand; the Captain of salvation keeps
them, and guards his flock; and through his

strength the weakest saint shall win the day. I could now see that if my religion were in the hands of Mr. B. it would soon be annihilated. I could praise God that I hoped the support of it was in infinitely better hands.

Mr. B. further said to me; (for it seems he was not without fears, that I should dishonor him in Whitestown, or detect the folly of some of his stories;) When you come to Whitestown, I would not have you tell any body that you have more than seven children. For that is the number that I have told them I have; viz. four sons, and three daughters. And I have never allowed Asa to tell of any more. I asked Mr. B. what I should say, if any should ask me how many children I had? He said, I might tell them that it was none of their business. I told him that was a civil question; and hence would seem to demand a civil answer. I added, that my troubles were such, that I surely should not wish to converse with any strangers upon my family or our affairs. But if I should be asked the number of our children, I should not tell a falsehood; nor yet give an uncivil answer. Well, said Mr. B. if you tell them you have seventeen children, I will still say that I have but seven. And you may be answerable, at the expense of your character, for the other ten. I replied, that I wished to have no occasion to say any thing upon the subject. But if I had, I should tell the truth, even if it were at such a risk of my character.

We arrived at Mr. Payn's. Here I met my dear son Asa. I praised God in my soul, that he had preserved my son, and me, thus far; and that we could see each other again in the land of the living. Thus my joy and sorrow were anew excited. For while I had joy in beholding this son; my grief for the deserted state of his little brothers and sisters, at so great a distance, was inexpressible.

This son soon expressed his anxiety for me, relative to the small pox; and asked, what I designed to do? For he said it was in almost every house for miles round; and was then in Mr. Payn's house. I told him, that his father said I should not be in danger: He said he could not tell why he should say thus; for the fact was quite the contrary. And he begged of me to be innoculated immediately. For warm weather was coming on; and if I should take it the natural way, it would probably go hard with me. I was soon convinced that his advice was good. For people, broken out with the small pox, were in the house, and continually passing, going in and out. I hence applied to a physician, and was innoculated.

I took opportunity to converse with this son, with some degree of freedom, upon the occasion of my being there: how his father had decoyed me from home; and in what a situation I had left his young brothers and sisters, as well as the evils of my journey. I had ever been exceedingly cautious, as to conversing with my children upon my family troubles. It had seemed as though I could not enter into these things with them. But now it seemed necessary, and calculated to afford some degree of relief to converse with some freedom with this son, who was peculiarly understanding, and amiable, for one of his years. I seemed now to have *one friend*, to bear some small part of my burden with me; and who could give an explanation of some things to my friends should I never live to return to them.

Mr. B. had told me, just before we arrived at Whitestown, that he had bargained for some land, near Mr. Payn's on which he was going to work; and we were to board at Mr. Payn's. But I soon understood, after arriving here, that Mr. Payn did not intend we should board with him, nor live in his house. Mr. B. had agreed that Asa should live with him till May.

My situation was truly pitiable. I had but one dollar in money. When I set out from Bradford, I had two dollars. But Mr. B. had urged away one of them, just before we reached Whitestown. Here I was, among strangers, at this distance from home, and going to be sick with the small pox. I saw no way but I must be shelterless, and destitute of a bed to rest my head on, as well as destitute of all other conveniences.

I talked a little with Mrs. Payn upon my trying situation. I told her when I left home I expected to return again in a few days, and made no preparation to have the small pox, nor even to have come to that place. And now, as I knew not what to do with myself, I begged of her to take pity on me, and let me tarry some where in their enclosures, till I had got through with the small pox. She said she did truly pity me; but it was not in her power to help me; for her husband said he could not have us there. I learned (though not by her) that Mr. Payn did not like Mr. B. and would not harbor him. And verily I could not blame him for this. But they liked Asa very much, and were kind to him, and to me while I tarried. Mr. Payn would sometimes speak hard things against religion; which I suppose he did on my account. He knew nothing about religion; and nothing of my troubles. I conclude he thought, by what he saw in me, that I was what is called religious; and that he imputed my gloomy appearance to this; and hence conceived an unfavorable opinion of religion. Of this I was afterward informed. While I was here for a few days, I could find little or no work to do. I hence spent considerable of my time in reading. And as there seemed no place for retirement in the house, I usually walked abroad several times a day, to some retired place. In a few instances, when I

had a good opportunity, I said a few words to recommend religion. But I endeavored to be cautious
and prudent in relation to this, as I thought duty
required. It is an object of prayer with me, that God
will enable me always, while I live, to plead the
cause of true piety in heart and life, both by my spirit, words, and examples; that I may thus let my light
wisely shine before men. But I should be exceedingly sorry, if, by my sadness under deep affliction, or by my spending more time in religious duties, at such seasons, than is common for christians,
I should give a just occasion to any to think unfa-
vorably of true godliness.

I could now see no way to obtain a boarding
place. Nor could I do any thing, but cast my burden on the Lord, who hears the cry of the needy.
I remembered that God is my Rock, and my Helper; and that he is ever able and ready to help the
needy in distress, who seek his aid. And I desire
to adore the condescending aid of the Lord of glory. I again became a witness of his goodness, and
that his mercy endureth forever. He regards the
wants of such a vile worm; and his hand is never
weary of bestowing favors.

While I was thus at Mr. Payn's, in doubt what
would become of me; there came two men from a
new settlement, about twenty miles distant, called
Unadilla,—a Mr. Sikes, and a Mr. Culver. These
men seem to be led to feel interested in our affairs.
And they told Mr. B. that if we would go with
them, we might probably be accommodated. Mr.
B. concluded we would set off immediately with
them, and leave Asa here, till his time was out in
May. I seemed not to care which way we went.
For the people and country were all strange to
me. And I knew nothing what would be best. But
I was grieved to think of parting with my son. I
had hoped he might be with me, or near, during
my sickness with the small pox. However, this

seemed to be providentially denied; and I had learned to submit to the will of my heavenly Father. Mr. B. had exchanged the horse on which I rode to this place, for one that had but just lived through the winter, and seemed the poorest and feeblest horse I ever saw. On this I must ride twenty miles into the wilderness.

Wednesday, April 4, I parted with my dear son, and we set off with the two men. Every step my poor feeble beast took, she seemed as though she would fall to the ground. And she did indeed fall many times, in going these twenty miles. I did not dare to put my foot in the stirrup, but sat upon my guard every moment, ready to spring off upon my feet, as soon as I perceived she was falling. This new road was miserable at any time in the year. But now it was all mud and mire; a great depth of snow having just been carried off by a rain; so that the badness of the riding was dreadful, occasioned by stones, roots, and mire. It seemed as though I never could get through this twenty miles? or at least it seemed as though I could hardly hope to get through without broken bones to be added to my sickness with the small pox which was just before me. Messrs. Sikes and Culver were so kind as to keep with us, and pilot us along through the woods. Night came on. We found a house, and put up with such accommodations as we could find. The next day, as we moved out still further from the old settlements, the road, if possible grew worse. This day we met several men in company. One of them, looking earnestly on Mr. B. and on me, said with great emphasis, Friend, I fear you do not set highly enough by your wife! Mr. B. made no reply; but looked down; and moved on as fast as he could. I asked Mr. B. who this man was that thus addressed him? He replied, that he did not know nor care!

Just before night, we came to Mr. Sikes'. When we came up, I thought we had come only to some camp in the woods; and little thought of there being a family, or of its being his home. He had been there but a short time, and had fallen a few trees, just to set a log house and be able to see the sun. I thought I had great reason for gratitude to God, that he had brought me through, and I had no broken bones. I found here a kind woman, and a pleasant family, of one son and two daughters. I shall ever remember this family with tender respect.

I expected to be sick, in a few days, with the small pox. This poor log house was very open and cold. It was covered with bark, which shed but a small part of the rain. They had no chimney; and no door, but an old coverlet. The floor was bass timber split, but not hewed; so that it was uneven and rough. Here I slept on a poor bed, on this uneven floor. But I was so far from feeling as if I had reason to complain; that I thought I had great reason to praise God, that he had provided for me among strangers so good accommodations and furnished me with so good friends as I here found.

I found I was now at a great distance from any physician, and from any stores. I could find no common garden herbs, such as people usually keep by them. So that my accommodations for sickness were truly frightful. Before I was taken sick I found an opportunity to send to a store. I sent and procured a little wine. This, and a few pills, from the doctor, who innoculated me, is all I had for my medical aid in the sickness then daily expected. Truly I was shut up to the faith, to confide in God, as my Physician for the body, as well as for the soul.

Thursday, April 12, I began to feel the symptoms of the small pox, which came on with some degree of severity. After sometime I was sensible

I needed something to bring out the disease. Could I have had a chicken, or a small piece of fresh meat, I would have given any thing in my power. But no such thing, nor one spoonful of milk, could be obtained. I had a most distressing and sick night, and seriously apprehended it must be my last sickness. I thought my want of proper help and accommodations was probably to be the means of my death. My earnest prayer to God was, that God would fit me for his holy will. I was most feelingly sensible that my whole dependence was on him, in whose hands my life and breath are, and who could heal as easily without proper means, as with, when they are beyond our reach.

Sabbath, April 15, I began to break out. But the disease came out very slowly; and my case was lingering and distressing.

Mr. B. and Mr. Culver, soon after we came to Mr. Sikes's went a little distance into the woods, and united in their business, to clear a small piece of land, and erect a log house. After working there a week, Mr. Culver and his wife moved into their log hut, while yet it had no roof to shelter them from the rain. On Monday, the day after I began to break out with the small pox, Mr. B. came and told me that I must move to this hut of Mr. Culver's! I was astonished; and remonstrated against being moved at this time, and into a new log house too, not half finished, and the timbers green and wet! I found he was determined I should go. I pleaded and entreated that I might tarry where I was, till I had recovered from the small pox; or at least, till I was better than I was at present. But all was in vain. I must go on that very day. Not a word had ever been mentioned to me about changing my situation till now. And now it must be done at once. For a short time I sunk under discouragement. It seemed as though I must be destroyed; and as though this was Mr. B's object.

13

I was now in the most critical period of the whole disease. I told Mr. B. that it really seemed to me he had set out to put an end to my days; and that he was determined to pursue the matter, till he had effected it. While I was dejected under this trial, these words of Christ came to my mind with cheering power. "The foxes have holes, and the birds of the air have nests; but the son of man hath not where to lay his head." I now felt a calm and patient resignation to the will of God. For the words had a transporting influence on my mind. I thought if the infinite Lord of heaven and earth would condescend to endure such poverty and sufferings for guilty wretched man, his enemies; why should I think much of my low and trying circumstances? If such a Saviour was given for God's chosen, what confidence might I feel in his wisdom and goodness? And how might I rejoice in resting all things in his hands? He could work wonders of mercy in my greatest trials.

I now, in my most feeble state, went with Mr. B. to Mr. Culver's, Monday, April 16. My strength held out to be conveyed there much better than my fears had been. The new green floor, and every thing being green and damp, made it very uncomfortable and dangerous. But the family were kind. As to conveniences for sickness, they were truly wretched. They had no bedstead. Nor could they get straw to fill any under bed. They laid my bed on the green split logs, which were very damp. The first night I was there, it began to rain just before day. We had next to no covering to the log house. It rained but a trifle before light. The two men went immediately to the woods, to peeling bark, to cover us from the rain. They began to place their barks over me, and then proceeded on, till they had covered the little hut all over. And they had nearly got it done, before it began to rain hard. Herein appeared the kindness of Providence; also in keeping me from taking cold in my miserable accommodations; which in former times it seems must have destroyed my life, had I been so exposed even in health. My soul was now full of admiring thoughts of God, for his merciful loving kindness.

After I had got considerably better, I was told that I needed something to take the disease out of my blood, so that I might afterward enjoy health. But I could have no help in this way. And I remained very feeble, having weakness and trembling in my stomach and limbs, shortness of breath, and general debility. These distressing symptoms continued for a long time. After vegetables appeared in the spring, I used to creep round in the woods, a little distance from the house, in hopes of finding some roots of a medicinal nature; but I could find none. But I found pleasing seasons of retirement in my frequent lonely walks. It was to me a delightful thought to consider the omnipresence of God, that no time, place, or thing, can hide from his all pervading eye: and that while I must mourn the absence of my earthly friends, I could rejoice in an Almighty heavenly Friend, without whom all other friends are but empty names; and whose loving kindness is better than life.

I here was struck with my change of affairs. When in my family, I had much hard labour, and pressing cares daily for my children. Here I had nothing to do; alas no child to call upon me! Nor could their exigencies reach my eyes or ears; nor my hand administer to their relief. But oh, their wants could reach my heart. Poor, dear creatures! What can be their present situation? What may be their distresses? What must be their views and queries, relative to my having thus left them? When, or how shall I reach them again? Oh, am I 270 miles from those dear forsaken and suffering parts of myself? and I in so feeble a state; and the way between me and them so bad and gloomy! The thought seemed enough to destroy nature! Oh God of mercy, may thy time of relief soon arrive! May the door be opened for me to escape from this dismal captivity, and be found again in the bosom of my dear, dear family!

I feared my anxious and creature fondness would rise too high, and place idols between me and my heavenly lover. I feared my own heart in this respect. For though I loved my children as my own life, yet I could not bear to have any creature, even my own line, interfere between me and my eternal All.

Mr. B. was now at work in union with Mr. Culver, to prepare a small piece of land for tillage. From this I joyfully inferred that I had reached my journey's end; that I should be carried no farther from home. I now set my heart on some hopeful turn to my captivity; and to think what plan I might devise for the purpose.

Mr. B. probably never designed I should return again to my family. He dropped some words from which I learned that he designed to return in May, to sell our farm in Bradford, and get his property there. Now, I thought, if ever I return, it must be while he is gone. But how could I accomplish such a journey? I never rode a journey of 20 miles alone; and this was 270 miles, among strangers, and a way which seemed to my imagination most formidable. And I was left by the small pox so feeble, that had I been at home, I should have thought it a great undertaking to have ridden out two miles, without some one to wait on me. All the money I had, was less than a dollar. Where could I get a horse? What could be done? I believed that God could provide, and carry me home; and this was all I could say. I could see no way how such an event could be effected. But my thoughts, and my prayers were hovering upon the subject. I was sure if

God opened the door, and enabled me to make my escape, and reach home, it would indeed be a remarkable providence. I could have no doubt of the expediency of my fleeing from my present captive state, if God should afford me opportunity. I earnestly besought the Lord that he would interpose for me, and open some door for my return. I really thought my truly difficult case required an unwavering confidence in God, an extraordinary faith in his providence and mercy; even such a faith as the martyrs had in times of persecution.

I expected, that when Mr. B. should go to Bradford, he would dispatch his business as fast as possible—and probably it was already in train by the agency of his accomplices in those parts; that he would aim at taking all the interest into his own hands; and perhaps would take the children, and be gone. Where he would go with them, or how dispose of them, I could not conjecture. But, from many things he had said and done, I was confident he had no notion of bringing them to this place. I hence thought I had much reason to fear, that if I did not return to Bradford soon after Mr. B. I should never again see my children. I therefore felt willing to undergo any hardships, if I might but arrive in time to save my family. My great bodily weakness appeared very formidable in the way of my journey. But I hoped God would restore my health. I pondered these subjects, and endeavoured to weigh every thing maturely. I thought I must carefully eye the hand of God, and learn what he would have me to do.

Should Mr. B. ride his horse to Bradford, which I thought it most highly probable he would do, then it seemed as though no way was left for me to go. And I did not dare to ask him, or say a word upon the subject, lest he should suspect my designs, and defeat them. But I carefully watched his words with Mr. Culver, in order to learn his designs. I

13*

had hoped that Providence would so order, that Mr. B. might go this journey on foot, that I might have the horse. And to my joy, I heard him one day inform Mr. Culver that he designed to go on foot. I thought this a small token, at least, that God would prosper my designs.

About the first of May, my son Asa's time being out with Mr. Payn, he came to us; and went to work with his father. As he was very feeble when he went from home, a year before, so he still remained feeble. Now I could again praise God that I might see one of my children, and have him in the house with me. Now I had one friend in whom I could confide. I queried in my mind whether he could afford me any help in my getting home. But could see no way how he could; for he was too feeble to travel such a journey. And to obtain another horse would only increase my difficulties, and expenses.

I wished to learn the names of the towns, through which I must pass, in returning home; for I did not remember them. And I did not dare to make, or have any inquiry concerning this, lest Mr. B. should suspect my intentions. He was speaking, one day, of his bringing some of the children over with him, when he should return. I now conceived I might lay a plan to learn the road from him, without exciting his suspicion. I told him I had thought much upon the long and tedious road I had travelled; but I could not recollect many of the towns' names. And, as he talked of bringing some of our children the same way, my mind must of course be held on the road; and it would be some pleasure to me to know the names of the towns, through which they must pass. I wished he would just name them to me. He cheerfully began. I told him, my memory was poor; I wished he would just write them. He did so; and wrote me all the towns from Unadilla to Bradford. I wondered his sagacity did not sus-

pect my design. But God mercifully prevented it.
This I construed as a little token, that God would favor my premeditated escape. I thought how easily
God could turn the counsel of Ahithophel into foolishness, when he was determined to deliver David
from the power and craft of a vile usurper. With
infinite ease, I was sensible, God could turn the
crafty and wicked designs of my present oppressor
into foolishness; and deliver me, and an injured family out of his cruel hands.

My thoughts and hopes now rose high. It seemed as if I could already praise God for a begun deliverance. I rejoiced that he could most easily defeat the plans of his enemies, and bring them into
their own nets; and cause his afflicted children to
escape.

Just before Mr. B. set off his journey, he told me
I must let him have what little money I had; for
he had but one dollar to go his journey. I replied,
that he knew my feeble state, how much I needed
something for my nourishment; and I had only a
part of a dollar. I wondered how he could think
of asking for that. I told him I thought he ought
to leave a number of dollars with me, rather than
take any thing from me. He made some flattering
promises of Asa's getting me some money, if I
would let it go. But I had no confidence in his
words; and I did by no means give up my little
treasure.

Mr. B. now inquired whether I should run him
in debt, while he was gone? or whether I should
tell any bad stories about him? I queried, by way
of reply, whether he had ever found me unjustly injuring him? Whether he had not confided in me in
days past? I told him, I believed I was still the
same person I had been ever since he had been acquainted with me, however much he had altered.
I told him, that his guilty conscience predicted evil,
and led him to imagine that I must, after all his

horrid treatment of me, do something in self defence.—That this moved him to wish to obtain a promise from me, on which he knew he could rest secure. As to exposing his wickedness in these parts, I told Mr. B. I should not do it, unless I saw some special occasion for it. But as to feeling (as I used to do,) under obligations to obey and please him, I really did not; and he well knew the cause, and the propriety of my feeling thus. I told Mr. B. I saw not much temptation or opportunity of running him into debt in those parts; and I should not do it, unless I found real need of so doing.

Mr. B. was then anxious to know of me, whether I would tarry at Mr. Culver's, till he should return? I replied, that I could not tell how that would be. For I knew not that he would ever come there again; and if he should, I knew not when; or whether I should live till that time. He said, he wished to know whether I intended to be there? I asked, where he thought I should be able to go? He said he wanted I should promise that I would not go from that house. And without such a promise, he could never go his journey. I told him I was under no obligations to make him such a promise. And if I should humor him in promising, when there was no need of it, he might increase his demands of promises, and lead me into some snare. I asked Mr. B. what he intended to do, if I would not promise? whether he would stay there and watch me forever? and thus let all his interest go. He said he must stay; for he could not go, unless I would tarry. I put him off from time to time. At last he said to me, may I depend on finding you here when I come again? Said I, *You may if you please.* (meaning, he might do as he pleased about it; but I would make no such promise!) He then tried to make me think I had *bound myself;* and therefore must and would certainly stay. I thought if he was willing thus to deceive himself, in attempting to

make a simpleton of me, he might act his pleasure.
I wished to get rid of him, and have him go on his
journey. And I should take my own time to feel
myself under any such obligation, as he attempted
to persuade me I was now under, to tarry till his
return.

Mr. B. made preparation for his journey. Now
I hoped the time of my deliverance drew nigh. I
hoped that God had heard my groanings, as he had
those of Israel in their Egyptian bondage, when he
said, "I have surely seen the afflictions of my people; I know their sorrows; and am come down to
deliver them."

Lest I might not live to reach home, I prepared
a number of letters to my children and friends,
giving directions how I wished to have my children
disposed of among their connexions. I shewed
them to Mr. B. and induced him to promise, that
he would deliver the letters; and would endeavor
that things should be with the children as I had
prescribed. But my private hope was, that I
should soon be there, and be able to controul my
oppressor, and to see to these concerns myself.

May 9, 1792, Mr. B. set off his journey on foot.
Now I viewed the time as come, for me to bend all
my attention to a preparation for my tour. I was
still very feeble. But I felt that I must trust Providence for strength to perform this journey. My
first object was to decide upon the time when I had
better set out. I determined on the one hand, to be
sure and let Mr. B. have time enough to get home;
and let it appear what he would wish to do: On the
other hand, to be sure and be there before he
should be able to dispose of all his interest, and be
gone. Relative to this, I exercised the best of my
judgment; and in my own mind fixed on the day,
when by the leave of a kind Providence, I would
set off. I then carefully watched every providential event, which might seem to have the least

bearing on my proposed journey; and labored to learn the will of my Heavenly Father, to whom earnestly sought in prayer, for *direction* and *success.* I most sensibly felt I was whollydependent on him for these. I feared I should take some wrong step, and dishonor him. That this might not be the case, I daily and hourly made the word of God my study; and I spent much time in retirement and devotion. Though I had a most anxious desire to return home, yet I felt that if it were not the will of God that I should now return, he would some way hedge up my path, and I was determined humbly to acquiesce.

Friday, May 11, I set apart for special prayer and humiliation; that I might confess and bewail my sins before God; might plead for pardon through Jesus Christ; and for direction and needed help in the object before me. I did attempt, by faith, to set myself and my children before the Lord; to plead our distresses before him; and that all my hope and expectation was only from him. I pleaded his covenant mercy in Jesus Christ; that he would own me as one of his dear children; and though I was the most unworthy of all his blessed family, yet that he would not suffer a cruel enemy any longer to prevail against me, and my poor helpless children; but that God would now plead our cause as his own. I pleaded the argument of Moses, when he besought the Lord that he would, for the glory of his great name, pardon Israel's sins, and bring them into the promised land, lest the wicked should speak against God. And also as Moses prayed for the divine presence, saying, "If thy presence go not with me, carry me not hence." My soul rested on such passages as the following; the Lord said to the people at the Red Sea, "Fear not; stand still and see the salvation of the Lord." "The Lord shall fight for you." "Dread not, nor be afraid; the Lord, he it is that shall fight for you." "This day, I will begin to put the dread of you upon your enemies." "And the Lord said—Fear him not; for I will deliver him into thine hand." With Joshua, I fell to the earth before the Lord, and pleaded in his words, "Alas, O Lord God, what shall I say, when Israel turn their backs before their enemies? For the enemies of the Lord will hear of it; and what wilt thou do unto thy great name?" The subsequent promises of God to Joshua enlivened my soul. And by these and many sacred passages of the like import, my mind was wonderfully enlightened, and my heart enlarged, to plead and to hope for delivering mercy from God to me and my children.

I had no idea of giving information to the all-knowing Jehovah. Nor did I expect nor desire that any of the purposes of the infinitely wise Sovereign of the universe should be changed. But I thought as God had made it the duty of such an inferior creature as I to spread my wants and desires before him, so it was my great satisfaction humbly to accept this infinitely precious privilege, and to plead the wants of myself and children. I did plead before God, that now it was a critical and dangerous time with me and my poor little children; that the present seemed like a turning point with us. And if our cruel enemy now prevail, how would transgressors be encouraged in their injustice; oppressors be emboldened in their wickedness, and say, It is vain to trust in the Lord; and how would the hearts of good people be rendered faint? I viewed Mr. B. a very wicked man, and intent now on cruel designs against his own family; and that I was in duty bound to plead against him. But, O my own unworthiness! I had no claim upon the righteous Judge of all the earth, on the ground of any merit in me. No! I cast myself at the feet of sovereign mercy, and prayed for free grace in Christ. No words can express the view I had, at this time, of my own unworthiness before God. I knew if God did work deliverance for me, yet the remark made to Israel would be true to me, "Not for your sakes do I this, be it known unto you." I saw in my heart such deformity, such unlikeness to God, and to what I ought to be, that I was utterly unworthy of the object, for which I interceded; unworthy of the least mercy; and I wondered I was out of a miserable eternity, and in a region of hope. I could not accuse myself of having lived in any wilful sin, or of having fallen into known transgressions. But it was the depravity of my nature, which was my source of guilt and trouble before God. The more I felt my need of help from God, the more I felt utterly unworthy of it. And it seemed as if I might shrink into nothing before the great Jehovah. These views, however, gave me no discouragement. For I was not pleading or hoping upon a footing of merit; but of free grace in Christ. I expected mercies according to God's nature and promises; and not according to my deserts.

In those days I thought it my duty often to examine myself, both my heart, and life, and see wherefore it was that God had dealt so peculiarly with me? And on this day, thus set apart, I attempted to examine peculiarly how it was between God and my soul. I looked back upon past times, and endeavored to examine all by the word of God. And I was led to apprehend that, through fear of Mr. B. and the delicateness of my situation, I had treated him with too great lenity. And I found various errors in judgment, into which I had fallen, even while I had been hoping that I was actuated by holy motives. But, as Peter appealed to his Lord, "Thou knowest that I love thee;" so I thought I could appeal to God, Thou knowest all things; thou knowest that ever since thou hast, in thy righteous providence, called me to the management of such difficult affairs in my family, I have

never meant to do any thing contrary to thy mind
and will. That I have sincerely desired to know
my duty, and to do what would be for thy glory.
My conscience testifies that I have not knowingly
erred from thy ways.

But I sensibly felt, at the same time, that my being in my then present situation, demonstrated, that
I was a very imperfect creature, and had much
erred in the management of my difficult matters.
And I thought that if I could bear the evil of this
error merely as a creature, and not as a professor
of religion, my trouble would have been small, compared with what it now was.

My hope was in the mercy of God. I renewedly dedicated myself to him. I could rejoice in his
grace. And I moreover had a strong confidence
in God, that he would soon deliver me from my
present state of exile, and restore me to my friends.
That as he caused the fish to throw out Jonas upon
the dry land, so he would prepare the way and set
me at liberty again among my friends. For any
prospect of this, I could already praise him. "Salvation is of the Lord."

My attention was now fixed upon my preparation
for my journey. But I kept my designs to myself.
For I thought if any thing should prevent my going,
it would be best for me that Mr. B. should never
learn what I had designed.

As to bearing my expenses by the way home, I
had about two thirds of a dollar in money. I had
also a piece of cloth for a gown, which Mr. B.
gave me, at my request, when he sold a horse on
the way as we came over. He had repeatedly tried to sell it; but was unable. I had the extra
clothes, which Mr. B. had taken privately from
home. These I thought I would sell, if necessary.
And I thought I could sell my gold beads, my silver
shoe buckles, and my stone buttons from my
sleeves, if needful.

14

My remaining in a feeble state, seemed a great difficulty in my way. But whenever my heart seemed discouraged and gloomy, I fled to the throne of grace for help. I felt that my all-wise Heavenly Friend alone could prepare the way, and carry me through. I expected no miracle to be wrought in my behalf. But I felt confident, that if I made the best arrangements I could, and did all in my power, God would bless and succeed my endeavors.

Sometimes, when contemplating my undertaking such a journey alone, difficulties in the way would appear extremely formidable. I thought, what if I should fall in company with drunkards or robbers, or other ruffians or wicked men? At taverns, I should not know the characters of people, or my dangers from them. I thought it was so uncommon to see women riding journies alone, that I should naturally be taken for some base contemptible creature, and people would not think it much matter how I was treated. But in all such fears, I found relief in flying to God my refuge.

One day these hosts of dangers rose in my mind, and I felt as though I must sink under them. But I bethought myself, It is not a common providence, that has brought me here; and has made this premeditated journey necessary. And as the occasion is extraordinary, so God will afford extraordinary aid and protection. I took my hymn book, and lifted my desire to the Father of mercies that he would graciously condescend to meet me with a blessing in these spiritual songs. I opened my book and lit on the following hymn; which it seemed to me I had never seen before, though I had so long had a most familiar acquaintance with the book:

"*The darkness of Providence.*   ▸

Lord, we adore thy vast designs,
Th' obscure abyss of providence!

Too deep to sound with mortal lines,
Too dark to view with feeble sense.

Now thou array'st thine awful face
In angry frowns, without a smile:
We, through the cloud, believe thy grace,
Secure of thy compassion still.

Through seas and storms of deep distress
We sail by faith, and not by sight;
Faith guides us in the wilderness,
Through all the terrors of the night.

Dear Father, if thy lifted rod
Resolve to scourge us here below;
Still let us lean upon our God,
Thine arm shall bear us safely through."

Every word seemed wholly for me, as though
God had overruled the penman to write this hymn
for my sake. I felt as though I could now truly
adore the Lord in his vast designs, though his
abyss of providence toward me was too deep and
mysterious to view with feeble sense. And while
God saw fit to hide his awful face in angry frowns,
yet through all this dark cloud I did very confidently believe in his grace, both for time and eternity.
My circumstances were all right. If my way led
through seas and storms of distress, so that I could
not walk by sight, I may and must go by faith; believing that God will guard and guide me in the
wilderness by day and night, from all my fears and
terrors. I therefore earnestly desired, that I
might henceforth lean wholly upon God; and never again indulge a doubt. And never after, during
my preparation for my journey, or during my per-
forming it, was I *much* troubled, but once. Just
before I set out, I was thinking of crossing the
Green mountains. I thought I must expect to find
the riding very bad, over those heights. And I recollected there were places where there were no
inhabitants for four and five miles. I thought,
what if I should be thrown off my horse there, and

my bones broken, or I so injured, that I could not go forward! Or if, among the rocks or roots, my horse should break a leg, and I should remain so feeble that I could not walk to any inhabitants! Yea, I thought, what if I should in these difficulties, or without them, be attacked by wild beasts, on those lonely and lofty wilds! Bears, wolves, and catamounts, I concluded were sometimes found upon these mountains. And how terrible for a lonely woman to be attacked and devoured by them! With such thoughts I once got my poor wandering imagination wrought up to a terrible height. But I soon recollected the folly of it; and at once felt guilty and ashamed before God. I looked to him for pardon and direction; and took my Bible, breathing a devout desire that I might there find something to cure my folly. I opened to the 78th Psalm, containing the story of God's wrath against the *incredulous* and *disobedient*. Here I found matter of much conviction. The story of Israel's unbelief and rebellion against God, I found very interesting. God wonderfully provided for his people, and saved them from their enemies; and yet they were almost continually distrusting his goodness, and turning aside from the right way. When God brought them into the wilderness, and there made miraculous provision for them, he required that they should constantly believe in God for the supply of their daily wants, and for defence against their enemies. And God complains that Ephraim turned back in the day of battle; because they kept not the covenant of God; and forgat his works. Marvellous things he had done for them. He divided the sea, and caused them to pass through. He led them by a cloud, and by fire. He gave them drink from the rock. Yet after all, they were full of distrust, and spake against God. "Can God furnish a table in the wilderness? Alas, had they not seen that he could? And yet they tempted him,

They grieved him in the desert. They limited the
Holy One of Israel. They stupidly forgat what he
had wrought in Egypt, and at the Red Sea. God
was angry with them, because they would not confide in him, after all they had seen of his power and
faithfulness. He was as much displeased because
they would not confide in his miraculous power,
when their needs required such a power, as he was
for their distrusting his common mercy in common
times.

The instructions of this Psalm were strikingly
impressed on my mind, and seemed to come to my
case. I saw my base ingratitude, in fearing to trust
myself, in my peculiar trials, in the hands of God.
I saw that God did call me to cast my whole care
upon him, even in the wilderness of my greatest
trials; and to expect that his mercy would be as
singular, as were my needs. I was grieved and
ashamed, that I had been so deficient in this duty.
And my earnest desire was, that I might limit the
Holy One of Israel no more, nor prescribe how
God should work.

I took my psalm and hymn book in my hand,
hoping to find something there to impress these instructions still more upon my mind. I opened to this
hymn, and read,

> "'Tis by the faith of joys to come
> We walk through deserts dark as night;
> Till we arrive at heaven, our home,
> Faith is our guide, and faith our light.
>
> The want of sight she well supplies;
> She makes the pearly gates appear;
> Far into distant worlds she pries,
> And brings eternal glories near.
>
> Cheerful we tread the desert through,
> While faith inspires a heavenly ray;
> Though lions roar, and tempests blow,
> And rocks and dangers fill the way.

14*

> So Abrah'm, by divine command,
> Left his own house to walk with God:
> His faith beheld the promis'd land,
> And fir'd his zeal along the road."

I presume I had often read this hymn before; but it seemed to me as though I had never seen it; and I was amazed at its contents. It seemed most strikingly to apply to my case. It gave me light and joy. I now felt a solid peace in God. I thought now I could cheerfully move forward in duty, though my way should lie through deserts and wilds. I would not fear rocks, nor lions, nor any other evils. I did now believe that God would soon bring me home to my friends, who had seemed at a world's distance; that the doors of his house would soon be opened to me; and I should find myself among my dear worshipping christian friends in Haverhill, who kept holy day. I thought more of Haverhill, because there had lately been a great revival of religion there; and I had a pleasing acquaintance with many of those christian friends. And the thought of meeting them, in sacred ordinances, seemed almost like the pearly gates, of which we read.

I took my piece of paper, on which my directions for the way home were written, and transcribed these two hymns, which have been noted, that I might commit them to memory, and have them often before my eyes, while on my journey.

I now took my son Asa, and informed him of my plan to go home. He thought it a great undertaking, and had tender concern for me, and especially on account of my feeble state of health. He said it would be most grievous to him to part with me. Yet, as things were, he rejoiced to have me go home, if I could possibly do it. He would willingly part for a while with me, that I might go to the little children. We now had free and affectionate conversation upon the dreadful state of our family, which must be finally broken up. He was a poor feeble youth, and needed the tender care of a mother. But I must now leave him in this wilderness among strangers, under the care of a father, who was far worse than a stranger; and where there were no such conveniences as he needed. These things were exceedingly distressing to the heart of a mother. O God of salvation! I have given my children up to thee. Be thou their Guardian and their Saviour. I gave my son the best instructions I could, relative to body and soul. I gave him written instructions, relative to many things; and hoped they might be a lasting benefit to him.

I then conversed with Mr. Culver and his wife, relative to my returning home. I was cautious as to saying any thing of our peculiar family trials; but let them know that things were so with me and my family, that I must now return home; and must take the horse left in their care. I tenderly expressed to them my gratitude for all their kindnesses, and hoped God would amply reward them. As to the pecuniary part, Mr. B. must reward them, upon his return. They were very friendly; and were tender at the thought of my leaving them. They wished me prosperity, and a safe return to my friends. I affectionately commended my son Asa to their tender regard and care; entreating them to be kind to him in his feeble state of health.

Mr. Culver gave me some additional directions relative to the road, and put me in a better way in the first part of my journey, than the one in which I went with Mr. B. He told me for what places and names to inquire; and gave me some information relative to taverns, and other things. This was a great service. I thought of the words of Abraham. "My son, God will provide." And when God did indeed wonderfully provide, Abraham called the name of the place, Jehovah Jireh, which is said to mean, God will see, or provide. I could now, in heart, sing,

> "My shepherd is the living Lord;
> Now shall my wants be well supplied.
> His providence and holy word
> Become my safety and my guide."

I formed my schedule of the way home, like a little map, for my guide. My weakness and bodily infirmities were distressing, and seemed sometimes as if they must, after all, prevent my setting out. I had symptoms of peculiar weakness, to which I had been incident, and which must have been a fatal obstacle in the way of my journey. I familiarly pleaded with my Heavenly Friend in relation to these trials. And he did remarkably interpose for me. After having reason, for several hours, to believe that I was attacked with a difficulty, with which I had, within several years, been repeatedly viewed in a very dangerous state, and once was thought to be dead; this difficulty was removed. But I felt reminded by it of my peculiar dependence on God, in my lonely journey, in relation to this threatening evil, as well as others. I seemed to hear God saying, in this providence, "Be still and know that I am God." For when this evil attacked, I was usually very sick at once. And riding was bad for it. But all was in the hands of infinite wisdom. God had showed me that he could controul this and every difficulty. "Bless the Lord, O my soul, and forget not all his benefits;—who forgiveth thine iniquities; who healeth all thy diseases; the Lord executeth righteousness and judgment for all that are oppressed. The Lord is merciful and gracious. He will not always chide. Like as a father pitieth his children, so the Lord pitieth them that fear him. Bless the Lord, O my soul."

Thursday, May 24, the day which I had appointed to set off upon my journey, arrived. It was

fair and pleasant. I had made the best provisions
I could for my comfort by the way. I took an affectionate farewell of Mr. and Mrs. Culver. I truly felt grateful and tender toward them. And I
never expected to see them again in this life. My
son accompanied me a few miles. For I had gloomy woods to pass, four or five miles between houses.
While my dear son moved on with me, I improved
my time, in the best manner I could, to instruct
him in the great things of religion. And now that
I must leave him, I begged of him to give himself
up to God, and live near to him. We parted in
the woods. None but parents, and not many of
them, can conceive of my feelings on turning my
back upon the dear boy in this gloomy situation!
Oh! how little do people prize the blessing of union
and peace in their families, and the presence and
enjoyments of their children at home! My children
were dear to me as my life. But how trying my
lot, in being parted from them! I renewedly gave
up my son to God, and cast all my burdens on his
arm; and said, with Moses, "O Lord, if thy presence go not with me, carry me not hence."

I went on according to my directions; and the
Lord led me in the right way. I rode seven miles,
and stopped to rest; for I was very weary. After
resting some time upon a bed, I again moved forward. My travelling to day was almost wholly in
the woods. But I got along comfortably. The sun
an hour high I found a tavern. The next was four
miles ahead. I therefore put up. For I had feared being overtaken with night in the woods. Here,
for the first time in my life, I called for entertain-
ment at a tavern.

I immediately got leave to lay myself on the bed;
for I was extremely weary. The landlord asked
if I was sick? I told him, not very sick, but very
feeble. He asked, how far I expected to ride alone?
I replied, that I hoped a kind providence would

enable me to ride as far as the eastern extremity
of Vermont.   He said, I was a person of great
courage.   I told him I had need of courage; for I
had not much else.   He said it was not good to
have more courage than conduct.   I replied, that
my doing as I did seemed necessary; and I hoped
I should be provided for.   He appeared very kind,
and said, he hoped God would take care of me;
and that I should meet with no harm in his house.
After he got to bed, I over heard him ask his wife,
what she thought of that woman? He said, she appears very clever; but it looks strange to see her on
such a journey alone.   His remark gave me such a
view of my situation, that I felt my hair rise on my
head.   But I remembered my help was in God.   I
fled to him; and prayed that as my day is, so my
strength may be.   The Lord was gracious.   I had
a comfortable night's rest.   So that in the morning
I could say, "I laid me down and slept; I
awaked; for the Lord sustained me."

The landlord expressed much concern for me,
when he saw that I was feeble, and ate but little.
He urged me to eat some veal, which they had prepared, or to take some of it in my saddlebags to
eat by the way.   But I had no occasion to accept
his kind offer.   I could not eat meat, at that time.
I was obliged to live very sparingly.   His bill for
my expenses was very low.   And he kindly took an
article which I had for sale, and which he did not
want; merely to favor me, giving me some money
for the article more than my reckoning.   This I received as a great kindness from him; and a token
for good from my Heavenly Father.   When I was
about to depart, this man presented me with refreshing things, of his own kindness; appeared very
pitiful; wished me prosperity; and directed me on
my way.   The weather continued fine.   These
things gave courage to my poor drooping heart;
they strengthened my faith in God.   I rode on,

through the woods alone. And yet I could say, I am not alone; but my Father is with me. His comforts delighted my soul. I saw him in every tree, and every shaking leaf. The little birds seemed to sing his praise. This day I reached a larger road; and passed by old farms and houses. I had been so long shut up in the woods, that these things appeared strange and pleasing. I rejoiced that "the earth is the Lord's, and the fulness thereof; the world, and they that dwell therein." The weather was warm, and I was faint and feeble. I found the people kind. I often wanted drink; and rode up to doors, and asked for beer, or milk and water; which they readily gave. I had taken a gown, (which Mr. B. had taken privately from Bradford, as before noted,) and made a loose gown of it to ride in, of which I now found the great advantage. The event therefore, of Mr. B's taking it which I had seemed to think was all against me, proved much in my favor. It now seemed as though I could not have done without it. "God will provide."

I came to German Flats about the middle of the day. I had here a meadow of several miles to cross, which lay flat, and wholly exposed to the sun. It was clear, and no wind stirring. I feared I should suffer with the heat. I thought, if I could stay till toward night, it would be much better. But I could not take the time to lie by. I entered the gate, and set forward. It was soon ordered so by that God, whose word the winds and clouds obey, that there sprang up a fresh breeze of air, and the sun was overcast with light clouds; so that my feeble frame was most comfortably sustained. Such common providences seemed to be ordered mercifully in my favor. I was delighted with the mercy of the Lord in all things to me this day, that so vile and obscure a worm should share so largely in needed blessings. To note one more instance;

—I was thirsty and faint. I thought I would ride up to a house, and ask for some beer. Before I reached the door, there came a young woman out of a cellar door, which opened into the road, and met me with a cup of a peculiar nourishing kind of drink. I asked her for a little of it, which she most pleasantly gave; and I was greatly refreshed. Truly the God, who numbers our hairs, and provides for insects, does not forget his needy followers. I considered these things as merciful providences; and they strengthened my confidence in the Lord. Night overtook me, and I put up at a Dutch tavern. They could talk English; and the woman was kind to me, and shewed much concern for my being alone, on so long a journey, and in so feeble a state, much more fit to be under the care of a nurse, than to engage in any business. She took particular notice of my being able to eat but little, and that my living was chiefly on milk and water mixed. She urged me to eat of her more hearty food; but I could not taste of it. I felt grateful for her kindness.

In the room where I slept, which seemed at a distance from the family, some time in the night I was waked by the opening of this door. The house being still I could hear the screaking of this door, it being evident that some one was opening it very slyly. I had not much doubt but some person was intent on mischief; and I knew not how far I was from any help. But I knew the Watchman of Israel (who neither sleeps nor slumbers, and is the keeper of his people) *was near*. This thought prevented my being much alarmed. I spake with an audible voice, and demanded, who was coming in at the door? No answer was given, but the person speedily retired. I arose, and went to the door, found it unlatched, and partly brought to. I secured it; stirred up the coals in the fire, and searched the room to see that no one was in it; and retired again to rest. A sense of the presence of the blessed God prevented my fear. I felt that nothing could injure without his permission; and therefore I could say, "Of whom shall I be afraid?" and could add, "I will both lay me down in peace, and sleep; for thou Lord only makest me to dwell in safety."

When I came to pay my reckoning in the morning, I paid in a little family article, which Mr. B. had put up among the other things, which he took off privately, when we came from Bradford, as before mentioned. The landlady gave me its worth, more than the reckoning, in money; and urged upon me some of her cake to carry with me; expressing her anxious and warm desire that I might have strength to perform my journey, and might be prospered in it, and in life. And in return, I did truly desire that she might know God, and be blessed of him, in time, and eternity.

Saturday, May 26, I again moved forward. Though I was very feeble in body, I had gained a little strength. And my hope in God was strong. This day I was hindered some with the rain. I crossed the Mohawk at Winecup's ferry. I well remembered my feelings when I crossed here a captive to Mr. B. And now I think I had a grateful sense of the tender care of my Heavenly Father over me, from that hour to the present. I praised him, that he had brought me so far and so safely on my way toward home; and had set me again on my homeward side of the Mohawk. I gave thanks at the remembrance of his holiness, and of his loving kindness. Soon after crossing the river, I closed the third day of my journey, and put up. This day I had witnessed some unkind things in a tavern, to shew me the great difference between kind and unkind treatment in this journey; and to make me prize the mercy of the Lord in the former. In the tavern where I put up, I received kind treatment.

15

I rose in the morning; it was the Lord's day. Oh, how I longed for Lord's day privileges; but I found there were none in this place. Neither did any seem to know it was sabbath, unless their knowledge of it appeared by renewing their recreations and vanities. I tarried till toward noon. Company was in and out, all the morning of this holy day; and nothing was to be heard, but worldly conversation, noise, or nonsense. I learned that this company were people of the place; and that it was customary there to spend the sabbath in visiting and vanity. I found this tavern was probably going to be thronged all day in this manner. I was led to query, whether it would not be duty for me to move along on the road, and enjoy my mind alone free from this noise and disturbance? I finally was induced to conclude, that, as things were with me, as the abominable customs of this part of the country were, and as there would be none to be offended, I had better move a little forward, than to remain in this tavern, a seat of confusion and folly. I accordingly set out. This day I had some alarming symptoms of a bodily infirmity, with which I had repeatedly, within a few years, been attacked. This led on to another series of trial. I was led greatly to doubt whether I had done wisely in setting off this journey in so feeble a state. It seemed to me my situation at Mr. Culver's, might in some respects be compared to the situation of Christ on a pinnacle of the temple. Satan tempted him to cast himself down thence, confiding in God to uphold him. And I had obeyed just such a direction; had cast myself down, in venturing on such a journey. But Christ had repelled the temptation, by saying, "It is written, Thou shalt not tempt the Lord thy God." It was now injected into my mind, that I had tempted God, in making such strange reliance on his signal interpositions. These things came like fiery darts. After riding some hours, I saw a house. I had a

strong desire to call at it. It was not a tavern. I
called. I found the family sitting in a room together. They appeared serious, with books in
their hands. I felt struck and pleased. I wished
I could tarry with them, and ride no farther on
this holy day. The man immediately asked me to
put up with them, and said he would put up my
horse, and I might tarry with them through the
day, and over night, in welcome; and perhaps I
should feel more comfortable in my mind, than I
should at a tavern. Oh how wonderful is the mercy of the Lord! I thankfully accepted his offer.
I told the man I did not love to travel on this holy
day. But from all circumstances, I had thought it
my duty to ride on from the tavern where I had
tarried till toward noon. Here I found a pleasant
English family. They treated me not merely with
common kindness; but as though I had been a most
respected friend, or sister. Nothing could be done
too much. Their victuals tasted good. I had felt
no relish for any meat, till to-day. Now I was
pleased and nourished with it, and thus gained
strength.

I here saw that God could indeed provide friends,
This woman told me her husband said, that as soon
as he saw me, he thought I appeared like a person
in trouble; that he felt a pity excited; and wished
to do something for my benefit. Truly I had no
doubt but it was that God, who was with Joseph in
all his afflictions, who moved upon the heart of this
man.

I had much serious conversation in this family;
I did not gain full evidence that either the man, or
his wife was a real christian. But they were serious, and exceedingly amiable and kind. The woman conversed with great freedom; told me many
of her afflictions; and she had been a woman of sorrows. I pitied her. But I thought I could have told
a long story, which would have far outweighed hers!

But upon this subject I held my peace; remarking
only, that I had been exercised with troubles, great
troubles, and such as infinite wisdom had seen fit to
lay upon me. I made such remarks to this woman,
as I thought would be for her benefit, and as might
profitably improve my time with her.

My alarming symptoms of sickness disappeared.
And my temptation, relative to my having, as it
were, cast myself from the pinnacle of the temple,
in setting out this journey, was controuled and gone.
And I had some comfort, as well as distress, on
this holy sabbath day. God showed me that he
could contract every difficulty. I rejoiced that I
had set out this journey. I believed God had called me to it; and would carry me safely through;
and I found it easy, as well as comfortable, to cast
my burden upon him.

I sensibly felt for the miserable people, whom I
had seen, this day, visiting, feasting, and carousing,
in the houses, by which I had passed. O poor
creatures, my heart exclaimed! How little do you
know what you are doing! What blessedness you
lose; and what guilt and wretchedness you incur!
My soul was drawn out to God for them. I longed
for their reformation, and salvation. I had never,
till on this journey, had an idea how many wretched beings there are, ignorant of God, and perishing
in sin. Oh, can nothing be done for such wretched,
wretched people? Is there no way for the leaves
of the tree of life to be applied for the healing of
such perishing multitudes? Will not the set time
to favor Zion soon come, When God will be glorified in the salvation of the dark corners of the
earth? I had now a great feeling for children and
youth, who are growing up in ignorance of God,
and in vice; and preparing an awful harvest for e-
ternal ruin! I longed that the God of heaven might
be worshipped more in spirit and in truth, in our
highly favored nation; and also that the whole fami-

ly of man on earth, Jews and Gentiles, might see the light, and obtain salvation. But my most earnest desires were, that God's professing people might be kept from dishonoring his name. Here I feared I discovered a deficiency in the conversation of my kind landlady this day. In all her accounts of her afflictions and trials, I did not discover that she had been tried with fear of *dishonoring God*. I was sure this had been among my greatest trials and fears.

Monday, May 28, I set out again with good courage. My horse's back had, for several days, been pretty sore. Notwithstanding all the precaution I could use, it had been growing worse: Now it was so bad, it threatened to stop my progress. What could I do? I must look to my Heavenly Father for help. My whole dependence was on him. I was among strangers, with but a few shillings in money, and a feeble woman who knew nothing about trading in horses. My desire and prayer to God was, that he would lead my mind to plan wisely concerning this matter; and that in his marvellous goodness he would help me to such an horse, as might carry me safely home.

With great difficulty I crept along the road this day, on account of my poor horse's back. I thought if I could get to Mr. Smith's of New-Galloway, where Mr. B. had left his sleigh as we came over, possibly Mr. Smith would assist me in relation to exchanging horses. I recollected hearing him say, when I was at his house, that he had three horses. I hoped I could reach there by night.

In the afternoon, through mistake I took a wrong road. After going some ways in it, I found my mistake. I inquired, and was told where I might go to regain the road I had left, without going all the way back. This cross road I took, and followed the direction as well as I could. A mile or two before I expected to reach the road that I sought,

15*

the cross way led me into a dark woods. Here my
small path grew blinder and blinder, till I thought
I should soon find no track to follow. I hence suspected I must be out of my way, and had indeed
got into the *woods!* I stopped, to consider with myself which way to turn, or what to do? In the space
of a minute, I heard a man riding in the woods.
He came out of the bushes against me and stopped,
and inquired if I had seen any stray sheep? I told
him I had not; but that I seemed to have got astray,
and wanted direction. In a very obliging manner
he gave me ample directions; and then turned back
again into the woods. The seasonableness of this
kind aid afforded led me at first almost to query
whether it was a man or an angel. I believed a
watchful Providence sent him to direct me, as soon
as my mind became alarmed. And I know not
but I was as much affected with the divine goodness,
as though I had known he was an angel from heav-
en! I thought the mercy of God was really visible
in sending this man. He came the moment I needed direction. He came in no path, from the woods;
and he immediately returned the same way. I was
affected with a view of God's constant and partic-
lar care over me in every thing. My soul was
melted with love and gratitude to my Heavenly
Benefactor and Guardian. The sense I had of my
own unworthiness, was inexpressible. And the
condescension of God filled me with admiration. I
thought I would never again distrust God's goodness. And I went on, with my heart lifted up to
him, in prayer and praise.

I arrived at Mr. Smith's in good season that
night, and put up. They received me very cordially. As they found I was riding such a journey
alone, they were the more tender and kind. I related to them some of the merciful providences,
which had attended me on my journey. And they
seemed to be animated as the true friends of God.

I really trust they were true helpers of each other in the journey of life. Here I enjoyed family prayer for the first time since I left home. Oh, how good it is to come around the family altar! Alas, how few comparatively know this blessedness! How few houses are houses of God, as was Joshua's, who with his house, would serve the Lord.

I informed Mr. Smith of my necessity of changing horses, on account of mine having a sore back; and asked if he could not assist me? He said he would with all his heart. But he had no horse that I could ride. He told me of a neighbor, who lived a mile and a half on my way, who had a horse that would suit me, and he believed he would exchange. He said he would go on with me to this man, and aid me in the business. But he was called another way, and could not go with me, having some public business on hand. Before I set out in the morning, he looked out, and saw the horse, which he had recommended to me, in the road. I saw the horse and liked it well. I asked him how he thought we ought to trade? He said, *even.* He thought they were about of equal worth. But for the sake of being accommodated, he thought I might give two dollars, if the man would not trade short of this. He gave me a line to the man; and I went on; but not without regret that he could not go with me. Before I got out of sight of Mr. Smith, I heard a horse running after me. I looked and it was this horse, which I had hoped to obtain in exchange for mine; and which had been wandering in the woods and ways, coming after me. It came up and then stopped to feed. I thought this was favorable, as the man might be more likely to trade, if his horse were at home; and I could the more readily go on. It was now my desire that my Heavenly Father would, in his merciful providence, accommodate me with this horse, in exchange for mine. While I was speaking in my heart, the horse came running as before, and followed me home. I with pleasure recollected the words of God by the Psalmist, "For every beast of the forrest is mine, and the cattle upon a thousand hills." I went into the house; but the man was not at home. I found by inquiring I could not see him, unless I should lie by perhaps all that day. Now I thought my hopes were frustrated. I informed the woman what I wanted, and what Mr. Smith had said, about exchanging horses; also gave her his letter. She thought it probable her husband would accommodate me, if he had been at home. I asked her, if she would not run the venture to accommodate me? She said, she never meddled with any such business in her life; and knew no more of the value of horses than a child. I replied, nor I neither. And it is necessity alone, which drives me now to make the attempt. I told her, my case was not a common case. It was very singular and required haste. It seemed as though I could not stay till her husband came home; and yet that I could not go without their horse. In short I pleaded my necessity, and the *peculiarity* of my case, yet without unfolding the particulars of my trials. Her attention was excited, and her pity moved. I asked her to call some of her neighbors for advice. She did so. One told her, he thought her husband would trade if he were at home; and that she might safely do it. She seemed first almost, and then quite willing to accommodate me. So I took the new horse, and left mine; giving her the value of two dollars for her kindness. Now I was excellently accommodated indeed. The new horse was kind, surefooted, easy, and good. I thanked God, and took courage. I thought of Joseph; how it is said, "The Lord was with him." And how the Lord was indeed with Israel in the wilderness; and with that cloud of witnesses in Heb. 11th chapter. It seemed far more astonishing, that God should thus aid so vile a being as myself.

I proceeded on till noon, and then called on a friend of Mr. Smith, where he directed me to call. Mr. Smith had not only kept me over night gratis, but told me to call and dine with this his friend, where I should also be welcome. Here I found good friends, and christian treatment. Now things seemed to go well with me. My new horse carried me on faster and easier than the other. And my health was much recruited. This sixth day of my journey brought me near the North river.

The next morning I crossed the river; not as a captive, or in fear of falling through the ice, as when I came over it before. I well remembered the wormwood and the gall, when I was dragged over it by the man who vaunted over me, and seemed to rejoice in the imagination, that no power could take me out of his hands. I now saw it is safe trusting in that God, who, when the wicked deal proudly, is above them. Finding myself safely on the east side of the North river, I felt a confidence that God, who had thus far delivered, would, in due time, bring me out of all my distresses. This passage run delightfully in my mind; "Blessed be God; even the Father of our Lord Jesus Christ, the Father of mercies, and God of all comfort; who comforteth us in all our tribulations, that we may be able to comfort them that are in trouble, by the comfort wherewith we ourselves are comforted of God. For as the sufferings of Christ abound in us; so our consolation also aboundeth by Christ. Who delivered us from so great a death; and doth deliver; in whom we trust that he will yet deliver."

This day I must get my horse shod. I had set out from Unadilla with less than one dollar in money. While I was thinking of this subject, a young gentleman rode up and went on with me with naked hands. I told him I thought he needed a pair of gloves. He said he did, and meant to have a pair as soon as he could find them. I took a good pair out of my saddlebags, which I had provided on purpose to help bear my expenses in the way. They just fitted his hand. He paid me a generous price for them, and some refreshment beside. Now I had plenty of money for shoeing my horse. I called and got it done. The blacksmith asked but a moderate price; and gave me a dinner. Thus I lived on a series of mercies. From Sabbath morning till Wednesday night, I had been kept, nights and days, without cost, for me or my horse. Wednesday night I put up at a tavern near Salem court house. Here they were so kind as to take for my reckoning such articles as I had to spare.

Thursday, May 31, I set forward. I crossed the line of the state, into Vermont. I remembered the terrors of my mind, when I was told, that now I was in the state of New York, and was threatened with horrid treatment. I rejoiced that God had thus far broken the rod of the oppressor; and I gave him thanks for his great goodness.

I this day called at a house, and obtained what I needed for myself and horse. I asked the man what was to pay? He replied several times, he did not know, nor care. I replied that if he would tell me, I would pay him. Or if he meant I had nothing to pay, I thanked him; and if ever I got home, and saw a woman riding alone, and thought her as needy and as honest, as I knew myself to be, I would give her as much, if I had any thing to give. He seemed pleased, and said I was quite welcome. This eighth day of my journey brought me to Pollet. Here again I met with most kind treatment.

Friday, June 1. As I rode on this day, I was struck to think how different every thing appeared now from their appearance when I was dragging along this road four months ago with Mr. B. Then every thing seemed full of terror and gloom; and every body looked like an enemy. Now God smiled upon me. His providence smiled. And all his works and creatures seemed to smile.

I recollected, this day, the mercy of God to me in directing me on this long journey. I had to inquire abundantly for my way. And I had scarcely ever been obliged to go one rod out of my way to inquire. Some person seemed to be placed directly where I wanted him. Sometimes, when I wished to inquire, I would meet some one upon the road. Sometimes a man would be mending his fence where the road turned, or where I wanted direction. And sometimes a person would be standing where I wanted direction, and I saw no business that called him there. Thus through the wonderful mercy of God, I seemed to myself to be guided and guarded as by a heavenly guard. This ninth day of my journey brought me near the western side of the Green mountains. Here I found good treatment. And they cheerfully took for my reckoning such articles as I had.

Saturday, June 2, I ascended the Green mountains. Here is the part of my journey, concerning which my terrors, on one gloomy day, rose to so high a pitch. But I now considered that as my kind Preserver had brought me on thus far, in so much safety, I could still trust and not be afraid. I passed on over the bad roads and wilds in safety. God kindly guarded and upheld me. I came at night to a Mr. Osgood's on the height of the mountain. I hoped I might find some conveniences to be accommodated over the sabbath, that I might keep this holy day of rest. But alas, I found it was impracticable to put up here. This poor family were almost wholly destitute of provisions. I had to divide my own little stock of cake and biscuit among them, to make out our supper and break-

fast. I was hence under necessity of going on in
the morning, with all speed, to find the necessaries
of life. And it took me a considerable part of the
day to get over the mountain, where I could be accommodated. Sometime in the afternoon I came
to a house, where it seemed as though they might
permit me to tarry with them, though it was not a
tavern. I called. The people were sitting in a
room, with books, and their appearance was such
as became the day. I felt greatly pleased. I petitioned for leave to put up with them the remaining part of the day, and the night; and obtained it.
This had been to me a lonesome gloomy day, trav-
ersing solitary wilds, with much bad road, and some
extremely bad places. But I was able joyfully to
say, "Yet I am not alone, but the Father is with
me."

Monday, June 4, I again set out homeward, in
hopes of reaching Mr. Warner's of Hartford that
day. Here I hoped I might meet my son Samuel;
as we left him here when we went over. I had
been, for some days, in a degree of fear of meeting
Mr. B. on the road. Yet I could not believe God
would suffer me to fall again into his hands.

Just before I reached Mr. Warner's, Mr. Warner himself met me, having another man in company with him. He rode directly up to me, with
his hand extended, to shake hands, and calling me
by name. I took hold of his hand; but begged of
him not to call me by name, till I might have opportunity to converse with him. For I was in trouble; and did not wish to have it known that I was
in those parts, till I could converse with him. He
told me to go to his house, and he would shortly be
at home. When he came, I laid my troubles before
him. His feelings and pity toward me and my family were much moved. He said he could not go
about his business, and leave me in such trouble,
with none to assist me; but he would put his affairs

in order at home, and would accompany me, and
see what could be done. Mr. Warner now charged all, that knew I was there, to say nothing of it,
even if they should see Mr. B. Thus the close of
the twelfth day of my journey seemed to promise
me some assistance.

Tuesday, June 5, I went on in company with
Mr. Warner. I now had one to comfort me, and
to take my part. This seemed to me a token for
good from my Heavenly Father. We put up at
night in Thetford.

Wednesday, June 6, we again moved forward.
About ten o'clock Mr. Warner advised me to
cross Connecticut river and go up on the east side,
and he on the west, lest we might meet Mr. B. or
some, who might give him information of me. I
was pleased with this. For I wished to get round
and consult my friends, before Mr. B. should know I
had returned. Mr. Warner directed me to go to
Rev. Mr. Richards's of Piermont, and tarry till he
should come to me. He would go to our house at
Bradford, and see Mr. B. who would be glad to see
him; and whom he could induce to unfold all his affairs. Mr. Warner would learn also the state of
my poor motherless children, and how they had got
along; would go to my brother Brock's in Newbury,
and inform them of my return, and would then
come to me. This plan we pursued. Mr. Warner found Mr. B. at his house, and the children
alive, and as well as could be expected. Mr. B.
was glad to see him; but told him that he now felt
very poor; for he could not get along with his business at all to his mind. Every thing seemed to
work against him. Mr. B. had called on Mr. Warner, as he came over, several weeks before, and
told him that he had left me at Whitestown very
well contented, and pleased with living there. That
he was now going on to Bradford to sell our place,
take the money, and return. Mr. Warner had in

16

formed me of this, and that Mr. B. had a man in company with him, called Capt. White, whom he had brought over to assist him in his business, and help him move his family. Capt. White had furnished Mr. B. with a horse, while he rode another. And Mr. B. had thus gone on in good spirits. But now, when Mr. Warner came to see Mr. B. he felt very differently; and felt poor and dejected. He could not sell his place; and every thing seemed to work against him. Mr. Warner went on to Mr. Brock's, and came round to me, and gave me the information, and related the state of my family. He told me they were all alive; but appeared indeed as though they needed their mother with them. He had given them no hint of my having returned.

Upon hearing that my poor children were alive, and in health, my heart was filled with gratitude, love and praise, to a kind and merciful God, for all his unbounded goodness; particularly to my children during my absence; and now to me, in having returned me to this region again, in so much safety; and in opening such favorable prospects of my relief. What shall I render unto God for all his goodness? I will take the cup of salvation, and call upon his name.

Mr. Warner and I came to Col. Johnston's in Haverhill. Here I tarried a short time, while Mr. Warner went on to Landaff, to see if the select men of that town would not come to my assistance, or afford their aid. Here I could see over into Bradford. Oh, my dear children, I longed to fly to them. But I must tarry away from them for a season longer, till our plans were matured, and something prepared to be done with Mr. B. I now felt that verily "I am a pilgrim and a stranger on the earth." I have no more a pleasant home like other women. My family is broken up. Our domestic peace is ruined and gone. I felt like one returned from a state of captivity, and who had no home, to which to repair. I felt as much at home at Col. Johnston's, where I now was, as any where. For I viewed him a most excellent man of God; and his house as a Bethel. Here I tarried a few days, while consultations were held among my friends in my behalf. After two days I went to my brother Brock's, in Newbury. Here I found my dear little Judith, (my youngest child but one, nearly three years of age.) She was asleep. I took her in my arms. She waked, and clasped her arms round my neck, in a rapture of joy on again seeing her ma'am. She had told her aunt, that she must call her ma'am, for she had no own ma'am. And she had been greatly grieved with the idea of my being gone. She now called me her own ma'am. We slept together. She would wake in the night, and cry out, Where is my ma'am? She is gone away again, Oh my own ma'am is gone! I would take her into my arms and tell her I was here with her. She would reply, Is it my own ma'am? Are you that ma'am, that went away and left me? When I told her I was, and that I would not go and leave her any more, she would be easy, and drop to sleep. People may guess at my feelings. Words will not describe them. I praised God that he had brought me so near to my dear children, and that one of them was in my arms.

The next day some of my brothers went with me to Bradford, that I might embrace my dear children once more; and that before any more decisive measures were resorted to, Mr. B. might have one more opportunity of making a fair settlement of our matters. None can well conceive of the surprise and shock of Mr. B. when he found I had returned! He was beat and amazed; but tried to appear friendly. He pretended he thought we parted in good friendship when he left me.

Now I had one more opportunity to see and embrace my children, Dear creatures! Yes, I saw

them, and could once more clasp my little ones in
my arms. I felt that I could never render sufficient praise to God, that he had returned me to see
them once more in the land of the living. My heart
desired to ascribe glory to the name of my gracious
God and Redeemer!

But oh, it was a melancholy visit, both to me,
and to the dear children. Perhaps never did children appear more as if they needed a mother. And
I could not now tarry with them. Nor could I yet
tell what could be done with or for them. They—
poor children—felt so much of the wretchedness of
our domestic affairs, that they could enjoy no comfort. And their appearance was solemn and gloomy,
as if they were attending a funeral of some dear
friend. My dear babe had forgotten her ma'am and
was afraid of me.

I asked Mr. B. upon his pretending that he
thought he left me on good terms at Whitestown,
and confiding in each other, how then it came to
pass, that he had never delivered one of my letters
to my children and friends, but had destroyed them
all? This, to be sure, was a tough question. He
was silent, and looked guilty and ashamed. I reminded him how he had promised to deliver them;
and how very desirable it must have been, to my
friends, and me, that he should have delivered
them; how easily he could have done it; and what
a total and cruel breach of trust and of promise it
was to destroy such a packet of letters from one
situated as I was to her friends.

I had labored so much with Mr. B. in times past,
to convince and reclaim him, and with so little success, that I should not have expostulated at all with
him, at this time, had it not been that my brothers
might hear and judge for themselves. But with
this view, I now conversed considerable with Mr.
B. upon his treatment of me, and upon his deceiving
me, and leading me off this journey. He seemed to

be at a loss what to say. He appeared very guilty.
And it appeared evident to all, that he knew he had
done very wickedly.

I now asked Mr. B. what he would do as to forming a settlement with me? For something effectual
must now be done. He said he would do what I
would say was generous. He meant to be fully reasonable towards me, and the children. But he
seemed to neglect to say what he would do. I pressed him to come to a point, and say what he would
do, at this time. He said it was now Saturday afternoon, and it could not be convenient to finish any
thing at this time. But he said he would engage that
by the sun an hour high, on Monday morning, he
would do that, relative to me, and our interest,
which all my brothers and friends would say was
honorable. Mr. B. said there was business to be
attended to between him and me, it was suitable
that we should attend to it alone, and not among
a room full of company. And he tried to induce me
to talk alone with him. I told him I should not be
alone one minute with him; that I had tried that
way too long already; and now I would try some
other way, as the Lord should direct.

My brothers and I were now about returning.
Mr. B. affected to be surprised to think I was going
away. He asked me, if I did not intend to stay
with my children? I replied, that it was grievous to
me to leave them again for the shortest time. But
I could not stay now with them. He asked, what I
intended to do with them? I replied, that I could not
tell, till our affairs were brought to a close. But I
intended to trust, in their behalf, in that God, who
had most mercifully preserved them and me hitherto; and who, I believed, would still take care of
us. He insisted on my tarrying there till Monday.
When he saw that I was going, he said, in a stern
manner, I forbid you, who are brothers to my wife,
and every body else, harboring my wife one night!
No reply was made. And we retired to Newbury.

*16

Now I thought I had done my private errand to Mr. B. I had labored many years with him in vain. And had now given him a fair opportunity for a peaceful settlement, which he had declined. As to his promises, what he would do on Monday morning, they were all idle. I had no confidence in them.

I now went with my brothers, to a justice of the peace, and swore the peace against my poor husband. A warrant was issued, and put into the hands of an officer, with order to have Mr. B. forth coming, early on Monday morning.

Mr. B. after we left him on Saturday, said, that my brothers and I would doubtless be there again on Monday morning, as earnest as ever, expecting that he would then give up a part of the interest; and do something very noble. But he said he intended to shew us a trick, and a manly one; but such an one as we did not expect. For we should not find him nor the children there, when we came. And we might settle matters as we could. And he went immediately to making preparations for a removal. All the sabbath he employed in this manner. He repeatedly jeered, and pleased himself with the idea, that my brothers and I should come on Monday morning, and be finely disappointed; finding him and all the children gone, and the property taken good care of. The oldest son spake to his father with concern for the little children, telling him, that the babe especially could not live to go through such a journey, and the others must greatly suffer. But Mr. B. replied, that he need not fear, for he never intended to carry the babe to Whitestown. But he should know what to do with her, and with all the rest of them, when he had got away. But he did not wish to talk at present upon this point. The children were terrified and distressed. They knew not what was going to become of them. They talked among themselves, that their father had first carried off their ma'am; and now as soon as she had returned, he was going to carry them away; and they knew not where. They said they did not want to go with him. They longed to live again with their ma'am.

Monday morning very early, Mr. B. was surprised by the officer, who went and took him. He found him in the act of putting his property into such a situation, that he thought we could not get hold of any part of it. He was taken immediately off, before he had accomplished the wicked object. Thus God taketh the wise in their own craftiness.

As soon as Mr. B. found himself a prisoner, he told Capt. White (the man who had come over with him, as noted before) to go on with his business, as he had been designing;—to take the team, to put into the cart the things which had been packed up, together with all the children;—and drive on as fast as he could. He said he would take the horse, which he let him have, and ride up to Newbury, and see what they wanted of him there; and would be back and overtake him in a few hours.

"A man's heart deviseth his way; but the Lord directeth his steps." The heart of this man thus cruelly devised to send away his poor little children in such a terrifying manner; and that he himself would soon be after them. But the providence of a merciful God took them eventually out of his wicked hands.

I was at Gen. B.'s, when Mr. B. was brought there under keepers. It was indeed a solemn sight to me. Here was the man, who had been the husband of my youth, whom I had tenderly loved, as my companion, in years past, now a prisoner of civil justice, and at my prosecution. But his most obstinate and persevering wickedness had rendered it necessary. And I thought I might hope that the situation of my family might now be altered for the better.

Mr. B. asked me what I intended to do now? I replied, that I hoped to find men wiser than I, who would determine what was to be done. He said he knew I wished to have him give up to me a part of the interest; and that he had told me on Saturday that he would do it, and do what should be called honorable. He pretended he was now willing to do any thing that was right. He talked thus for a long time; but told nothing what he would do.

While we were waiting for the arrival of a brother, Mr. B.'s brother in law informed me that he had a piece of news for me. I asked him what it was? He answered, that all my children at Bradford, and as many things out of the house as was thought proper, were now under way for Whitestown! I asked, who had taken them? and how they had gone? He said, Capt. White, a man whom Mr. B. had employed, had gone on with them, this morning, in a cart drawn by oxen. I replied, if it was really thus, I was glad to come to the knowledge of it. He said it was a fact, for he saw them go.

It is impossible for words to express my grief on this occasion. Poor children, hauled away in such brutal cruelty. They had long been suffering for want of a mother. And now, that they had just had sight of her, and she of them, and hoped their relief was at the door; they are gone in this wretched manner;—hurried away;—totally unprepared!—the days were long, the sun hot, and those poor little lonely lambs bruised along in a cart, with only a stranger to take care of them! The babe I thought must certainly die. My mouth was shut with astonishment. But I endeavored to look to God to interpose and help in this scene of affliction. I walked the room with my eyes fixed upon the floor, but my soul lifted up to God, attempting, with humble confidence, to cast my burden upon him.

Mr. B. after a while, asked me, what I intended to do about the children, who were taken away? I

.replied, that I meant to trust them, as I had ever
done, in the hands of the Lord; and I doubted not
but he would take care of them. He asked if I did
not mean to go and take care of them? I was not ignorant of one design of this cruel subtle man, which
was to torture my tender parental feelings, by this
his conduct toward the children, and divert my attention from my prosecution of him; or get better
terms in our settlement, on his delivering up the
children. And this cruel purpose I was determined
to defeat. I told Mr. B. I had important business, on
which I must now attend; and I did not mean to be
diverted from it. I told him I had long viewed it a
great privilege to cast all my cares upon God. And
I believed God would give me firmness to pursue
my object with him; and also, that God would take
those children out of his cruel hands, and restore
them to me. Mr. B. appeared to feel mortified and
in some measure defeated.

I then and ever understood that trusting in God
implies the due use of all proper means. In the
present distressing case therefore, I was determined
to have all done that was possible, to recover my
children. Application was immediately made to
an attorney; to see what could be done. He said he
knew of no authority, by which I could take my
children back. The law had given a man a right
to move his children where he should think best,
and the wife had no right by law to take them from
him. But he said no law could prevent my attempting to alarm the man, whom Mr. B. had employed to take the children away, and to induce him
to return them to me.

In my perplexities, relative to the children, and
my affairs with Mr. B. nothing was done to bring
the children back, this first day. The next morning my brother W. was prepared to set out after
them. I wrote a letter by him to Capt. White, who
was taking them off, as follows:—

"Sir, I understand you have taken away my children, my clothing, and household furniture. As your friend, I advise you immediately to return them to the place whence you took them. If you do not, you may expect trouble.   A. B."

My brother went on inquiring for the load and the children; and found no difficulty in following their track. He came to a tavern in Thetford, where Capt. White and the children put up the first night, and inquired for them. The lady asked him, if he was the father of those children? He replied that he was not, but was a brother of their mother, and was in pursuit of them, to get them back. Then, said she, I will inform you concerning them. But if you had been their father, I would have given you no information. For I am sure that a man, who would send away young children in the manner those are sent away, is not fit to have the care of children. She then informed that they tarried there the night before; that the babe was so overcome with the journey, being out in the heat all day, and with most miserable accommodations, that she rested but little in the night, and cried chief of the time. She added, that the poor child appeared in the morning so unfit to be carried forward, that she begged of the oldest children to leave her with her, and she would take good care of her. And if she never saw their mother to deliver the infant up to her, she would take good care of her, as her own. For she really thought the poor child would not live through another day, to be carried on in that rough and cruel manner. They had complied with her request; and the child was *with her.*

What had rendered the case with the babe and the children more distressing, was, they had been so unfortunate as to take the itch, during my absence; and were now very bad with it. It was a dreadful trial to the children to give up their dear little sister, and leave her among strangers. But they had thought it best to do it; and had gone forward.

My brother W. now pursued Capt. White, and the children. He overtook them, and delivered to Capt. White my letter to him. He appeared troubled; and wished to know where Mr. B. was? My brother told him, he was in Newbury goal, in close confinement; and added, that he should advise him to look out for himself, and see what he was doing, in taking away a family of small children in this plight, and without father or mother to take care of them.—That, if he wished to avoid trouble, he had better take those children and that load of goods back immediately to Bradford. Capt. White was struck with fear. My brother informed him, that no person would wish to injure him, if he would now comply with his advice. He concluded to do it; and immediately turned his course. He was now much concerned for his own property in the hands of Mr. B. especially the horse he had let to him, and on which Mr. B. rode to Newbury. He wished to return immediately to secure this. The poor little children leaped for joy, as though they had been released from captivity.

After my brother had seen them safely retracing their steps, he returned and left them; taking the babe from Thetford in his arms, and conveying her to Newbury.

Thus a merciful God restored my dear children again. My soul praised and adored him for his goodness. I felt that peculiar gratitude was due to him, who has all hearts in his hands, that he moved the heart of that kind woman, to pity and interpose in behalf of my poor suffering child! I desired that I might ever have an affecting sense of God's marvellous kindness to the poor distressed babe, to all the children, and to me. And I felt very grateful to that kind woman who had acted so merciful a part, and it seemed to me had been the means of saving

the child's life. She had made an ointment; had
been applying it to the poor little creature; and was
doing all in her power for her restoration and comfort.

But to return to Mr. B. it was thought best, as
things were situated, that if Mr. B. would be induced to come to an honorable settlement, and give up
such a part of his property, as was deemed sufficient for his children, he might be permitted to do
it, and be gone forever from our sight. To this
point therefore our exertions were directed; and
the court was adjourned, from day to day, for several days; Mr. B. being as often remanded to close
prison. He still shewed his obstinacy, and exerted
all his intrigue to wring himself out of our hands.
He would pretend he was willing to do any thing,
and every thing, that was right. But when instru-
ments were written, he would pick some flaw in
them, or find some difficulty, and nothing could be
brought to a close. Day after day passed away in
this manner.

Sometimes he would try to excite my tender and
pitiful feelings, in hopes of finding some relief in this
way. On the third or fourth day of his confinement, my brothers and I thought we would go once
more, and see if he would come to terms. Mr. B.
looked through the small window in his prison
room, and seeing me in an adjacent room, with my
brethren, he desired me to take my seat by that
small window near him. He then began to try to
work upon my tender feelings. He said, it was a
great pity that he and I should set ourselves against
each other, and maintain our contention. He said
it was costly settling difficulties in the law. That
our interest was now wasting as dew before the sun;
and our poor little innocent children must suffer for
our folly. That if I would be persuaded to take
this matter out of the law, he would do what was
fully right; and our friends might assist in the set-

tlement, as well as the court. That it would hence be much better for our family to have it taken out of the law.

He seemed to think my tender feelings must certainly set him at liberty. He said, I could go home with my friends, and eat and drink with them, and sleep on a good bed; while he must be confined in that dirty, dark, and lonely room, with but little to eat; and with no better way to sleep, than to lie on the hard floor. He said he thought I was too tender-hearted to consider these things, and not feel for him so far, as to be willing to set him at liberty.

I replied that the considerations he had held up were not to me new. I had well considered and weighed them. I had done nothing without mature deliberation. I had done nothing against him from perverseness or stubbornness; but, as I trusted, from a sense of duty, and with Christian firmness. I sensibly felt for him in his wretchedness. He had ever well known my tender feelings. And he well knew I was the same now, that I ever was. His perfidies and wickedness had rendered these steps indispensable; and I should not now foolishly relinquish them. He well knew what he ought to do, and must do, in order to be set at liberty. And while he should refuse to do this, I trusted God would enable me to pursue the process, commenced against him with firmness.

But all my talk was in vain. Mr. B. would not come to any reasonable terms. It was determined therefore, by my friends and myself to take another course with Mr. B. We would take him into New Hampshire, and let the law have its course; and let it be ascertained whether he had, or had not, committed any capital crime. It was concluded that an officer should take him to Connecticut river, the line of the State; and that an officer, and proper assistance from Haverhill should meet him there, and take him into custody; and he should be brought to trial, according to law and evidence.

17

When I came again into the sight of Mr. B. he, not knowing what conclusion had been formed relative to him, began again to try to flatter me to set him at liberty. He said he had been trying but could not do any thing there a prisoner; he could not do business in such a situation. But if I would set him at liberty, he would do whatever I desired of him. I informed him of the conclusion we had made of taking him forthwith over the river into New Hampshire; and added, that I believed we could do business with him there to more thorough purpose, than any thing we had yet done.

This gave him a shock. He was utterly unwilling to go over the river. He now wished there might be one more trial to settle the business here. I consented. An attorney was called in; and he with my friends, and Mr. B. now soon settled the matter to our mind. Mr. B. made a legal conveyance of such part of his property, as we claimed and he was set at liberty.

The officers of the court, also my attorney, and the high sheriff, kindly gave me in all their fees. Also the selectmen of Landaff, who were down, and Mr. Warner, (who came home with me from Hartford, who had ridden fifty or sixty miles, and had been from home about a week,) all made me welcome to their kind services. Much gratitude I felt to them for their kindnesses. And much praise I was sensible, was due to God, that in his merciful providence, he had brought my long and sore difficulties to so favorable an issue.

Mr. B. appeared as though he sensibly felt himself to be beaten and defeated. We went to Bradford. My friends accompanied me, to see my affairs with Mr. B. finally closed. Many other people were present. Our effects we divided. Mr. B. relinquished to me all the children, but our three oldest sons. These he would take with him. I hoped these three sons would afterward be able to return; as they indeed did. In the parting of the children, and bringing our affairs to a close, my trials were inexpressibly severe. Numbers of men present remarked, that this was the most affecting sight they ever saw! Mr. B. insisted on taking several more of the young sons. They pleaded and begged to stay with their ma'am, and their sisters; and turned their attention to me with the most earnest entreaties. This was enough to break the stoutest heart. Mr. B. finally concluded I might take them. His self-interest here wrought in my favor. He knew not what to do with them.

Mr. B. and I parted. I had no expectation, or wish ever to see him again in this life. I petitioned for a bill of divorcement, and readily obtained it.

I now disposed of my children in the best way I could. The three oldest sons were gone with their father. The three oldest daughters were gone for themselves, one in the family state, as mentioned before. I had six younger daughters under my care, the oldest of whom was fifteen years of age; and the youngest upwards of a year old. Also several young sons, the oldest of whom was in his twelfth year; and the youngest in his fifth year.

I thought it best that most of these children should be put out, in regular and good families, where they might be well brought up to business. Such places I readily found; and had many more applications for them, than I could supply. I was urged to give up even my youngest, beside the babe, who should be well brought up, without any cost to me. But I hired a room, and chose to keep some of the youngest with myself. The property which Mr. B. conveyed to me and the children, was, in process of time turned into money, and delivered to me; which I disposed of in the best manner I was able, for the benefit of my family.

Thus I have sketched some of the most important events of my life, through which God, in his deep and holy providence, caused me to pass, from the time I entered the family state, A. D. 1767, in the twenty-second year of my age,—till A.D. 1792, when I was in my forty-seventh year. Great trials, and wonderful mercies have been my lot, from the hands of my Heavenly Father,

APPENDIX.

THUS the narrative of Mrs. Bailey is closed. I shall add a few things, relative to her, and the miserable man, from whom she was separated.

As to Major Bailey, a son of his gives me the following information; that his father after the final settlement which has been noted, returned with two of his older sons to Whitestown, where the second son Asa already was; that he was peevish and unreasonable to his three sons then with him. That his credit sunk, and he became wretched. That in Dec. 1793, he found and married a vile widow,—a turbulent being, who in some degree repaid his cruelties to a better companion. That in Jan. 1794, his three sons left him, and returned to their mother and friends. That rumors have since reported him to be in extreme poverty, and disgrace;—to have become a methodist preacher; to have been parted from his new wife; and then to have lived with her again in poverty, disgrace and misery. And that the probability is, the latter is now his wretched case.

This son discreetly remarks, relative to the publication of the preceding memoirs,—that perhaps many will wonder how the children should consent to such a publication. Those of them, who have been consulted, sensibly feel the delicacy of the subject. But, viewing the finger of Heaven in these distressing scenes, and not knowing but the narrative of them, which their venerable mother has left, is calculated to do good, they have endeavored to lay self out of the question, and to submit the matter to other judges.

*17

Relative to Mrs. Bailey, she came to Haverhill, after she was released from her cruel companion; hired a house, and lived with her four youngest children, four years, she then thought it best to put out these small children; and to go herself into some good family. She went and lived with Deacon Andrew Crook, of Piermont, a member of the church in Haverhill and a constant attendant on public worship in Haverhill, till their religious order was interrupted. Here she lived to the great comfort of the family, and her own comfort ten years.

After this it was thought best she should go and live with her children, who had families. With one and another of them she lived about eight years till her death. She died in the family of her son Asa Bailey of Bath.

This pious lady had a constant rule, to which she conscienciously adhered, never to make, or to receive a visit, without having some pious conversation. In this way she made all opportunities afforded by visits improving to the best interest of the soul.

In those days, and where she lived, in the earliest state of her family, schools were miscrable. All the literary, as well as religious instructions of her numerous family, devolved on her. And none of them failed of being very decent, and some very excellent readers.

After her husband left her, and while she lived in a family state, or wherever she resided in a family, if the man were absent, and the family were willing, she failed not to read God's holy word, and to pray night and morning, in the family. This was to her a delightsome employment, which long and pious practice had rendered most familiar, and in which she was very able.

As a reprover, she was very faithful, and very tender, and pungent. She would usually begin with unfeigned expressions of her own nothingness; and then proceed, either by some parable, or more literal expressions, to make the delinquent feel the object designed. On seeing a methodist use some impertinence, she pleasantly asked him, if he was a professor of religion? And being answered in the affirmative, she replied, it was not for her to say he was not a christian. But this she could say, he was not such an one as she wished to be!

To the church in ———, she wrote the following anonymous address, while she was residing among them, and feared they were something fallen from their first love. The pastor and good members could not but be delighted with it.

Aug. 31, 1798.

"To my Rev. Pastor, and beloved brethren and sisters, whom I love in the Lord. Dear Christian friends; I humbly beg your serious attention a few minutes, while I hint to you some things, which for considerable time have lain with weight upon my mind: But how shall I begin? For I find so much inactivity in myself, and find so much reason to be ashamed before God, and before all my acquaintance on earth on account of my leanness and unprofitableness in the things of religion, that I feel as though I might rather lay my hand upon my mouth, and cease at once from my object. But it appears to me a matter of such importance that I cannot longer neglect what appears a duty. And who can tell but the feeblest means may be blessed of God for good; and that the smallest spark may be made to kindle a flame of love to Christ, and of zeal and faithfulness in the hearts of his dear children.

We all well remember the goings of our God and King in the midst of us, in this place, a few years since, when it pleased the Almighty to awaken many among this people from carnal slumbers, to feel their lost estate, and to cry to God for mercy, We remember how our merciful God and Saviour did, by his almighty power, subdue many to himself, who were inquiring, what they should do to be saved? how he sweetly captivated their souls, and disposed them to yield themselves willing subjects to their rightful and sovereign Lord; having proper views of God, of themselves, of their duty, and of the worth of souls.

We well remember that while things were thus, great effects were produced on our hearts and lives. Our farms, our oxen, our domestic comforts, did not then have our highest attention, or stand between Christ's friends, and their God, or keep them from his worship. How few then appeared to be carried away with popularity, new fashions, or the things of this vain world. In those days Christ and religion were all our theme. We spake oft one to another; and the inquiry was for the prosperity of Zion; and whether any were newly brought to Christ? How careful were people then to receive instruction one of another. The subjects of grace seemed to take their greatest pleasure in doing something to build up the Redeemer's kingdom;— to enlighten and strengthen one another. When neighbors met even in the road, they could not pass, without something being said on the things of eternity. Prayer and reading the scriptures in families seemed a great delight. And how glad were we, when they said unto us, Let us go into the house of the Lord?

My dear friends, we then esteemed it our duty, not only to attend two meetings every Sabbath, but to have some religious meetings besides *every week*, that we might be acquainted with each other, and stir up each other's minds to the great things of religion. Was not this a great privilege? Was it not owned of Christ, and made a rich benefit to many?

But, my dearest friends, how is it with us now?

Does this life, this activity, still continue? Do we, as a church, maintain the life of religion, as in days past? Where are our religious conferences? Have they not been too much neglected, and the Holy Spirit grieved away? Has not occasion thus been given to the enemy? And are not Zion's friends left to mourn? Had we in those years of our attention seen another church do just as we have done, should we not have said of them, *"They did run well, who did hinder them?"*

. We had our two conferences in a week. But after some time it was said by some, that it might be more suitable to discontinue the Sabbath evening conferences; and *very faithfully* attend one conference in a week, on a week day. This expediency was adopted. After a while the week day conference began to be but thinly attended. I heard of no objection made 'to it by professed friends of religion. But it seemed to die away. Repeatedly only the Pastor and several others attended. And soon these pleasant meetings were no more.

. Upon one other failure, which appears to me still more unhappy, I wish to remark. It was once agreed in our church, that we would maintain a monthly church conference, beside preparatory lectures, for the sake of attending to church business; and especially to unite in prayer, and in free christian conversation with each other. To this appointment we long attended. And did we not find it very improving and pleasing? But after a while, (many of the members living at a distance, and much scattered,) it was proposed by some to discontinue these church conferences, and to have them absorbed in the preparatory lecture, and have *this* well attended. This after a while was agreed to; and thus those delightful church conferences were no more. Though the defect was *very much* made up, for a considerable time, in a church conference after our preparatory lecture; yet did not this too, after a while, much dwindle away? Have we not in these things, dear brethren and sisters, been too deficient, and too much inclined to turn back to the world? Is not that christian freedom, which used to be maintained among us, to so delightful and beneficial effect, now withered away? And are we not lean and dull, in proportion to this our unfaithfulness? Are not the pious grieved, and the wicked delighted with these things?

We are assured that those who love God will keep his commandments, and not find it grievous. Shall we not then, dearly beloved, give evidence to ourselves, and to others, that we have indeed risen with Christ, by seeking those things that are above! setting our affections on things above, and not on things on the earth. Shall we not hold fast our profession without wavering? Shall we not consider one another to provoke unto love and to good works, not forsaking the assembling of ourselves together, as the manner of some is, but exhorting one another daily while it is called to-day, lest any one be hardened through the deceitfulness of sin. A city that is set on an hill cannot be hid. Are we not as a city on an hill? Are we not under peculiar obligations to let our light shine before men, to the glory of God? Herein God is glorified, that we bear much fruit.

Do you not recollect, beloved friends, that some of us in this church left other places, and came by other churches, to join in christian communion with you, because we understood that God was singularly manifest among you? We understood that here were great christian freedom and christian faithfulness. Oh, ought not such members, who came from other places, as mentioned, to prove their godly sincerity in thus coming, by their persevering usefulness and faithfulness? And ought not the coming of such, to remind the church of the duty of faithfulness? Shall we not maintain the life of religion, and be valiant for the truth? Can we in any other way "be strong in the Lord, and in the power of his might?" Let us put on the whole armor of God, that we may be able to stand in the evil day, and to withstand the wiles of the devil. Does not the description apply to Christ's true church, "They all hold words, being expert in war; every man hath his sword upon his thigh, because of fear in the night?" Should we not watch and pray that we enter not into temptation? Ought we not to watch and pray always? O shall any of us be found sleeping?

I fear I shall intrude on your patience. But I feel as though I had you by the hand, or rather by the heart, and cannot let you go. My tender love for you, and for the cause which I plead, seems to demand a few words more. I know not how to think that we shall not immediately return, with warm and penitent hearts to the duties, which we have too much neglected:—to the duty of church conferences, and special seasons of prayer. We have found these a great privilege. Why then do we relinquish them? Can christians live in the neglect of duty? Shall not a sense of our ingratitude deeply affect our hearts, to think that after all the displays of sovereign love among us, and our great spiritual privileges, we are making no more grateful returns of love and obedience to God? Dear christian friends, I remember that while some were under your discipline, in times past, for irregular conduct;—in your kind intreaties and labors with them, this among other things was mentioned, that they had turned their backs upon your *church conferences*, and meetings. Now what will such persons think of you, that you have all relinquished those special meetings?

Think not that I have lost confidence in you, because I thus write. No, my beloved in the Lord, I have not lost confidence in you. If I had, I should not use such freedom. I have great confidence in you; and this animates me to attempt to stir up your minds by way of remembrance, in hopes you will become more engaged and heavenly; that God may be more glorified, and we comforted.

Nor would I be willing you should think that while I am thus addressing others, I feel whole in myself. No, my dear friends. My inactivity and great imperfections are my constant grief and burden;—far greater, than it is possible those of others should be. Yet I do think that the cause of Zion lies near my heart; that I do prefer Jerusalem above my chief joy. And the considerations I have suggested to you, I think, bind my own soul to live near to God. I humbly ask your prayers for me, that I *may* live near to him, and to his glory. I hope and am conscious that this epistle is the result of love, and of solemn prayer.

That God may bless us, and pour out his Spirit, and build up his kingdom, is the devout desire of
A SISTER.

I shall add one or two scraps, from the manuscripts of Mrs. Bailey.

"*Jan.* 1793. On the Holy Bible.

It is said of Christ, that his word was *with power.* I think I may say that the Holy Scripture is to me God's word *with power.* It is like apples of gold in pictures of silver. It is sweeter than the honey comb, or the honey. I do rejoice in God's word, as one who finds great spoil. I think I can say with David, I delight in the law of the Lord; and I meditate in it day and night. O Lord, open thou mine eyes, that I may behold wondrous things out of thy law. O let me not wander from thy commandments. Enable me to hide thy word in my heart, so that I may not sin against thee. Thy word is a lamp unto my feet, and a light to my paths. Thy word is very pure; therefore it is the delight of my soul. It is true from the beginning; and every one of thy righteous judgments endureth forever. I will never forget thy precepts; for with them thou hast quickened me. I have sworn, and through Christ will perform it; that I will keep thy righteous judgments. I love thy commandments above gold, yea above fine gold. Seven times a day do I praise thee, because of thy righteous judgments."

"*May,* 1793. On trusting God for my temporal support.

After a short season of melancholy, on account of my singular and trying circumstances, God did once more revive my hopes, and strengthen my faith in himself, and did lead me to the rock, which was higher than I. He did enable me to lift up my soul to God, and cast all my cares upon him. I thought I could take hold on his strength, and rest on his promises. So completely do I feel myself to be in his faithful hands, that I find no room to fear.

God's providential stores are without bounds. And it is as easy for him to provide for me, as for those, who now enjoy the greatest possessions. "The earth is the Lord's and the fulness thereof." And although I know not the farm, that will yield my food, nor the house that will long be my shelter, nor yet the kind friend, who will much interest himself in my behalf, from time to time, yet God knows my needs; he does care for me; he knows what will be most for his glory concerning me; and he has all hearts, as well as property, in his hands. And he can and will supply my needs, whenever it is best. God gives food to the beasts of the earth. He hears the ravens when they cry. And will he turn a deaf ear to the cry of his children? He will not. He will hear them....

I do believe, and hope, and trust in the same God, who made a way through the sea, to bring his people into the promised land; who caused the ravens to feed his Elijah; yea, and who sent this prophet to relieve the distress of the widow of Sarepta. God has been with me in six troubles, and in seven. And I now believe he will rever forsake me. I have enough to day. And I doubt not but I shall be able to say the same, every succeeding day of my life. The great God, after bringing me through the iron furnace of affliction, has done for me wonderful things. I am still in the same gracious hands; and it is enough. "It is the Lord; let him do what seemeth him good." God will provide as he sees best; and I ask no more; I desire no more. But I pray the Lord to make me truly thankful for his great goodness to me and others; and ever to hold my heart in a state of holy resignation to his sovereign will.

To be sure, God has seen fit to give me a very singular lot. He has afforded me signal lessons relative to my total dependance on him, and my duty of living by faith, and not by sight. But in my deepest afflictions, the word and grace of my heavenly Father yielded me such support and daily comfort, that certainly now I cannot sink; nor can I fear to trust my God in future. It is my natural inclination to wish to see my way through for a long time to come. But generally God has not suffered me thus to do. And I think he has given me that faith, which overcometh the world; and to feel as secure in him for my temporal accommodations, as though I had the greatest interests. The Lord reigns. In this I rejoice. My help is in him alone. And I need not fear, though the earth be removed. God spared not his only begotten Son. And shall he not with him freely give us all things. If the greater was not withheld, the less will not be withheld."

Mrs. Bailey died with a lung fever. For a year before her death she had been favored with very good health. About three weeks before her death he took a slight cold attending an evening lecture, which had been appointed on her account. Sabbath, Feb. 5, 1815, she was very comfortable through the day. At evening the was seized with sharp pains in every part of her frame. She remarked that she knew her last illness must come; and she thought this would probably prove her last. About the middle of the week her physician pronounced her case hopeless;—said she was sinking under the lung fever; and hoped she was resigned to her situation. She replied that she was entirely resigned. She thanked him for his kindnesses: hoped he would be well rewarded; and calmly bid him farewell. She informed her friends she had no fear of death, and no choice whether to live or die, but that the will of the Lord might be done. She regretted that she could say but little to her children and friends. Such was the nature of her disorder that she could say but little. She continued till Saturday night; and just before twelve o'clock she gave up the ghost, in calmness and peace, and began her new sabbath in heaven. She died Feb. 11, 1815, in the 70th year of her age. A sermon was delivered at her funeral, from the very appropriate text, Rev. xiv, 13; "And I heard a voice from heaven, saying unto me, Write, Blessed are the dead, who die in the Lord, from henceforth. Yea, saith the Spirit, that they may rest from their labors, and their works do follow them."

BIOGRAPHICAL SKETCHES,

OR,

RELATIONS OF THE CONVERSIONS

OF

SUNDRY PERSONS.

THE following original relations are here an-nexed. They are selected from a large number of relations of persons, with whom the editor has an intimate acquaintance. A few of those only are selected, where the subsequent life and conversa-tions of their subjects have well evidenced, in the eye of charity, the genuineness of the gracious op-ertions which they relate. Hence they may be read with a good degree of confidence, that they do exhibit the *turning point* from a life of sin, to a life of holiness.

Such relations of the works of special grace, in the conversions of God's chosen people, are very interesting. They give glory to the God of grace; and afford signal instructions to men, by exhibiting practical, and most solemn testimonies in favor of the peculiar doctrines of grace found in the gospel.

We find much, in the sacred oracles, fully in fa-vor of recording and prudently circulating such re-lations. The sweet Psalmist of Israel was much in writing relations of his own religious experiences. Many of his Psalms abound with these writings. Numbers of them present but little else than this. And David avowed his design to relate the wonders of grace in him, and toward him. "Come, and hear, all ye that fear God, and I will declare what he hath done for my soul." And other inspired writers of the Psalms do the same.

The penman of the Acts of the Apostles was inspired to record the particulars of the conversion of Paul. And from time to time Paul, in after days, repeated the relation of the joyful event. And Peter was inspired to leave the general injunction, "Sanctify the Lord God in your hearts; and be ready always to give an answer to every man that asketh you a reason of the hope that is in you, with meekness and fear."

Perhaps, by a too general suppression of the relations of the most evident and remarkable conversions, the glory of them has not been sufficiently given to their glorious Author; and the strength and comforts, which they are most happily calculated to afford, have been withholden from the children of God. If I know the experience of religion, I am sure that I have often found great quickening, instruction, and solemn delight, from *perusing*, and *re-perusing* such relations. But alas, I find but few of them to peruse, as given to the public.

The *writing* of such relations, is of service to the young convert,—to learn self-examination,—acquaintance with his own exercises,—and to obtain the confirmation of a good hope,—as well as to gain the confidence of christians, who hence form a better acquaintance with his gracious character.

As to an objection, that hypocrites may write good relations, it proves nothing, because it proves too much. For the same objection lies equally against the christian profession, and all religious conversation and practice.—Hypocrites may, and do, attempt the same.

I shall give no names of the subjects of the following relations. For a number of them are yet living; though some are dead. I shall call them by the names of the alphabet, A, B, C, D, &c.

*18

1. *Relation of Mrs. A.*

THE Spirit of God, I am now sensible, has been striving with me from my childhood. Many have been my checks of conscience, and fears of hell. But I often stiffled them. When I was married, and came to live with Mr. A., I found myself much tried with the sentiments, which were preached in this place. The doctrines of election, decrees, and divine sovereignty, were to me very disagreeable. But after a while I resolved to throw these things from my mind, and care no more about them. For such was my situation, that I knew it would be much against my interest, and reputation, to be found an opposer of such preaching. Upon this my feelings became very secure; and I was wholly taken up with the things of this life. I was greatly desirous of obtaining property; and could not endure the thought of being poor. Often when I saw the prosperity of others, and that their situation was more affluent than mine, my heart would rise against God, as though he were a partial Being, a hard Master. And I often felt disheartened and discouraged.

On a Sabbath, Nov. 30, 1801, God was pleased to call my attention to eternal things. I was reading the parable of the rich man, Luke 13. The words, "But God said to him, Thou fool; this night thy soul shall be required of thee; then whose shall these things be that thou hast prepared?"—took fast hold of my mind. I looked with amazement on my past life. I queried, what worldly interest would profit me, if my soul must be lost? I went to meeting with a heavy heart. The subject of the preacher was, the merchantman seeking goodly pearls, finding one of great price, and selling all his other property to buy it. The reading of the text much affected me. I felt that I was indeed undone, unless I could obtain that pearl. And how to obtain it, I knew not. I felt myself condemned; and thought I was going to eternal ruin. The sermon deepened my distressing impressions; and they continued for some time. But being much taken up in company, my distress of mind abated, and my convictions nearly left me; though I had intervals of terror.

On Lord's day, March 1, 1802, I was reading a funeral sermon of a minister. The preacher spake of the meeting, which ministers and their people must have before the bar of Christ, what an account must there be given of all sermons, and of praying opportunities; and that companions, parents and children must there have a most solemn meeting. The words were set home upon my heart. I was greatly shocked. I reflected how many sermons I had heard; and to how little effect. —How many prayers I had reason to believe had been made to God for me.—How highly I was exalted in privileges; and what wretched improvement I had made. I was thrown into great distress. When people came home from meeting, I endeavored to conceal my feelings, but I could not. When some came into the room, I thought they would rise in judgment against me at the great day. I knew not what to do. I tried to read my Bible; but it all condemned me. Great enmity now rose in my heart against God, and his law. I could not endure the thought of being in his hands, and of being disposed of as he should please. I was disposed to seek relief from the thought, that there is nothing in religion;—or that all men will be saved. But my conscience testified against these expedients. I felt the presence and terrible majesty of God. I saw that I was in his hands; depended on him for every thing; and had got to stand before him in judgment. The thought was insupportable. I saw that God was a Sovereign, and would have

mercy on whom he would have mercy; and would
dispose of me as he pleased. I imagined to myself,
that he was the most tyrannical Being; and had
placed me in a situation to be eternally miserable.
At times I labored to do something to recommend
myself to God. But here I could obtain no relief.
For I saw that my heart was utterly perverse; and
for my best performances I felt condemned. I felt
that I was an undone creature. What to do, or attempt, I knew not. But I fought against God with
all my might.

One day as I was walking the room in anguish,
I saw a man coming in, with a grave-cloth under
his arm. I concluded some person was dead. I
queried with myself, what must have been my situation, had I been thus called away! I was so shocked
with the thought, that my strength failed me; and
I dropped into a chair in silent astonishment. My
load of guilt and wretchedness seemed insupportable. The next day was the Sabbath. I attended
meeting, and heard a sermon from these words,
"Lord save me; I perish." On hearing the text, I
felt glad, and hoped I should now hear something,
that would afford relief. But O, my disappointment! Every thing that was said was against me,
and seemed to conspire to cut me off. In the afternoon, the minister being called away to attend a
funeral, at a distance, our deacons led in the meeting. One of them read Flavel's Husbandry spirit-
ualized. The author spake upon pruning orchards,
and cutting down those trees, which cumbered the
ground. This I saw was my case. I felt myself to
be a cumberer of the earth; and thought I should
not be suffered to live. Such was my view of my
wicked heart, and of my just condemnation, that I
felt myself to be ripe for destruction. Coming
home from meeting, and feeling my heart wran-
gling against the book which had been read, I asked the deacon, as he passed by with it under his

arm, to lend that book to me. The fact was, I wanted to read it myself, in hopes of finding it less terrible to me. He looked me in the face, and said he was glad to have me take it. I felt mortified, and was sorry I had asked for it. I read the pages, which I had heard at meeting. But I was so far from finding relief, that I was the more wounded and distressed.

I kept my troubles as much as possible to myself. I said nothing concerning them to Mr. A. For I well knew his strict evangelical sentiments, and what he would say to me. This I had no desire to hear. He had often attempted to converse with me; and I had as often evaded it. For I was utterly unwilling to make that surrender of myself to God, which I well knew he would press upon me.

At night I retired to bed; but I could not sleep. My anguish increased, till I thought I must speedily die. I could refrain no longer. I asked Mr. A. if he was awake? I found he was. I told him I was in great distress of mind, and I thought I must soon die under it. He replied that he had long perceived my trouble, and had tried to introduce conversation with me; but finding me utterly unwilling to converse with him on the subject, he had refrained. He then conversed freely with me, and clearly described my state, my duty and my only ground of hope. But the opposition of my heart rose violently against the truths urged upon me. I replied that I could not feel reconciled to God, unless he would save my children and friends, as well as myself. He told me this feeling was unreasonable and wicked; that my will must be bowed and made submissive to the will of God; I must unconditionally embrace Jesus Christ; or be unavoidably miserable. I then begged of him to say no more, and go to sleep; for I could hear no more of this. My enmity against God and all religion, at that time, was inexpressible. I lay and thought upon my dreadful case. I felt myself to be in the immediate presence of the Almighty God;—that he looked me through and through;—and I felt I was justly condemned to be forever miserable. I would fain have fled out of God's hands; but I was infinitely unable. It tortured my soul to think that I must be disposed of at his sovereign will. I rose from my bed, and desired Mr. A. to pray with me. He did. But alas, such was the bitterness of my heart, that I could not unite with him in prayer. My distress increased, till I thought I was actually going to die, and sink into eternal despair.

I now saw and felt that God had a perfect right to do with me as he pleased. And I was willing to give myself up into his hands, that he should dispose of me for time and eternity, as he should see fit. The following words slipped from my cheerful tongue, *I am willing to be in the hands of God, as clay in the hands of the potter!* My distress was gone. I fainted, and for some time lost my senses. When I came to myself, I found myself upon the bed, and in a most calm and peaceful state of mind. All my opposition and trouble seemed to be gone. I knew not the cause. I had no idea of having been made a subject of renewing grace. The thought turned in my mind, that I had lost all my convictions. This something alarmed me. But I felt delighted with the character of God. Christ appeared just such a Saviour as I needed, and altogether lovely. I felt a satisfaction in giving up myself into his hands, to be disposed of as should be for his glory.

Reflecting on my feelings and views, and comparing them with the word of God, I began to admit of a hope that I had passed from death unto life. I hope my heart is reconciled to God. And truly I am convinced that the salvation of lost man is wholly of the Lord, and according to his own sovereign will; and not for any thing in the creature,

I now desire to own my glorious Saviour before men; to walk in the order of his kingdom; and to partake of the rich benefits of his gracious ordinances.

---

2. *Relation of Miss B.*

Not two years ago, an incident alarmed my mind. I saw that I was a great sinner, and feared I should be forever lost. Soon after, our minister visited my school. His conversation and prayer much affected me. I was led to feel myself to be in a very guilty and dangerous situation. I resolved to reform, and read, and do all the good I could; and I hoped this would cancel some part of my debt to divine justice; or induce God to save me. Soon after, old Mrs. M. was drowned. I was struck, and led to inquire, why I was spared? My trouble now became so great, that my sleep, was much interrupted. And many times I knew not how to get through with the business of the day. I wickedly attempted to get relief from my tortures of mind, by mingling in company. But those tortures would return with fresh vigor, after being thus interrupted. The death of one of my scholars (he being drowned) increased my alarms. I then attempted to obtain relief by embracing the scheme of universal salvation. For I found my heart full of enmity against the scheme of doctrines preached in this place, and by all regular ministers. I wished to disbelieve those doctrines, and to think all men will be saved. I accordingly conversed with a teacher of universalism. He was very confident in his scheme, and conversed very freely. But I was now thoroughly cut off from the belief of it. My conscience roared upon me, and thundered in my ears, that what he held up was but a *perversion* of the word of God. The truths of God were now set home upon my soul with unutterable power; and my horror of conscience was very great.

Hearing one day of a person hopefully converted, my heart rose in great enmity against christians. This enmity became so powerful, that for several weeks I said many things (and all I could well conceive of) to their disparagement. A young woman died suddenly. This gave me a new alarm and stopped my clamors against the people of God. The words seemed to sound in my ears;

> "And are we wretches yet alive?
> And dare we yet rebel?
> 'Tis boundless, 'tis amazing love,
> That bears us up from hell."

I now thought I must fly from the wrath to come, and do something to obtain salvation. I attempted to retire, and call upon God for mercy; but repeatedly was I driven back from my closet, without being able to say a word. For a considerable time I thus remained almost in despair.

One sabbath morning, I had a lively impression of the day of judgment, and of sinners calling to the rocks and mountains to fall on them, and hide them from the dreadful presence of their Judge. My distress of soul I cannot describe. The words struck my mind, "Stand still and see the salvation of the Lord." I recollected not *what* or *where* they were. But they seemed to afford some mitigation to my despairing tortures. I went to meeting. Our minister preached from these words, "For the Lord hath chosen Zion to be an habitation for himself." Never did I hear a sermon before. The scheme of sovereign grace opened strangely to my view. I now saw and loved the doctrines, which I before hated and rejected. I saw that this scheme of grace was not only taught in the Bible, but was the only door of hope for such beings as I saw myself to be. I seemed to realize that if God had chosen me in Christ before the foundation of the world, he could and would convert and save so vile a wretch. If he had not, he had a right thus to decide, and to leave me to perish in my sins, rejecting his salvation. And I could with cheerfulness leave myself in the hands of God. I felt such a calmness of mind, as I never felt before. God and divine things appeared ineffably delightful.

I have never since that day heard the doctrines of divine sovereignty preached too forcibly. The scheme of free grace, which I used to hate, is all my hope. When I hear people converse upon it as I used to converse, it is to me matter of most serious grief. I am sure they are very wrong, as I know I myself was, when I conversed thus; and they will one day see it. And I hope and pray it may be before it is too late. I have been troubled, relative to baptism. But I have become fully sat-isfied with the order of this congregational church, relative to this, as well as other things. And I am sensible it is my duty, and is my desire, (though I feel most unworthy,) openly to unite with God's people here, to walk in his gracious ordinances.

---

3. *Relation of Mr. C.*

I LIVED an impenitent sinner, till last spring. I then became more attentive to reading and religious meetings than before. For six weeks my serious impressions increased. One day, attending a religious conference, at the house of a neighbour, our minister held up the depravity of the human heart in a clear and forcible manner. I was exceeding vexed and agitated. I went home in great distress, and had feelings of violent opposition. I wickedly resolved that I would no more attend meetings to hear such sentiments; nor should my family attend. But I found it hard to kick against the pricks. I found that the enmity, which was at first excited against a teacher, was indeed against the word of God. This enmity, and my horror became terrible. I would read my Bible, and then throw it by; I could not endure it; nor hear it read. I labored to conceal my agitations and distress. I could not endure that any should know my situation.

My distresses continued. I could not get rid of them. I became fully convinced that I was a great sinner; had broken the whole of God's law, and was justly condemned. And I concluded eternal misery must be my portion. I finally was tempted to think, that the sooner I knew my woful torments in the world of despair, the better. Yet, I was tempted to destroy myself, and thought I must do it. Night after night I was kept awake, ruminating upon the terrors of my case, and the horrible deed in expectation. Just before the period arrived to execute so fatal a purpose, I was enabled to exert mental power enough to change my purpose from the design of destroying myself, to that of flying to some distant part of the world. As well as I had loved my dear family, this I resolved so to do. Never before did I know the feelings of distress and anguish. Guilt, madness, and despair, seemed to combine for my ruin. I felt undone. One night as I lay waking, thinking upon the horrors of my case, new views of the word of God shone into my soul. Passages full of salvation came with force to my mind; such as, "Son be of good cheer; thy sins are forgiven thee." I had such views of the way of salvation, as I never had before. My purpose of fleeing to some distant region was laid aside. I felt I could be very happy where I was. Fears of being deceived rose in my mind, and I had again great darkness. But the passage, "Come ye blessed of my Father," occasioned the return of light and comfort.

The Bible, and the preaching of the gospel, have since appeared to me entirely new. They form the sources of my delight. The doctrines of grace, against which I had the most decided enmity, I now love as the blessed truths of God; and as unfolding the only door of hope for fallen man.

I am satisfied with the order of the kingdom of God in this place; and desire to give myself, and children, up to God, according to the institution of his grace.

4. *Relation of Miss D.*

WHEN I was young, my mind was often impressed with the solemn things of eternity. But the vanities of youth, and the hope that I had many years to live, would soon remove such anxieties. Hearing our minister converse, some time ago upon the peculiar doctrines of grace, I found my heart utterly opposed to them, and determined never to believe them. I thought if they were true, they were inconsistent with my being criminal for neglecting Christ. But it was not long, before I was constrained to believe the truth of these doctrines. I saw the Bible did absolutely and abundantly contain them. But I could not perceive why they should be said to be desirable. They were far from being thus to me.

But I began to feel, from a view of the doctrines of the gospel, that I was in the presence and hands of a holy God, who would dispose of me as he pleased. And I felt that, notwithstanding the sovereignty of God, I was a sinner, and inexcusable. My sins began to appear awful; and my condemnation most just. I then formed resolutions to live a very moral and strict life; and hoped that through the mercy of God this would be sufficient. But alas,

I reaped continual disappointment. I could not heal my wounded conscience. Our minister preached from these words, "Choose you this day whom you will serve." My false refuges were gone, and I was deeply alarmed. The following text, (not long after illustrated,) "Ye cannot serve the Lord; for he is a holy God;"—filled me with great dismay. I labored to quiet my mind with general indefinite ideas of the mercy of God. On a Sabbath the text gave me great uneasiness, "What is the hope of the hypocrite?" I tried to banish it from my mind. But it returned with new force. I threw it off again. These words then forcibly arrested me, "Wo to them that are at ease in Zion." I now felt myself a great sinner in the awful presence of God; and that I had been thus all my days; and without his rich mercy I was forever undone. I could not pray. My heart was as hard as a stone. I felt that the prayers of such a heart were sin; and God would not hear them. I felt that if I should never obtain mercy, I must entirely justify God.

Remaining some time in this dreadful suspense, I was brought to say, in the deepest sense of my unworthiness, "God be merciful to me a sinner."

I became joyfully convinced that God was on the mercy-seat, inviting sinners to come to him. I saw there was enough in Christ for so great a sinner as I. But it seemed as though, if God should forgive me, I never could forgive myself, for my vile treatment of him, and living so long in the rejection of Christ. The invitations of grace looked to me wonderful and glorious. I thought I could forever sing the song of redeeming grace, let what would become of me. I felt that it was a great privilege to give myself unreservedly, and unconditionally to God. And I longed to have all do the same. But I could leave myself and friends, and all things, in God's faithful hands.

I was, after a season, led to inquire, Shall I now profess Christ and his religion, and take my lot

with his followers? Or shall I seem to take my
part with the stupid world? These words occurred
to my mind, "Esau for a morsel of meat sold his
birth-right." The interests of this world appeared
to me like Esau's mess of pottage. And surely I
thought I felt the most decided preference of the
lot and inheritance of the followers of Christ, above
Esau's mess of meat, or the vain influence and interests of the people of the world. I feel determined, in the strength of divine grace, to follow
Christ. And I desire to unite with his followers in
this church.

5. *Relation of Mr. E.*

I HAVE been a subject of some serious impressions from my early days. But my heart ever said,
"Go thy way for this time." Last winter hearing
our minister preach on family religion, and the
great duty of training up children in the fear of
God, I found myself condemned. My conscience
plead guilty. I found myself deeply arrested with
the thought, that the Spirit of God was now
calling me; and probably it was the last time.
My heart began to complain of God's government. I thought I was willing to come to him;
but he was unwilling to save me. I feared I was
made for misery. My heart quarrelled at the
thought, and said, "This is a hard saying." I
punctually attended divine worship, and heard many excellent sermons. But I found nothing in my favor. I had much distress concerning the decrees of
God. I feared he had called in all his chosen, in
this place, and I must perish. I was tempted to
shake off my convictions, and take what pleasure I
could in this life, as being all the good I could ever
enjoy. But the thought of this appeared to me horrible. I attempted to pray that God would have
mercy on me. But I dared not to say to him, "Thy
*19

will be done," lest God should take me at my word, and cast me off. I felt myself to be in a very dreadful case. I must have faith in Christ, or be forever lost. Yet faith was the gift of God. I thought with myself what can be done? What shall I do to be saved? Worlds would I have given, had they been in my power, to have found the way of salvation.

My heart rose against my Maker for placing an event, to me so momentous as my salvation, in the hands of Adam, when he knew he would fall. I would have given the universe to have died in infancy, or even to have been made a brute. And I thought the sooner I died, the better.

The thought now occurred with awful force to my mind, that I was in arms against a holy God, whose almighty power had hitherto kept me out of hell, which I fully deserved. I wondered he had not sent me thither. I saw it would have been just; and that God was just in saving whom he would, and leaving others to perish. For all, by nature, are fighting against him; and deserve eternal death.

I now saw that if ever I was saved, it must be by the free grace of God. I hope that I was then stripped of self-righteousness, and made to rest on the sovereign mercy of God in Christ. I began to feel pleased with the divine government, and could cordially say, "Thy will be done." I longed to be able to glorify God. Though I had then no idea of having been born again; yet I felt an unusual and delightful composure. Hearing a sermon upon being *followers of them, that by faith and patience are inheriting the promises*, I received light, hope, and comfort. One Sabbath morning I waked with these words powerfully on my mind:

"Hark! the Redeemer from on high,
Sweetly invites his fav'rites nigh!
From caves of darkness and of doubt,
He gently speaks, and calls us out."

After such views and feelings, I could not but hope in the mercy of the Lord through Jesus Christ. The invitations and promises of grace are precious to my soul. I have many and distressing fears. But my hopes prevail. And I think it my duty to own Christ before men.

6. *Relation of Mrs. F.*

From the time I was twelve years of age, I had serious impressions. But I lived without God in the world. Ten months ago I was sick. I was alarmed from a consciousness that I was not prepared to meet my Judge. After health was restored, the solemn impression remained, and gradually increased. At a lecture at a private house, upon the whole needing not the physician, but they that are sick;—I thought the preacher had discovered something singular in my case, and his object was to point it out to others. I felt myself undone. My pungent distress continued. I seemed to be held out of the bottomless pit only as it were by a single hair. I saw I deserved to go thither. I seemed to feel myself arraigned at the bar of my angry Judge, and only waiting for the sentence, "Depart ye cursed."

On one Sabbath morning I waked, and found my burden gone. My mind was calm in the view of God and divine things. But I was terrified from a view that I had lost my conviction, and had become stupid. My spirit of bondage had fled; and I thought I was delighted in the view of God, and the way of salvation. Hearing, at a preparatory lecture, a description of the *christian warfare*, I thought I could witness in myself the feelings of the new-born soul. But I discovered such vast deficiency and depravity in my heart, that I thought it could not be that I was interested in Christ. My fears prevailed, till the next preparatory lecture.

Hearing then a description of the *good hope through grace*, salvation by Christ was so opened and presented to my view, that I thought I had substantial evidence of having passed from death to life. But my fears have since been distressing. It has seemed impossible that such a heart as I find mine to be, should possess the least degree of the grace of God. I find myself at a vast distance from being what I used to apprehend true christians to be. And at times I greatly fear that I am in the gall of bitterness and bonds of iniquity. Never did my heart appear to be so wicked, as at present. But I think this is my great burden and grief. And I long to be reconciled to God through Jesus Christ. I should account this my greatest happiness.

I know it is my duty to own Christ before men; to come visibly into the bonds of his covenant; and walk in his ordinances. And I am induced to venture forward, hoping in the mercy of God through Jesus Christ.

7. *Relation of Mrs. G.*

AFTER I was two-and-twenty years of age, I had deep impressions of mind concerning my future state. But I continued for years impenitent. Last spring, hearing a sermon from these words, "Behold, now is the accepted time,"—I was struck with conviction and distress. I thought, if I neglected my salvation any longer I could have no hope. The thought of my being left to perish, sunk deep into my heart. I was much affected; but labored to suppress and conceal it. My distress continued. I could not wear it off. Sometime after, hearing our minister preach from these words, "Behold the Lamb of God, that taketh away the sin of the world," the sermon most deeply arrested me. The sacrament was administered. My being separated from the people of God, on this solemn occasion, led me to look forward to the time, when the wheat and the chaff shall be separated; the wheat gathered into Christ's garner; and the chaff burned with unquenchable fire. I felt myself to be among this chaff; and that I was undone. I retired home with a heavy heart. Monday was a distressing day. When I sat to eat, I felt myself to be most unworthy of such bounties of providence. I could not refrain from weeping. But I retired to conceal it. My distress seemed insupportable. But I was unwilling it should be known. O, I thought, I would gladly have exchanged situations with any animal, or reptile in creation. I thought I had liked our minister, and liked his distinguishing preaching. But I now could not endure either. The doctrine of election tortured me. My heart rose against the doctrines of grace. The next day I thought my conviction had left me. Now I thought, I must surely perish in my sins. I retired to my chamber. And truly I found my distress was not gone. It seemed as though I must have been overpowered, and destroyed. I begged of God for mercy. I could conceal my anguish no longer. I made it known to my husband, and the family. I tried to go to the Bible for help: but my heart alas, at times, would not suffer me thus to do. A professor conversed, and prayed with me. But no relief appeared, I walked my room in anguish. The sun shone; but the day was to me darkness; and the whole world appeared a gloomy prison, and good for nothing. Such were my views of my guilt and wretchedness, that I thought my nature must sink under them, and that I should live but a short time. My sins, especially unbelief, appeared of the deepest die, and unpardonable. My bodily strength failed. I threw myself upon the bed, and saw nothing but darkness and despair.

The thought now struck my mind with great force, that I could not save myself; but God could save. And whom he loves, or means to save, he rebukes, and makes them see their guilt and wretchedness. My soul was calmed. I felt willing to resign myself, soul and body, unreservedly, into the hands of God my Saviour. From the depths of distress and terror, I obtained the sweetest composure, and inexpressible joy. My feelings since have been various. But the Bible is to me a new and glorious book. I long to have all men discover and embrace its excellencies. And I desire to walk in all its commands and ordinances.

8. *Relation of Mrs. H.*

Four years ago, my attention was called up to the things of religion. I felt a desire to meet with christian people, but I feared the ridicule of the the ungodly. And I feared to attend conferences, lest I should be questioned, and the wretched state of my mind exposed. The relations given in by professed converts much affected me. But my wicked heart suggested that God was partial in taking one and leaving another. I was displeased with this; and concluded I would not go to meeting. I thought if God saw fit to give me a new heart, very well. If not, I could do nothing. And I would wait for him to do his own work. My anxiety abated. I grieved away the Holy Spirit and became stupid.

Six months ago, God was pleased to lay his hand upon me in the sudden death of a child. Upon this my heart rose violently against God. I mourned; and my heart wrangled with my Maker, as though he had dealt very unjustly and cruelly with me.

God was pleased now to shew me the wickedness of my heart. I saw that I was fighting against God, and was extremely wicked. I was greatly confounded: I clearly discovered that I must have a new heart, must cast myself upon the mercy of

God in Christ, and be reconciled to his character;
or be forever lost. My past sins rose like mountains before me. I saw how obstinate I had been in
neglecting and despising so many offers of mercy.
The trouble of my loss, in the death of a little son,
was swallowed up in my far greater anguish for
my soul.

A religious meeting was appointed at our house:
but I thought none would attend it; for they would
not come where there was so vile a being as I. To
my surprise people did come. Then I was distressed
for the consequence. For I thought, now I must not
only hear those dreadful truths, which are so terrible to me; but by questions and conversation, my
wretched character and situation must be unfolded.

The religious meeting was opened. To my amazement, no such evils, as I had anticipated, occurred.
The singing and prayers were excellent, and most
delightful. I could join in every word with all my
heart. The discourse of the minister was plain,
important, and to me most lovely. Never did I see
such a meeting before. I could pray with him,
who led in prayer; and sing with those, who sang, I
felt a sweet composure, to which my heart had ever
before been a total stranger. I could praise God
for every thing;—could bless him for afflictions, as
well as mercies. Duty appeared easy and most delightful. I had no idea of the cause of this alteration.
After meeting, I longed to talk with my friends.
I knew not how to retire, and lose my time in
sleep. The next day I could take my food and go
about my business with alacrity. I had before
been afraid to eat, feeling so utterly unworthy of
every divine bounty; and had no heart to attend to
any business. Now I could labor, with the greatest cheerfulness, to get my business out of the
way, that I might have leisure to take my Bible,
and have comfort in reading and devotion. A

christian friend, the next day, suggested to me a
hope that I was reconciled to God. I was surprised at the suggestion. I had apprehended no such
thing. But I truly felt myself in a new world. I
have since entertained a hope that I have experienced renewing grace. My hearts desire and
prayer to God is, that I may daily die to sin, and
to this vain world, and live to God, and be prepared for the world to come. I desire to have Christ
for my Saviour; to be taught by his word and
Spirit; to own him before men as my Lord and
Master; and to walk in all his commands. The
kind of preaching, which I used to hate, is now
my delight. And I rejoice to unite with the people
of God in the assembly of the saints.

9. *Relation of Miss I.*

I LIVED a careless impenitent life, till last spring.
Attending the death of old Mr. J., I was solemnly
impressed with the query, what must be my case,
were I called hence? The death, and funeral sermon, of Mr. T. S. soon after, deeply affected me.
A sermon soon after from the words, "I came not
to call the righteous, but sinners to repentance,"
made me greatly to tremble. At a lecture the minister conversed with me. I tried with all my might
to appear indifferent to what he said, and to shake
off all my impressions and distress. But I could not
do it. I was mortified with the idea, that I should
be no company for my mates, if I should become religious. Also my heart rose against the doctrines
of the Bible. I could not endure them. I returned
one day from a private lecture, highly displeased
with the preaching I had heard. The minister and
other people stayed to converse; but I fled from the
place. Being in trouble I read my Bible. I lit upon the
passage, "Give glory to the Lord your God, before
he cause darkness, before your feet stumble upon the

dark mountains, and while ye look for light, he turn
it into the shadow of death, and make it gross darkness." I saw that I had not given glory to God; and
was utterly indisposed thus to do. I hence thought
God would soon take me away, and plunge me in the
darkness of despair. I was filled with great terror.

I now attempted to pray, to read, and reform,
and do something to recommend myself to God.
But alas, I clearly saw I could do nothing. One
night, after retiring to bed, my horror of soul was
so great, that I could not sleep. In the course of
the night I rose, and walked my room. I saw that
I was exposed to hell, and fully deserved to be sent
thither; that nothing held me out of eternal burn-
ings, but the brittle thread of life. And I wondered
I was not there. I attempted to beg for mercy,
but my prayers appeared full of sin and pollution;
and they but added to my guilt and wretchedness. The next morning my distress left me.
The Bible, the way of salvation, and the things of
God, appeared in a new point of light. I saw a
beauty and fulness in Christ. I thought I could
commit myself into his hands; could leave all things
for him, and commit all my cares to him.

Not long after I was taken sick. I now set myself to serious self-examination, to learn what was
my state?—and why I was so free from my former
distress?—when perhaps I was now going into eternity. The verse of Dr. Watts passed through my
mind with exquisite delight;

"Jesus can make a dying bed
Feel soft as downy pillows are;
While on his breast I lean my head,
And breathe my life out sweetly there."

I could not refrain from prayer and praise with
an audible voice. I thought I found it delightful to
give glory to God.

I afterward greatly feared I was deceived by
him, who transforms himself into an angel of light
20

to deceive and ruin souls. I was much afflicted
with temptations. I read the eighth and ninth chapters to the Romans; the latter of which I had before hated and neglected. The truths here contained now appeared to me good and delightful, and
the only door of hope.

After I recovered, I heard a sermon on being
slain by the law; another on redeeming the time.
The door of gospel salvation seemed in a clear
manner set open to me. It was indeed a new and
living way. I felt constrained to hope in this salvation. A sermon afterward from this passage,
"Jesus Christ came into the world to save sinners,
of whom I am chief," confirmed my hope and comfort. I have since continued to hope, but with
many fears. And though I feel myself most unworthy of christian fellowship;—yet I am sensible
it is my duty and privilege to bear my public testimony for Christ and his religion.

10. *Relation of Mrs. J.*

I LIVED a stupid life, till within one year. My
attention was arrested to serious things by the entreaties of a brother, who lives at a distance. I
visited my friends in my native place who ex-
horted me to attend to the state of my soul. I
returned home determined to work out my salvation. I went several times to meeting; but I could
not endure the preaching. I was extremely offended to hear the distinguishing doctrines of grace, and
of the divine government. I resolved I would not
hear such hard things; and I absented myself from
the house of God. But I was far from feeling easy.
I searched the scriptures, to see if those hard doctrines were indeed there. And to my astonishment
I found they were indeed. My heart rose in enmity
against them. At this I was much alarmed. I
clearly saw that the enmity I had indulged against
the preacher, was against God! I turned to the

invitations of the gospel. But I found my heart full of enmity even against them; and I was utterly indisposed to accept those invitations. I now saw that I could never be saved, unless the power of God should subdue my obstinate heart.

My husband, who had been under distress of mind, told me one one day, that he began to see into the doctrines of the gospel, and to be pleased with them. This threw my heart into a violent rage. I thought I never would attend at the same meeting with him any more; and I begged of him to procure me a pew in the other meeting house.

In this distressed, wretched state of mind I continued for some time. I felt myself guilty and lost. I well knew that all the evil and blame existed in myself. And I saw I must become the subject of a great change or be eternally undone.

I attempted to pray that God would change my heart. But O, such prayers! They looked to me awful! At meetings, (which I now punctually attended) all the public prayers and preaching seemed to strike with a dreadful power against me; and they heightened my distress. I clearly felt that I deserved the eternal wrath of a righteous God.

After a while, my load of distress was gone. I knew not why. But the scheme of gospel grace began to appear to me very pleasant, and inviting. It seemed to me very strange, that doctrines and things, which had looked so wrong and terrible, should now look so perfectly right. I was led to query, can this be a change in my heart? It became an object with me solemnly to examine. At a lecture at our house, those things were wonderfully cleared up to my mind. And I saw the consistency and glory of those holy doctrines of salvation, which I before had hated. The word of God sweetly opened to my view. Soon after our public teacher presented in a sermon, the false ideal gods, which sinners form to themselves, while they hate and reject the doctrines of the true God. With great

clearness I saw that this had been my case, I had
formed my own imaginary god; while I had rejected the true God, as presented in his word. I
thought I could now hate and renounce such a false
ideal god, as heartily, as I had before hated the
true God. I have been led to hope and feel that all
my comfort and salvation are now derived from the
view of the great and sovereign God, whom I have
hated and rejected. Christ appears to me a wonderful Saviour, in whom I think I sometimes have
joy and peace in believing. I have desired to own
and obey this God, who has done such wonderful
things for the children of men; and to come publicly under the bonds of his covenant.

11. Relation of Mr. K.

'Till middle age, I lived an enemy to God. I
usually attended divine worship. Often after hearing a sermon, I would go home with a heavy heart,
But in the course of the week I could wear off all
my serious impressions. My worldly business would
always affect this. I formed many resolutions; but
always broke them. Never was I ready to carry
any of them into effect. Last spring, after a lecture in my neighborhood, our minister asked me if I
ever attended to the state of my soul? I replied that
I thought of it at times; but my pressing worldly
cares drove it from my mind. Mr. H. who had
preached the lecture, replied, "If you keep on in
that course, you are forever undone, soul and body!"
The words went through my heart! Never before
did I know the irresistible power of truth. I was
now made to feel the sentiment expressed, in such a
sense, as I never knew any thing of before. I retired, and tried with all my might to divert my
mind, and get rid of my pungent distress. I plunged into business, and worldly conversation. But
my load still continued. I was pressed down and

distressed under a sense of guilt. Sometimes I found myself crying; and sometimes begging for mercy. But nothing afforded relief. I was bound under my load of guilt and misery, as in bands of iron. I attempted to do much to recommend myself to God. But I saw that all I did was selfish and perverse. It availed me nothing. I now felt myself a poor wretched, undone sinner, a rebel against God; condemned and lost.

On a sabbath, as I was returning from meeting, feeling as though nothing could ever afford me relief, the verse of Dr. Watts occurred to my mind, with strange light and power;

> "Why was I made to hear thy voice,
> And enter while there's room?
> While thousands make the wretched choice,
> And rather starve than come!
> 'Twas the same love, that spread the feast,
> That sweetly forced us in;
> Else we had still refus'd to taste,
> And perish'd in our sin!"

I had a view of the way of salvation, different from any thing I ever before apprehended. I thought it a lovely and good way;—every way adapted to my miserable case. I felt astonished at the grace of God in the salvation of miserable sinners. And from my heart I could pity those, who were still rejecting this salvation. From this time I found the Bible to be a new book.

The preaching of the gospel seemed entirely new. I was astonished to think that I had so long heard such preaching as *this*, and saw no beauty in it, but was opposed to it. I saw that I had been a most guilty, vile creature.—That I had indulged a most perverse enmity against the doctrines of grace, and hence had disbelieved and rejected them. I think I loathed myself for such ungrateful wicked-

*20

ness; and longed to live, for the time to come, as the
grace of God, that bringeth salvation teaches.

I see so much imperfection in myself, that at
times I have great darkness. But sometimes I find
a little light and comfort. It is my wish to glorify God
by a public acknowledgment of his religion, and
walking in all his commands and ordinances.

12. *Relation of Miss L.*

I THOUGHT I had lived a very inoffensive moral
life, and had not much to fear. One sabbath day
I saw one of my mates, about my age, walk up the
broad alley to give herself up to God in covenant.
She had set out alone, in a time of general inatten-
tion to walk with God. It gave me an unusual
shock. I went home troubled to think she was taken,
and I was left. Soon after, the minister preached
relative to baptized children, that they were dedicated to God, had the seal of his kingdom upon
them, had been blessed with a great privilege in
having been thus given up to God by pious parents,
and in a gracious ordinance.—That they were under great obligations to give themselves up to God;
and were in great danger, if they violated them.-

My conscience testified against me. I knew I had
been a subject of these privileges, and alas, had
been disposed to make little or nothing of them. I
went home with a full determination to set immediately about the work of religion. But my resolution
amounted to but very little. Another sermon soon
after renewed my alarms. I now saw myself to be
a sinner, and felt as though I should sink under the
load of my guilt. I attempted to get relief by prayer,
and begging for mercy. But my prayers appeared
so vile, that they seemed to increase my distress,
which now seemed insupportable. I betook myself
to the Bible. Here I seemed to get some light, and
a glimpse of hope, which held me up from despair.

But I was still stout-hearted, and far from righteousness. My heart murmured against God for the fall of Adam, and the consequent depravity of my nature, and my deplorable state. In this distress, (sometimes to a greater, and sometimes to a less degree,) I continued through the winter. The thoughts would often be forcibly injected into my mind, "*O you have been very moral; your sins are nothing to what others have committed!*" But alas, I felt the falsehood of all this.

In the spring, a sermon from these words, "For to be carnally minded is death, but to be spiritually minded is life and peace," much increased my distress. I saw my heart was indeed carnally minded, and totally dead in sin. And my whole life, (which I before had deemed very moral,) appeared to me to be one continued series of wickedness. All my best deeds were defiled and sinful. And I felt undone. My heart began to murmur against my father, (who is a lively professor,) for not having done more to awaken me from my wretched state. I thought, surely he must have known my wretched case, and ought to have been most abundant and earnest in labors with me, to aid my salvation from such deplorable ruin. But when I came to consider, I found he *had* abundantly labored with me; and I would not obey him in this thing. Oh, I thought, was this what he *meant*, when he used thus to converse with me? I then had no idea of it. But I now could no more cast the blame upon parents. I saw that the guilt all lay at my own door. And I wondered that God had suffered so vile a wretch to live, and remain in a region of hope.

I became sick of sin. It looked most vile. And I seemed to be afraid to *move*, or do *any thing*, lest I should sin against a holy God. One evening as I came home from lecture, the ideas struck my mind with an overcoming force, "Lord into thy hands I commit myself!" I felt inexpressible joy in God.

But I was unable to indulge the thought that this
was conversion. I dared not, for a long time, to
admit this idea. I was much troubled at the thought
that my convictions had left me. But I found different and new views of God. He had before appeared to me the most *dreadful* Being. I *feared* and
dreaded the thought of him. But now I could *fear*
and *love* him. Christ was now to me the chief of
ten thousands, and altogether lovely. I found joy
and peace in believing. And it is my desire to follow Christ all my days, and publicly to own him
before men.

13. *Relation of Miss M.*

THOUGH I was dedicated to God in baptism, and
was blessed with much early religious instruction,
I lived a careless life, till I was nineteen years of
age. I was then some alarmed at the funeral of a
child, and by the warning of a brother. But I opposed and much abated my conviction from an idea,
that I was too young to be perplexed with these
things. With this thought I became again so easy
in sin, that I could neglect the house of God with
but little compunction. Six months ago I was again
alarmed, on hearing of the serious impressions of
some young people. But I dreaded to hear any
thing upon the subject. Some in our family became
serious. I felt my heart rise against them, and
wished I could see them lively as before. A pious
parent spake to me upon the importance of religion, and of my attending to it; of the present
time's being a sealing time, and that doubtless some
would have the dreadful occasion to lament, "The
harvest is past, the summer is ended, and we are
not saved." My mind was solemnly alarmed and
affected. The sabbath arrived. My mother, sus-
pecting that I did not intend to go to meeting, asked
me, if I designed any thing should prevent my at-

tending at the house of God that day? I waved a reply. A tide of opposition was swelling in my heart; and I determined I would not go to meeting. She asked, what it would profit, should I gain the world, and loose my soul. These words came with such power, that I was forced to leave the room. I found myself in great trouble; and felt as though I was undone. I dared not to neglect attending public worship. I felt that I was a great sinner, and that death was nigh. The thought, that "except a man be born again, he cannot see the kingdom of God," greatly overwhelmed me. Our minister preached upon the words, "That the thoughts of many hearts may be revealed." And truly I found my heart and my wretchedness *revealed*, by the truths of the gospel. The world appeared a wilderness. And so great did my sins appear, that I seemed to be sinking under the wrath of the Almighty. I longed to be out of his sight; but I felt that it was infinitely impossible. As we left the meeting house, and the minister passed by me, I longed to have him know my distress, and pray for me. Alas, my distracted eyes were looking round for creature help! The thought occurred, that my sins were so great, and I so vile a wretch, that no prayers for me could be of any avail. At every step, as I returned home, it seemed as though I must sink. Finding at home one, who had not attended meeting, this added to my distress. I felt as though I must warn him of his danger. I retired to my chamber, where I walked the room in anguish, I read my Bible. Something I discovered in the cxvi Psalm, which seemed to afford a glimpse of hope, and to keep me from sinking. My past life was presented in a dreadful light to my view. I found that my carnal mind was indeed enmity against God. My distress continued from day to day. I often attempted to pray; but my prayers appeared vile and most ineffectual. I read ——

and attended on meetings; but the preaching seemed all against me. At times I thought God was unjust, and demanded of m e what I could not perform.
I labored to reform, and to do all in my power to be
saved. But I was living on my own strength and
good works. At the close of a lecture one asked
me, if I was willing to be left, while many were tak-
en? I felt unwilling. But I feared there was no
mercy for me. I seemed to feel as though the sentence were already past, "Depart from me ye cursed." This sharp distress continued more than a
week. Upon a sabbath the preaching was upon
Herod's hearing John; "And when he heard him,
he did many things, and heard him gladly." This
sermon fully convinced me that I had never heard
preaching with better motives, than those of Herod
in hearing John, while he still lived in sin. I clearly
saw that I had never been willing to give myself up
to Christ, and give up all for him.—That I had
been depending on works. But that they were utterly ineffectual.

I now found myself disposed to say, "Here Lord,
I give myself away; 'tis all that I can do." Upon
which the following verse of Doctor Watts occurred to my mind, with a powerful and pleasing sensation;—

> "Our guilty spirits dread
> To meet the wrath of heaven;
> But in his righteousness array'd,
> We see our sins forgiven!"

I felt myself to be in the hands of a just and holy
God, who would do me no injustice, if he cast me off
fovever. I felt grieved to the heart, that I had
been fighting against so holy and good a Being.
Every thing, except my wicked heart, appeared to
be praising God. And I felt an ardent desire and
prayer, that I might praise him too, and be reconciled to his will. After this, I had some comfort;

but many fears. Alas I was far from feeling as I
had ever imagined true converts feel. I longed for
the day of a preparatory lecture. It arrived. But
I was unable to attend. I believed that God gov-
erns all things, and knows best how to deal with
me. I was now made to feel, that God knows the
secrets of my heart, and that all my excuses for my
sins are vain. The words of Christ, "O ye of little
faith," shewed the great sin of unbelief, and that
my heart was full of it. The following passage
came with light and power to my mind; "Cast
away from you all your transgressions, wherewith
ye have transgressed; and make you a new heart
and a new spirit; why will ye die, O house of Israel.
For as I live, saith the Lord, I have no pleasure in
the death of him that dieth." My views of the passage, and indeed of every thing else, seemed new.
Christ appeared a glorious Saviour,—just such an
one as I needed. The Bible I saw to be indeed the
word of God, and most excellent. I was constrained to hope in the mercy of the Lord. That preaching of the Gospel, which I once hated, now appears
to me worthy of all acceptation. I think I ardently
long to be holy and obedient to God.

14. *Relation of Miss N.*

ATTENDING at the house of divine worship, one
day my attention was much arrested, and my conscience alarmed on perceiving that a number of people
were distressed for the state of their souls, and their
eternal welfare. The thought occurred with power,
surely my soul is as precious as theirs; and I have not
less reason to be troubled than they. Why am I so
unconcerned. I resolved to attend to this important
business.

i carefully attended meetings, in hopes of hearing
something for my good. But though I heard solemn
sermons, and most pathetic addresses, yet I found

my heart hard as a stone. But I was deeply troubled. A pious man addressed me, apprehending me to be under trouble of mind. He expressed a great desire that I might become reconciled to God. But alas, I felt that instead of being reconciled, I was utterly opposed to God, I could not endure his character. These words continually haunted my troubled mind; "I form the light, and create darkness; I make peace, and create evil. I the Lord do all these things." My impious heart replied, Where then is man's transgression? Why is he to be blamed? How then can the fault be in me? But these words confounded me, "Except ye repent, ye shall all likewise perish." What, (replied my wicked heart,) perish for what God says he himself has caused to be done? This is a hard saying indeed: Who can hear it? My mind had become greatly distressed. I opened my Bible, and these words first presented to my sight; "Wo to him that strives with his maker. Let the potsherds strive with the potsherds of the earth." I strove to reason myself out of my impious cavils; but it was reasoning with a heart of stone, and of perverseness.

But it pleased God to confound my cavilling heart, by shewing me the unreasonable nature of my objections. He shewed me that he is mighty to save, by breaking the strong hold of Satan, and discovering to me the inexcusable nature of my sinfulness, and my need of the Saviour. I saw that I was voluntary, and most unreasonable, in all my wicked treatment of God and his salvation. I felt no more inclination to charge my sins upon God. I most clearly saw, that notwithstanding all the divine decrees, I was the criminal cause of all my own wickedness.—That I was voluntary and perverse in transgressing the greatest obligations.—And that God would have been just, had he, long ere this time, numbered me with the damned. Every refuge failed me. The plain truth had stripped me of all my excuses. I could see nothing but a dreadful life of sin; and the dreadful consequences which justly awaited it. I attempted to pray for mercy, and to lay my most wretched case before God; —that against him, and him only I had sinned, and been most perverse. I tried to plead his promise, that those who come unto him, he will in no wise cast out. I felt an unusual and delightful sensation in my soul, in these views of God, of myself, and of my sinfulness. My distress was gone. I inquired with myself, what had produced these strange alterations in my feelings and views? I thought it could not be regeneration. For my sins appeared far greater than ever;—piercing like pointed arrows. I dared not hope. And yet all my slavish fear, my spirit of bondage, was gone. I went to meeting. Our minister preached upon the warfare in the christian; "For the flesh lusteth against the spirit, and the spirit against the flesh; and these are contrary the one to the other; so that I cannot do the good that I would." I thought my inmost soul could witness to every word in the sermon. My evidence was brightened; I dared to hope in the mercy of God through Jesus Christ. I think I have since had joy and peace in believing. Sure I am, that I now approve and love those distinguishing doctrines of the gospel, which I once abhorred. These words of sovereign grace, "I will have mercy on whom I will have mercy,"—(a sentence once as terrible to me, as, Depart ye cursed!) are now full of consolation. Were it not for the most blessed sentiment contained in them, sure I am, that I should never have been saved, nor any other soul of fallen man. These great alterations, which I find in my views, feelings, and pursuits, have excited in me a steadfast hope that God, in his infinite mercy, has brought me up from the horrible pit, and miry clay; and set my feet upon a rock; and put a new song into my mouth of praise to God. I desire to give

21

God all the glory, and to walk with him in all his commands and ordinances.

15. *Relation of Miss O.*

As long ago as I can recollect, I had many serious impressions relative to my soul's concern. But I most erroneously imagined the christian life to be gloomy and unhappy; and I decidedly preferred my youthful vanities to it. Seven years ago the death of a dear sister greatly distressed and alarmed me. But I cautiously concealed my distress, lest I should be despised by my vain companions. I feared the face of a christian, and hence opened my troubled thoughts to no one. And I soon was able mostly to dimiss my serious thoughts of religion. Conviction, however, at times returned, and armed my conscience against me. At such times I tried to comfort myself, that I could and would do something, by my own exertions, to better my situation. But finding that this desire did not accord with the plain language of the Bible, my heart rose against God; and I endeavored to lay the blame upon him. I thought with myself, God has commanded me to believe; and condemned all, who do not; and yet Christ says, "No man can come to me, except the Father, who hath sent me, draw him." This, I said to myself, is like *reaping where he has not sown!* In these alternatives of carnal security, and of cavilling, and conviction, I remained for years.

Last spring, at the meeting house one Lord's day, a person, whom I had supposed to be as careless as myself, introduced conversation with me respecting the things of the future state. This somewhat alarmed me. In the afternoon, the sermon from the text, "I came not to call the righteous, but sinners to repentance," was powerful upon my mind. No words can express the views and feelings, which it excited. But my cavilling heart took the lead. I knew the gospel taught that Christ died for sinners, and came to call them. But I knew it taught also, that there is an elect number, whom only God will save. And I thought it was not at all likely I was one of them. And it would hence be presumption for me to think of being saved. I found my heart harder than a stone; and my mind a chaos of darkness. In this state of confusion and distress I remained several weeks; sometimes wondering why God should contend with me, as I had not been the greatest of sinners; and at other times wondering why he had not cut me off, and sent me quick to destruction.

One day, as I was going to a lecture, the thought seemed to be injected with force into my mind, that I was a *fool* for wasting my time in such a manner, as it would be no use to me. I was tempted to resolve I would never attend again. But afterward hearing a sermon, which pointed out the way of salvation for sinners, my troubles were greatly increased. This sermon, instead of affording me relief, almost drove me to despair. I believed that there was a way of salvation in Christ;—and that Christ did invite sinners to come to him. But alas, *I had no heart to come!* This I clearly saw; and felt that I was utterly undone. If I looked forward I saw nothing but an infinite, and justly incensed God, whom I had been provoking all my days. To look back I dared not. Darkness and death appeared on every side. Oh, I thought how gladly would have fled out of God's hands, had this been in my power! I even wished for mountains and rocks to fall on me, and hide me from the divine presence. I then saw my heart to be full of all manner of evil, and to be such a sink of pollution, as I believed no one ever had before. I clearly perceived that I every day grew worse and worse. I felt great opposition to the doctrines of the Bible; and finally I

was left utterly to doubt of the divine authority of
it. Now I thought christianity is without founda
tion. The thought drove me almost to distraction.
Our minister conversed with me upon the subject.
And my unbelief relative to the divinity of the Bible,
was removed. But I was fully convinced that I
could do nothing of myself; and that if ever I was
saved, it must indeed be by sovereign grace.

I began after a while to perceive a change in my
feelings. The word of God, which had been to me
a sealed book, began to open in a strange and lovely manner. And on hearing a sermon upon the evidences of the good hope through grace, I thought
I perceived some evidence of a saving change in
my heart. I had intervals of distressing darkness.
But God was pleased to bring me out of it into his
marvellous light. I think I do rejoice in Christ, as
my Prophet, Priest, and King. I am sensible that
the things I once loved, I abhor. And that scheme
of gospel grace which I hated, and long rejected, I
now love, and desire to embrace. I consider it as
a bounden duty, and a great privilege, to own Christ
before men, to covenant with his people, and to
obey his commands and special ordinances.

16. *Relation of Mrs. P.*

THREE years ago, living single with my parents,
I was deeply impressed with a sense of my guilt and
danger. For several months the Spirit of God
strove with me. But I proudly resisted his kind
motions, and labored to persuade myself, that my
gloom and distress arose from bodily infirmity. For
the thought that I was a sinner in the hands of an
angry God was so mortifying to my proud heart,
that I could not endure it. I in vain attempted to
get relief from mingling with friends and the world.
No ease did I hence obtain to my troubled conscience. My peace was disturbed by day; and my

sleep and dreams by night. But I with much difficulty kept my distress concealed. I thought that
to make the inquiry, "What must I do to be saved?" was too much for my proud heart. I fondly
hoped. however, that by doing some things myself,
I could render my situation more safe. I hence attended meetings and religious conferences. But I
was very cautious where I placed myself. I did not
mean our minister, or any other person should
have the opportunity of interrogating me as to the
state of my soul. Thus resisting the Holy Spirit, I
became more easy and stupid.

Last Spring, it being a season of sickness, and
some sudden deaths, the troubles of my mind returned; my conscience was again alarmed. I heard
a sermon, in which the sovereignty of divine grace
was illustrated. I felt much offended, and thought
that if ever I found comfort in religion, it must be
in some other way beside this. I could never submit to such a system of salvation. I was beset with
a tide of passions and temptations; and Satan, I believe, was very busy with me; although I then knew
it not. My heart complained and wrangled against
God for not saving me.

I was led to be sensible that the difficulty was all
in myself; that I was utterly unwilling to become a
subject of grace;—had resisted the Holy Ghost;—
had rejected all his calls and invitations;—and now
did fully deserve eternal banishment from God. I
saw I had been flattering and deceiving myself, in
thinking I had done all I could, and hence ought to
be saved. I found, I had no heart to do any thing
aright; all I did was rebellion and sin. I now found
my situation was too serious to be trifled with any
longer, or to be kept concealed. It was no more to
be treated thus as a matter of little importance. I
was no more afraid to have my trouble known.
My great inquiry was, What must I do to be saved? How shall I become reconciled to God, whose

*21

law I have violated, and whom I have so grievously offended? I now saw that I had never performed a good deed in my life; had never done a single thing that could or ought to be acceptable to God. I felt astonished at his forbearance with so vile a wretch. I depaired of ever doing any thing to recommend myself to him. I was in his hands, as clay in the hands of the potter. And I trust "it pleased God, by the foolishness of preaching, to save" so great a sinner, and open to my view the great atoning sacrifice, the righteousness and salvation of Christ. I think I rejoiced to embrace him, and to embrace him in those doctrines of sovereign grace, which before I had violently opposed and rejected. I saw that this was the only way of salvation for lost sinners. And I could rejoice with wonder, that such provision was made for them. Surely if God had not, of his own free mercy, made me willing in the day of his power, I had perished in my opposition, pride and impenitence.

────────

17. *Relation of Mr. Q.*

I HAVE been a great opposer of the doctrines of the gospel all my days, till last spring. It was seldom that I paid any attention to the preaching of the gospel. Our public teacher once asked me, why I did not attend meetings? I replied, that it was because I could not endure his preaching.

Last spring my wife was in distress of mind relative to her salvation. And some others I found inquiring what they should do to be saved? This gave me a shock. My conscience waked up and testified against me. I thought my soul was precious, and needed attention as well as others. I was called to attend the funeral of a man about my age. The sermon and the occasion added to my troubles. Soon after, a sermon was preached upon the text, "It is hard for thee to kick against the pricks,"

This sermon was to me full of solemnity and terror. I found I had all my days been kicking against the pricks, or opposing divine truths; and that it was indeed as unavailing, as for one to attempt to batter down a strong and sharp spike with his naked foot. I was now sensible that something must be done, or I was forever lost. I flew to works. I tried to reform; I read, and heard preaching, and prayers. But I found no relief. I was led to see that all my doings were ineffectual, and I could never save myself. I found trouble and sorrow, such as I never before apprehended.

After considerable time I found myself possessed of new apprehensions of God's pardoning grace. I saw there was redemption and forgiveness with our God. The passage, "Though your sins be as scarlet, they shall be white as snow," came to my mind with light and power. This excited some hope that my case would not prove utterly desperate. But I still viewed myself to be as in the gall of bitterness.

One morning as I waked, I found myself sitting up in my bed, and uttering these words;

"Lord, in the morning thou shalt hear
My voice ascending high;
To thee will I direct my prayer;
To thee lift up mine eye."

I found myself possessed of delightful views and feelings concerning God and divine things. I perceived a glory in them which I never saw before. I walked abroad, and seemed to feel myself in a new world. Christ appeared like a Saviour indeed; —mighty to save; and altogether lovely. With some painful reverses my apprehensions of the beauties of holiness continued. I heard a sermon which described the feelings of the new-born soul. It was to me a delightful one. I thought I felt the witness of the truth of it in myself. I hope I was sealed with the Holy Spirit of promise. I have found myself possessed of new feelings of soul toward God, his people, sin, holiness, and the way of salvation. I think I abhor myself, and my past opposition to the gospel. What I hated and rejected, now appears to me most excellent. It exhibits the only way of salvation, and a way of salvation worthy of God. Christians, whom I before wished so shun, are now to me the excellent of the earth. I think I am disposed to take up my cross and follow Christ in all the duties of his religion.

18. *Relation of Mr. R.*

THOUGH I was dedicated to God in infancy, and early taught the things of his religion, yet I led a very stupid life, till I reached the age of manhood. I was in some respects a leader in fashionable vanities. I was not a total stranger to reflection. I knew I had a very hard and wicked heart. But to get rid of the painful apprehensions of this, I mingled in vain company, and led them in vanity.

On a certain day, I heard there was to be a religious conference, that evening, in the vicinity where I lived. I resolved to attend; but I confess my motives were very unworthy of a rational soul, that is accountable to God; and such as I hope I shall ever, in future, hold in detestation. With some of my companions I set out for the meeting. When we came to the house, we found that for some reason, but few were there. We hesitated about going in; but finally mustered courage enough to enter.

When I came to hear the conversation of the minister present, I lost all inclinations to make light of religion. My mind was involuntarily solemnized. The conversation took a turn upon the inexpressible joys of the inhabitants of the celestial world; and the intolerable miseries of those, who are lost. My mind was forcibly arrested with the consciousness, that I was going to the wretched situation of the latter class. I retired home deeply wounded. I was led to see that I was indeed a great sinner; that I must embrace Jesus Christ, or be forever lost; and that I had no more time to lose. For a number of weeks my distress continued, and increased. I strove to do something to conciliate the divine favor; but alas my views and feelings were wholly legal and selfish. I hope I was led to feel that I could do nothing without the regenerating grace of God. I think I obtained new views of the way of salvation by Christ, and a totally new estimation of it. I thought I could rejoice in bowing at the feet of Christ. I have since found my heart extremely wicked. And at times I much fear that no grace can be found in such a heart. But I find myself possessed of a prevailing hope, that I am fully determined, in the strength of divine grace, to follow the Lord Jesus Christ in all his commandments.

I now desire that the rest of my days, and all my talents, may be unreservedly dedicated to God. Hence my request is, that I may be admitted, unworthy as I am, to the fellowship of this church of Christ.

19. *Relation of Mr. S.*

FROM my early youth I had, at times, pungent impressions, which constrained me to weep. But my wicked heart found means to resist them, till I had been for several years settled in a family state. Last spring I became more deeply troubled than ever. It was a time of general stupidity. But I felt as though I could no longer follow the multitude in the neglect of salvation. I attended meetings, and visited our spiritual instructor; and he visited me. My troubles increased. I considered that I had lived under the gospel; had enjoyed great privileges; had heard much solemn and good instruc-

tion; but I had ungratefully and wickedly misim-
proved those blessings. I now became sensible that
my heart was utterly depraved, full of real enmity
against God, and was haughty and perverse. I
saw that I had been displeased with the doctrines
of the gospel; and utterly unwilling to submit to
God, and obey him, as his word demands. I could
no longer treat these things with indifference. I attempted to seek God by prayer and reformation.
In this way I sometimes would obtain a degree of relief, upon what I now am sensible was legal ground.
Then again my distress would return; and I saw
that there was no goodness in my prayers and performances.

In the course of the summer I began to have
views, which led me to hope God had mercy in
store for me; though I did not dare to hope I was
then converted. At times my heart in my secret
devotions, was drawn out, in a way wholly new to
me, after God. My soul overflowed with gratitude
to him. This often filled my eyes with tears, and
my soul with comfort. These views and feelings
increased, and rendered my closet to me a desirable place. I was afraid to hope this could be from
a gracious heart. I became convinced that God is
the only source of rational enjoyment. At times I
was beset with violent temptations to let all these
things go, and return back to to the world. But I
was enabled to decide that I could not and would
not do this.

One morning as I lay in my bed, I had such an
apprehension of Christ, as I never had before. He
appeared glorious and lovely. I was filled with a
great degree of joy. It seemed as though I could
doubt no more. But darkness and doubts afterward returned, and I have from time to time, had
to struggle with temptations and fears. My views
of Christ, and of the way of salvation by him, have
I think been more and more clear. At times they

have appeared to me full of glory and inexpressible excellency, so as to carry me above all doubts and fears. But such views are not continual.

I have become more and more sensible of the total and dreadful depravity of my heart by nature. I clearly see that it is a sink of dreadful wickedness. The views, that I have had of this, have sometimes so overpowered my strength, that I felt I must certainly sink, were not for the upholding power and grace of God. I think this dreadful wickedness of my heart is my greatest burden. I long to feel the life and power of religion, and to be conformed to God.

I desire to bear my testimony for Christ. His cause is glorious, and infinitely worthy of the attention of all. I firmly believe in the doctrines and system of religion, which are taught in your solemn assembly. This scheme of salvation by sovereign grace, I think, is precious to me. It is all my salvation, and contains all my hope. And I desire to be admitted to the fellowship of this church.

20. *Relation of Mr. T.*

Six years ago, my mind was much alarmed with a sense of my lost state. But I stifled my convictions, and again went to sleep in impenitence. Last July, on hearing the hymn read,

"Behold the Potter, and the clay," &c.

I was deeply troubled. The words were made sharp and powerful upon my heart. I saw that God was a Sovereign, in choosing the vessels of his mercy; and yet this implied that all men were in themselves sinful, wretched and undone. In this wretched condition I viewed myself. I felt that I was a great sinner, and was lost. I was led to feel that I truly deserved to be left of God, and to be made a vessel of wrath; and I expected that this must be my lot. Having been one day to meeting, my distress was much increased. I thought no human being was ever in such a case as I found myself to be. I viewed my day of grace as over. I had out stayed my time. It seemed as though my harvest was past, my summer ended, and I not saved. I saw the blame was all in myself. My heart was so hard, opposed, and wicked, that it never would come to Christ. I was in a degree of despair.

In the evening as I was thinking upon my dreadful case, this sacred passage occurred with unusual power to my mind, "Turn ye, turn ye; for why will ye die?" This seemed to divert my attention from my wretchedness. I found myself possessed of new views of Christ, and of the way of salvation. I felt delighted with a view of his glory. He appeared to be altogether lovely. His condescension to guilty worms appeared most wonderful. My tongue was loosed to speak his praise. The things of God furnished a new theme of wonder. I walked abroad. I seemed to behold a new world. Every thing was full of God. Every thing spake his Godhead, and his praise. The heavens declared his glory; and the earth the work of his hand. I thought I could unite with the creation in praising its adorable Author. I continued thus all night. I could not be willing to lay these glories aside for sleep. About day I thought it might be duty to try to take a little rest. But sleep could not prevent my hearts being wrapped up in praise to God and the Lamb.

This frame of mind continued for several days. Then I experienced a sad reverse. God seemed to be withdrawn. He hid his face, and I was troubled. I most sensibly felt the wickedness of my character; and felt undone. I could not behold the beauty of Christ. I was again almost in despair. The thoughts were strongly excited in my mind, that I had better now turn back to the world, and give up all religion. But this appeared indescribably horrible. The world appeared to me good for nothing. Ten thousand of it would be no compensation for the loss of Christ. I cried to God for mercy and salvation. I found I had no where to go but to him through Christ. The thought struck my mind that others had been in as great distress as I; and yet had been brought to the light of salvation. I then felt, that I would hope in God, and wait patiently for him. Soon after this, my clouds of distress again gave way, and the beauty and loveliness of Christ appeared to me as before. My spirit of bondage was gone; and I could rejoice in the Lord.

Reviewing these things in the light of the word of God, I am led to hope that sovereign grace has plucked me as a brand from the fire, and given me a saving faith. Darkness and light, hopes and fears, have struggled in my breast, but I desire to own Jesus Christ; and practically to give him all the glory of my salvation.

------

21. *Relation of Miss U.*

My mind was arrested a number of years ago, with the thought that I must die; and that if I died as I then was, I should certainly be sent to misery. My sins appeared very great. I appeared to myself to be the greatest sinner on earth. And I wondered God had spared me so long to rebel against him in this world of hope. I searched the Bible; but it was all against me. I went to meeting; but found no relief. My distress increased. I saw nothing but hell before me. I saw my sins to be so great, that I thought God could not be just in saving me, and he ought not to do it. Still I could not endure the thought of being a monument of divine justice. I labored to do something to make myself more worthy of the mercy of Christ. But I found no relief in this. I was brought to despair of all help or hope in myself. And I almost despaired of help in God, and thought there could be no mercy for me. In this most painful state of mind, I continued for considerable time.

At a certain period these words came to my mind, with light and power, "My grace is sufficient for thee." I found great relief; and thought I rejoiced in being in the hands of God. I felt that if he sent me to hell, it would be fully just. And if he saved me, it would be of his mere mercy; and I should praise him. The way of grace in the Bible appeared to me new, lovely and excellent. And I thought I took more comfort in a short time in religion, than all I ever enjoyed before.

But alas, I afterward got too much into the world and did not unite with the people of God, as I ought to have done, in walking in the ordinances of grace.

Our public instructor came into our district, to catechise the children. He talked solemnly with me upon the state of my soul, and my neglect of gospel duty. The words fastened conviction upon my conscience. I was deeply wounded and greatly distressed. I saw I had wickedly backslidden from God. I was overwhelmed with guilt, distress, and shame.

But the astonishing mercy of the Lord again appeared, in applying to my heart these words of grace, "Though your sins be as scarlet, they shall be as white as snow; though they be red like crimson, they shall be as wool." I had again most delightful views of the mercy of God in Christ, and the excellency of his perfections. I felt and was grieved that I had sinned against him, and was utterly unworthy of the least mercy. But I could rejoice in God, and in being in his hands, let him do what he would with me. I felt that salvation was wholly of the Lord, and that no part of it ever originated in the

guilty creature. Jesus Christ I saw to be most glorious, and I longed to have all the world see his glory, and embrace him. I saw a fulness of salvation
in him, that he is indeed mighty to save. I have
since had many doubts and fears relative to myself.
But my duty now appears plain, and desirable, to
unite publicly with the people of God.

22. *Relation of Mr. V.*

WHEN I was about twenty eight years of age, I
was in great distress of mind relative to my salvation.
My proud heart was determined to suppress my
troubles; but it was with the utmost difficulty I did
it. But wretched being that I was! I succeeded
in keeping my trouble concealed, and in grieving
away the Holy Spirit. I then remained stupid, and
opposed to faithful ministers, for a number of years.
The peculiar doctrines of the gospel appeared to
me most mysterious, and disagreeable; especially
that of the election of grace. When I heard ministers
or people advocate it, I accounted for it in this way,
that they thought they were going to be saved, and
hence were partial to this doctrine. I was pleased
with our minister as a man; but I could not feel
pleased with much of his preaching. I was utterly
unreconciled to the sovereignty of God.

I began to feel uneasy; and wished to improve
every opportunity to converse with those people
who believed in the distinguishing doctrines of the
gospel. I much feared they would prove true. I
found the Bible did read in favor of them. I knew
not how to refute the arguments of their advo-
cates.

In May last as a person was laboring with me
upon these doctrines, my heart rose against them;
and I felt a bitterness against him, who was laboring to instruct me. I left the house, and went to
my secular business. My mind became greatly

exercised, till my distress seemed almost insupportable. I began to view myself to be God's creature, made for his purposes, and yet under obligations to him. My conscience testified that if I had no will to obey God, he was not hence deprived of his right to command; but he does command; and does condemn for disobedience. And consistently with this, he is, and must of necessity be, the sovereign Potter, and the Ruler of the world. He alone must save all who are saved. He must do it with design. And his designs must be, like himself, immutable and eternal. He from everlasting felt the same reasons, which he has in time, for saving whom he will of the children of men. Those, whom God does not save, are voluntary in refusing his grace. And they are under every obligation to embrace it. They have none to blame them but themselves. And if all are disposed thus to refuse salvation by Christ, as the Bible decides they are, then none would be saved, unless God had designed to save them. And when he thus saves some, while all are rejecting, those who are left to their own wicked choice, have no reason to complain.

I hope I was now brought to submit to God in this sacred doctrine, and to see and feel, that the preaching of it was neither unscriptural, dangerous nor unprofitable; but quite the reverse. And that it is the power of God, and the wisdom of God unto salvation, to all who believe.

From this time I endeavored candidly to search the Bible, and to read the most discriminating books; and I became attached to them. I read with solemn attention, books, which distinguished between saints and sinners; and I delighted in hearing preaching, which was the most searching. I found a solid pleasure in these things; and in conversation with good people; a pleasure, to which I was before a total stranger.

After a while I was induced to hope that a work of grace was begun in my heart; though I hoped with great fear. I found that my heart was treacherous, and extremely wicked. I had supposed that a change from death to life was of such a nature, that every subject of it must immediately and most clearly know it; but I at last concluded that I ought to try my exercises by the word of God, and abide the decision. In this way I thought I often found such evidence in my favor, as I should deem satisfactory in others; but I much doubted it in my own case.

I found that my heart was very deceitful; and I feared to confide in it. I saw that Jesus Christ was willing and mighty to save; and I endeavored to refer my cause wholly to him. I felt myself to be in the hands of a holy, sin-hating, and sin-avenging God; yet my mind was calm. I feared my calmness arose from my loss of conviction, and my stupidity. I hence endeavored to recover my fears by meditating on the wretched state of the enemies of God. But before I was aware, my mind would be taken up in contemplating the divine glory, goodness and mercy, and God's astonishing forbearance toward me. I wondered that my heart should not be captivated with love to so glorious a Being. I longed to love and adore him, to live to his glory, to obey him in every known duty, and to confide in him for strength to perform all his will.

For a considerable time I have been led to hope, that my views and feelings are gracious and sincere. I desire to give up myself and children to God, in the bonds of his covenant, and be a *visible* as well as *real* follower of Christ. I can only say, that, unless my heart deceive me, I have a real desire to walk as becometh the saints. If I be renewed, I am sensible God alone has done it of his sovereign mercy, and by the still small voice of his Holy Spirit.

*22

N. B. The subject of the above relation is *here no more!* He lived three years after uniting with the church, and most solemnly and amiably adorned his profession. He then was taken sick, and died apparently in the solid triumphs of faith. "The memory of the just is blessed."

Several of the subjects of the other preceding relations are likewise gone to their long home. They well adorned their professions while they lived; and died in peace.

23. *Relation of Miss W.*

ABOUT the beginning of the year 1801 I was much concerned respecting my future state; but I carefully kept it concealed. Not long after, I was called to mourn the death of a dear sister. I sensibly felt my heart rise against God, for calling her away, and laying so heavy a trial upon us. I was sensible that my murmuring spirit was very wicked. I was troubled in the view of it. My conviction increased in the course of the spring and summer, till I became exceedingly wretched, and felt myself undone. I attempted and labored with all my might to do something for my benefit, and to ease my tortured conscience. But I found myself continually growing worse and worse. My heart rose violently against God. I could not endure his sovereignty. It appeared a hard and cruel thing, I could not endure to be in the hands of such a God. Yet I found I was in his hands, and could not escape.

On a certain time I was struck with the idea that I had lost all my conviction. I seemed to be stupid as a stone. And my heart appeared far more wicked than ever. This gave me keen distress. I was affected with a view of the unreasonableness of my enmity against God. I saw his character was good, his perfections glorious. My enmity appear-

ed most unjust and hateful. I longed to be able
never to suffer this wicked temper to rise any more.
but to submit and acquiesce in God's will, let him
do what he would with me. I found from this time
new feelings of heart, and a calmness of soul. I had
not an idea of being a subject of saving grace, But
Christ appeared a glorious Saviour; and I had a
lively hope that I *might* be brought to embrace
him, and walk in him.

Continuing thus for a considerable time, I began
to indulge some hope that God had wrought salvation in my heart. But it was with great difficulty
and fear, that I could persuade myself that I might
hope I was a subject of true religion. I have gradually dared to hope, more and more, that this is the
case. I think Jesus Christ is altogether lovely. I
desire to adore, to confide in, and follow him, and ——
long to find my place in his church; though I feel
myself utterly unworthy of so great a privilege.

24. *A Narrative of the conversion of Miss X.*

THE subject of the following narrative is in her
long home; and, we may well believe, in glory.

This person was in low circumstances, and went
abroad to work, in different families. So poor
had been her advantages, that she was never learned to read. Repeatedly I had taken occasion to
speak to her, relative to her spiritual concerns.
But I found her ignorant and unconcerned.

One day at meeting, I perceived this girl was in
tears, and appeared very attentive. The same appearance was afterward repeated, and continued.
I conversed with her, to learn the reason of her
trouble. She informed, that death stared her in
the face. She saw she must die; and the event
seemed near and dreadful. I could perceive no
real conviction of sin. I endeavored to give her instruction.

She became a constant attendant on all religious
meetings; and was generally in tears while attending. Her views of death continued; and she
was more and more affected with the subject.

After a while, I perceived that she had a degree
of conviction of sin. She spake of being a sinner;
and was afraid to appear before God in judgment.
She continued thus, some months, with her conviction of sin increasing. She became greatly troubled,
as being a great sinner. Her convictions gradually became clear and rational.

On a Sabbath day, her distress had become extreme. At a conference, held just before night, at
a private house, I conversed with her, and found
her convictions deep and most pungent. She had
a great sense of the Majesty of God, and of the
wickedness of her own heart.

Returning home, with several in company, I conversed with her. Among many striking things, she
said, *O Mr. S. you have often preached to us on
the depravity of the human heart, and told us how
we all by nature hated God! I did not believe a
word of it. But O, you did not tell the tenth part
of the enmity I now feel!* Her expressions of her
views and feelings were extraordinary, and very
affecting. She cried aloud, wrung her hands, and
passed swiftly on before us.

The next morning I went to see her. She came
down from her chamber. I asked how she felt
now? She spake of her being a poor vile creature;
but went immediately on, to express a new source
of troubles. She said, she had been thinking and
looking abroad, that morning, and she saw God in
every thing. And every thing was praising him,
but she, and other miserable sinners! The birds
praised him; the trees, and the grass, every thing
spake God's glory. But she, a wretch, never
praised him. She expressed much grief and astonishment at herself for her never having praised

so great and good a Being, when his glory was so manifest.

I was informed, that she had been out abroad, that morning, to speak to her mates as they passed by. She would even lay hold of them, and tell them what a great, and good being God was; and how she longed that they might praise him, if she did not.

I found she had not the least idea of any saving change, as having been wrought in her heart. And did not suggest to her any idea that I thought her heart was renewed. I endeavored to give her such instructions as I thought best; and retired. She thought upon what had been said, and felt such an ardent desire to be able to praise God, that she went to converse with a very pious man, in the vicinity, with whom she had lived, to see if he could give any further direction how she might be able to do the duty, on which her heart was so much set. He told her she must pray to God that she might be enabled to praise him. She soon after retired, and attempted to comply with his direction. While on her knees in her closet, she found her difficulties removed, and found she could praise God. Her joys were inexpressible.

So remarkable were her appearance and conversation, that even despisers of religion were struck, and acknowledged that *something strange had taken place! For this person could never converse so before!*

She mourned and grieved for poor perishing sinners. She longed and prayed for their salvation. As to her own salvation, it seemed much out of her sight. She said little or nothing concerning it; but was wholly engaged for the glory of God, and the salvation of sinners. A minister in conversation with her, asked her how she should feel, if after all she should be sent to misery? She replied with the greatest readiness and simplicity, as though it was no matter what became of her;—that she should, delight in praising and adoring God, even should his glory require her destruction.

A female professor of religion had occasion to sleep one night with this young convert, and related, that she appeared in the highest strains of devotion, in the course of the night, even in her sleep. She prayed for sinners; and sung praise to God.

She joined the church; and as long as I heard of her, she adorned her profession. After this she lived at a distance from me, till her death.

———

25. *Relation of Mrs. Y.*

For about two years I was deeply impressed with a sense of my sinful wretched state. To give an account of all my distressing views and feelings, during that time, would take a large volume. I will hint a few things.

Soon after the death of old Mr. C. my conscience became alarmed with a sense of my lost state. But I labored, with all my might, to drive away these distressing feelings. I consented to go into company, and to scenes of mirth, to recreate my feelings. But while there, I was ready to sink with horror. I could not unite in the exercises, but (when speaking to others) I imputed it, and my depression (which was very visible) to want of health. At times I was under such terrors of conscience, as to be under necessity of keeping my bed for days together;—complaining of bodily indisposition; though I well knew this was not the cause. For one year I left no method untried, which I imagined would be likely to divert my mind, to wear off my conviction;—visiting, journeying, and social interviews. But all was in vain. I could not get out of the hands of the Holy Spirit, who had now taken me in hand. I kept all my trouble to myself. My proud heart would not permit that any person should know the cause, or existence, of my distress. I was utterly unwilling that any should suppose I had any concern about my future state. While visiting at Boston, I walked toward Cambridge, one day, with some young acquaintances. I was in such horror, that, every step I took it seemed as though I should sink into the bottomless pit. I soon left the town, and retired to a little distance, where I had other friends. There a pious lady suspected and suggested to me the cause of my appearance, that I was troubled for my soul. But I turned the conversation, and meant she should understand this was not the case. I returned home much disappointed; having obtained no relief.

A religious awakening commenced in this place. This led me to think I would open my case to some one. I made some attempt to do it; but my heart failed me. Pride overcame judgment, and kept me in silence.

I had always been a great opposer of the doctrine of the necessity of a new heart; and of the calvinistic doctrines. I had a kind of friendship for the person and family of our minister; but I could not endure his doctrines, and heartily hated his strain of preaching. But this strain of preaching has been made the means of sweeping away my false refuges;—tearing in pieces my obdurate and perverse heart;—and preparing it, as I hope, for the salvation that is in Christ. I have been brought to see that my heart is, by nature, a seat of all wickedness. I have been fighting, with all my might, against God, who might have cut me off in a moment, and made me a monument of justice. But his grace is astonishing, which I hope has made me a monument of his mercy.

The terrors which preceded my deliverance, exceed all my description. The word of God became to me sharper than a two-edged sword. It was indeed a discerner of the thoughts, and intents of the heart. For months together, it seemed to me our minister clearly saw my heart; and that one great object of his preaching was, to unfold it to others. This vexed, and astonished me. I knew not how to attend to such preaching; and yet I felt constrained to attend, I was eager to hear all that was said.

Whole nights my eyes were held waking. My distress baffles all description. My constitution appeared sinking. My strength so failed me, that for some time I could not attend meetings. Every limb and joint trembled. My pale visage partially depicted the horrors of my mind. And I seemed to see nothing before me, but destruction and despair.

One night, after setting up late, ruminating upon the horrors of my case, I thought I must retire to rest. I slept, (or partly slept) one hour. I then waked, and leaped from my bed in lively horror! I walked the room I thought I would open my Bible, which was lying on my bureau. But I dared not do it, lest something should there appear, which would sink me into total despair. I felt my strength failing, and my sight departing. I thought I would throw myself on the bed, if possible, before I should fall. While struggling for this, the words struck my mind with power, "Stand still, and see the salvation of the Lord." I found myself relieved from sinking. My mind was somewhat diverted from my wretchedness. I felt in a little degree calmed, and supported. I then went to my Bible. I read in Isaiah; and found something, which seemed to excite a hope that my case was not desperate. I dared not to hope; and yet could not despair. The next day, which was the Sabbath, I felt calm,

Silent, and solemn. After meeting our minister
visited and conversed with me. I hardly dared to
say any thing. But I thought I felt very sick of
contending with God. I longed to be reconciled to
him. But it seemed astonishing, that I might hope
for this. Yet I had some pleasing hope that I
might become reconciled through Christ. I viewed myself vile beyond description. I knew there
could be no hope for me, but in the astonishing
mercy of that God, against whom I had been contending.

The next morning I felt that I was in a new
world. I did indeed dare to hope in God through
Jesus Christ. My hope has since continued;
though with great reverses, and fears. The doctrines of salvation, which I used perfectly to abhor,
I found were not only true, but lovely, and glorious;
and presented our only foundation of hope. The
kind of preaching which I used to oppose with my
whole heart, I am now sensible is the only true
preaching of the salvation of God through Jesus
Christ. But I am so far from feeling as I used to
imagine true christians feel, that it seems impossible I should be a subject of grace. And at times
I truly and greatly fear I am not. But this I do
feel, that the things I once loved, I now detest. And
those, which I hated and rejected, I now ardently
desire. Nothing appears to me so desirable, as to
love, obey, and be like God, and enjoy his smiles.
I desire to own his cause; and unite with his followers.

---

26. *Relation of Mr. Z.*

It was my happy lot to descend from godly
parents. They gave up their infant offspring to
God in baptism; and took peculiar pains to train
them up for God. I well remember the abundant
23

and pathetic instructions, which I received, particularly from my pious mother; and I remember the deep impressions they made on my mind, when I was four years of age. I was then much troubled with a view of the importance of being a friend to God, and of being prepared for the judgment to come. Often would I leave the plays of the children, and come and set by my ma'am, to hear her solemn instructions.

My father died in my early youth. And it was my lot to be put out to one of my uncles. Here alas, I failed of enjoying much of that tender instruction, which I had enjoyed at home. I often, however, saw my mother, and heard the repetition of her kind counsel. And my mind was very tender, at times, and deeply affected with a sense of my sin and danger. I formed many resolutions of amendment; but like the dew they passed away.

So strange was the obstinacy of my carnal mind, and so infatuating the dangers of youth, and snares of sin, that I continued in impenitence eighteen of the first years of my life. In the fall, just before I was eighteen years old, I was deeply troubled in view of my sinfulness. I saw that I was a sinner; and was much confounded. Though I had pleased myself that I was moral; yet I had led a gay life; and had been very forward in the fashionable and alluring vanities of the times. These courses now lost all their charms; while I felt deluged in guilt. I resolved to relinquish all my vain courses; and to begin in earnest to seek God. It was a very stupid time. There were no young people in the church. And I knew of none in town, of the unmarried class, (according to my present recollection) who gave evidence of true religion. My setting out therefore must be alone, and against the strong tide of popular vanities. It was a matter of some notoriety among my young mates, (who were in the full career of sin,) that my place among them was vacant. And I had no desire to keep them in the dark upon the subject. I felt free to inform them, that I had pursued such vain courses long enough, and much too long; and that I was now determined to relinquish them forever.

I now formed my place of retirement under a sequestered hedge; to which I resorted, morning and evening, for meditation and prayer, and soon found a kind of delight in this employment; and most punctually pursued it. I hardly know that any thing could have induced me to neglect, even for once, this retirement; or to have been absent upon the Sabbath from the house of God.

I soon found myself possessed of a hope, and thought I was a very good christian. In the course of the spring, an awakening began among the young people in the town. I was informed that *such and such* young persons were inquiring what they should do to be saved? I thought I was very glad; and I said to myself, *It is time they were attending to religion. I have been attending for a considerable time. And I hope now they will set out to be religious!* My pharisaical heart, I believe, exulted in my superior goodness. Oh, if I had been left here, I might have been a very strict Pharisee all my days!—but certainly an enemy to religion.

One day the thought occurred, with much force, to my mind, that there was *such a sin*, to which I was exposed, against which I had formed no firm resolution;—(a sin, of which indeed I had never been guilty; but for the commission of which, I now found I had reserved a kind of liberty, to indulge it, if I pleased.) The question came to my conscience in a most decided tone, Are you willing forever to relinquish *this*, as well as all other sins? Can you pluck out this right eye? I saw, to my great discomfiture, that my heart was utterly reluctant. I hesitated, and wished to be excused from giving an immediate answer. My conscience then asked me, and pressed me with such queries as these, How then can you pretend to be a christian? What is your religion? Can you take up with a hope, that will allow you to live in sin? My dilemma was distressing! But I clearly saw I must come, to the painful conclusion which was pressed upon me; or relinquish my hope. I then did, with distressing reluctance adopt the resolution, *I will relinquish the design of indulging this, as well as other known sins, forever!* Now I blessed myself, and thought I had done well. Now I should be able to maintain my hope. Wretch, that I was! Little did I think that I was doing all this in my own strength!

Directly upon this, *all my hope was gone!* My self-righteousness was stripped off. And for the first time I saw what it was to be utterly *undone in sin!* Never before did I know myself, nor feel the power of conviction any way to be compared with this. The event seems to me much like an old building's being struck with lightning, being instantly demolished, and its rubbish hurled in every direction. I before had felt pungent convictions of some external improprieties;—and, generally speaking, of the importance of religion. But never before did I have any just knowledge of the sinfulness of my heart. Now I had a sense of it, which not only annihilated all my former goodness, but which shewed it to be most hateful hypocrisy. O, I thought, if I were now in the situation of those, whom I had viewed the greatest sinners in town, I could have had some hope that there was mercy for me. But now it seemed as though there could be none. I attempted to beg for mercy. I read the Bible; and attended conferences, which were now set up among the young people. But found no relief. Death, judgment, and eternity stared me in the face, in a manner which no words can express. I found I was a great enemy to God, and utterly unprepared to die. Eternal realities were uncovered to my apprehension. I viewed them to be as real as my own existence, and to be very near. Time was as nothing. I looked through it, as through a thin transparent column, through which I was swiftly passing into a boundless space; and felt astonished at the madness of being diverted with the things of the former, to the neglect of the latter.

My heart quarrelled with the doctrines of grace. But I was conscious of their truth. How to reconcile them with the free agency, and accountability, of which I was conscious, I knew not. But the fact, that both were true, I could not controvert; though I was displeased with it.

My troubles long continued. I lost my flesh. My spirit sunk. My visage became pale. And I went bowed down. I heard the relations of the experiences of my young mates, who professed to be brought into the light. I longed to feel as they felt; but alas, could not. I viewed myself to be left, while they were taken. I had formed my view of conversion. I struggled hard to come up to this mark; but was ever disappointed. Often have I since thought, that if Satan had been suffered to paint something on my imagination, similar to that, for which I was looking and longing, I should easily have been deceived with a false conversion; and have been undone.

I continued thus, through the summer. Usually when I awoke in the morning, my anguish would roll upon my mind with such lively horror, that I was forced to leap from my bed, to dress in haste, and to flee to my place of retirement, to beg for mercy. My distress seemed as great as my nature could sustain. It seemed a mercy that I was not utterly overwhelmed. One day the greatness and terrible majesty of God brightened in my view; my sins of heart and life all stared me in the face; I felt myself in the infinite hands of the omnipotent

23*

God; I felt that he was most justly incensed against me; that no creature in the universe was able to deliver me out of his hands, nor afford me the least relief; I seemed to view all good characters, (ancestors and ancient saints from the beginning,) as looking on, in silent awe, to behold the decision; and none of them able, or disposed, to say a word in my behalf; the infinite God alone would form the decision, whether I should sink to hell, as I felt I fully deserved. These things brightened in my view, till I dropped my business, and looked round in wild astonishment. It seemed as though my nature must sink. I believe I had a lively view of the feelings of the damned; and may say, with David, "The pains of hell got hold upon me." I seemed to be saved from sinking under it. These lively views, after a minute, abated. God held back the face of this throne, and spread his cloud upon it. I could learn nothing in favour of my salvation. The above view left an impression on my mind, which I believe will never, never be forgotten! It led me to know "the terrors of the Lord."

In the latter part of the year, I often found, in my retirement, and while pleading for mercy and salvation, a set of feelings and views, which led me to hope my case was not wholly desperate. I saw there was indeed a Saviour,—Jesus Christ; that he was glorious, and altogether lovely. I longed intensely to come to him, and be reconciled. It often seemed as though, were it possible, I would fly to the most distant region, to see, love, and adore God in Christ. My soul often seemed to be dissolved in the view of the glories of Christ. My eyes flowed with tears; and my mouth was filled with arguments. I thought it would be an inexpressible pleasure, if I might but enjoy God and the Saviour. And I felt much encouraged, in hopes that this might, sometime, be the case. I felt great encouragement to persevere in seeking God, in hopes I might be converted, and be prepared for his service. I imagined myself to be still unconverted. For I thought I discovered in myself none of those marks of conversion, which I had previously set up in my mind. My apprehensions, at that time, of the proper evidences of regeneration, were doubtless incorrect.

I continued for a considerable time in this course, before I had any comfortable hope that I was renewed. The process of my admitting a hope was very gradual. My hope came in a very different way, from what I had expected. And my evidence of it was admitted with great fear and caution.

After some time, I felt the duty of owning Christ before men, and coming publicly into the bonds of his covenant. I thought this was my indispensable duty. But I greatly feared to perform it, lest I should come unprepared. The following argument brought me to a decision. I felt that I never should make myself any better, or more fit to covenant with God. I had learned my help was not in myself. If ever I were made more holy, God alone must do the work. And I queried how God would be most likely to do it?—in my running away from him?—or coming to him, in the way of his ordinances? I could no longer hesitate. I knew I ought to obey, and leave all with God, hoping in him to enable me to do my duty. I united with the church. And never have I regretted it.

I found the word of God to be a glorious book, and took substantial delight in searching it. Its doctrines and truths opened delightfully to my view. Seldom did I open the sacred volume, but I found myself amply repaid.

I will suggest a few of the many passages, which unfolded to my mind with great light and comfort; as I searched the scriptures. *"In the Lord shall all the seed of Israel be justified, and shall glory." "And their righteousness is of me, saith the Lord."*

Oh I thought, how good it is, that God has provided a righteousness for his people! Their salvation is all of him; and it is a wonderful salvation. *"The eyes of the Lord are in every place, beholding the evil and the good."* How good it appeared, that God was always present; and I could set him always before my face.

"I will instruct thee in the way that thou shalt go; I will guide thee with mine eye." This promise looked worth ten thousand worlds. God would go with me, as an infallible Guide, through this dangerous wilderness. I had been tortured with a view of my exposedness to error, I saw that nothing but divine grace could prevent my turning aside into crooked paths, with the workers of iniquity. But in the above, and similar promises, God was ready to undertake for me. Here I found relief.

"The heart of man deviseth his way; but the Lord directeth his steps." *"There are many devices in a man's heart; nevertheless the counsel of the Lord, that shall stand."* Here I saw the divine government, and the agency of man, unite in the same thing, and in all the thoughts and ways of man. This view of the subject was to me delightful. This subject opened still more strikingly to my view in reading Isa. x, 5—9, 12. "O Assyrian, the rod of mine anger, and the staff in their hand is mine indignation. I will send him against an hypocritical nation, and against the people of my wrath will I give him a charge, to take the spoil, and to take the prey, and to tread them down like the mire of the streets. Howbeit, he meaneth not so; neither doth his heart think so; but it is in his heart to destroy and cut off nations not a few.—Wherefore it shall come to pass, that when the Lord hath performed his whole work upon mount Zion,—I will punish the fruit of the stout heart of the king of Assyria, and the glory of his high looks." Here the scheme of the divine government, and the agency

and accountability of man, in the same event, (and
'even in the most cruel acts of tyranny and oppression,) were, to me clearly ascertained. I could
doubt no more. God had decided the point. It looked to me deep as immensity; but true, and glorious.
The following texts came to my aid, with a pleasing power. "He that hath received his testimony,
hath set to his seal that God is true." "They that
have erred in spirit, shall come to understanding,
and they that have murmured, shall learn doctrine."
"I will bring the blind by a way, which they knew
not; and will lead them in paths, which they had
not known; I will make darkness light before them,
and crooked things straight." I thought I could receive these deep things, of the universal government
of God, on divine testimony; and could set to my
seal that God is true. These things had looked to
me dark and crooked. I thought they were now
light and straight. I knew I had erred in spirit, and
murmured relative to them; but I hoped I had now
come to understanding, and learned doctrine.

I fell into the following train of reasoning. It
must be that I am dependant on God. The hairs
of our heads are all numbered. In all my thoughts
and deeds, God's counsel shall stand, and he will
do all his pleasure. But I find it a fact, (what the
Bible teaches,) that this does not at all interfere
with my free agency and accountableness. Do I
not choose my own ways? May I not do one thing,
or another as I please? Can I not put forth my
hand to this wall, by which I am standing; or retain
it to myself as I please? Can I not put it forth once,
twice, three times, or not at all, as I will? I see I can.
And just so free I am, and ever have been, in all
my ways. Why then shall I complain of the divine
decrees? or of the government of the great King of
the universe, in fulfilling them? I can have no reason to complain.

The sacred Oracles decide that God has elected his chosen from eternity; and that it is God, who regenerates them. But all this is as consistent with the free agency of the creature, in the matter of his salvation, as are the divine decrees in other things, with my freedom in my daily actions. Why have I not sought and served God all my days, as he has commanded me? *I* know the true reason has been, *I would not.* Whom then, but myself, have I to blame? Such, at the same time, have been my pride and opposition of heart, that I never should have embraced Christ, had not God powerfully wrought salvation in my heart. And this God would never do, had he not designed to do it. The command now lies upon me, to seek the Lord with all my heart, and to work out my salvation with fear and trembling? Am I willing to obey? If I be not, then God may well deal with me as a vile rebel. If I be disposed to do it, let me do it with all attention. The doctrine of election or reprobation, no more stands in my way, in these things, than do the decrees of God in relation to all my voluntary motions or deeds.

I will then cease from my vile cavilling; and, by divine grace, will give all diligence to make my calling and election sure to myself, as God invites and commands; rejoicing that God works in his people, both to will, and to do, of his good pleasure. If I be willing to do my duty, let me give God the glory, for making me thus. And in all my performance of duty, let God be glorified, that he has led me to the performance of it.

The following passages opened to my view, with light and comfort.—*"Deliver thyself, O Zion, that dwellest with the daughters of Babylon!"* This address I thought applies to God's people, diligently to save themselves from all unchristian conformity to the enemies of religion;—to come out from among them, and follow Christ. *"Through desire a man having separated himself, seeketh and inter-*

meddleth with all wisdom." This gave me a lively view of the great excellency of devoting one's self to the service of God, and the study of his word. I found the Bible to be an inexhaustible source of riches. I thought I had a great desire to imitate David, who said, *"Thy word have I hid in my heart, that I sin not against thee."* This I conceived to imply, not only embracing divine truth,—but treasuring up, in our memory, directions and precepts of the Bible, which enjoin the various duties, and apply to the various circumstances, in life. In order to this, I attempted to form in a book, my rules of heart and life, which relate to duties toward God, toward men, and toward myself; and to annex to each of these rules those sacred injunctions, which enforce them. These I multiplied, as they occurred, in the course of my reading the Bible; and I committed them to memory; till I had hundreds of texts transcribed and committed. In this way I found great benefit, and great delight; and can most cordially recommend the same practice to all young people,

I have found continual occasion to mourn under a hard, wicked and barren heart; but I think I rejoice in the astonishing plan of salvation in the gospel. And all my hope is in the sovereign mercy of God, through Jesus Christ; who is of God made unto us wisdom, righteousness, sanctification, and redemption.

THE END.

Samuel T. Armstrong, Printer, No. 50, Cornhill, Boston.

VALUABLE BOOKS,

Which have been published, and are for sale, whole-sale and retail, on the very best terms, by SAM-UEL T. ARMSTRONG, No. 50, Cornhill, Boston.

Cambridge Platform of Church Discipline. This little work contains the constitution and order of the Congregational Churches in the days of our Fathers. Ought not every Congregationalist to be possessed of this book, to which constant reference could be had to determine what was the faith and practice of the Churches at their foundation—Milner's Church History—Smith's Letters to Belsham—Mason on Self-Knowledge—Hurd on the Prophecies—Taylor and Hampton on Atonement—Gospel Treasury—Evangelical Instructor—Smith on the Prophecies, 2nd edit.—Saint's Rest—Foster's Essays—Buchanan's Researches—Owen on the Hebrews—Watts on Communion—Province of Reason—Abbot's Sermons—Emmons's Sermons, *three volumes;* a *few* at $7 50, or single volumes at various prices—Lord's History of Missions—Minister's Companion—Thomas a Kempis—Sacred Geography—Life of Whitefield—Life of Mrs. Ramsay—Life of Harriet Newell—Life of Brainard—Life of Fanny Woodbury—Life of the Converted Jew—Life of Spencer—Life of Ruby Foster—☞Dr. Worcester's Christian Psalmody. To this work you are requested to pay particular attention. The whole work with tunes 1 31 single, 13 25 a dozen; without tunes, 1 12 single, 11 25 a dozen; Select Hymns 25 cents single, 2 40 a dozen; Select Harmony, i. e. the Tunes and Rudiments of Music, 37 cents single, 3 75 a dozen; some of all in different bindings at various prices. Any minister who intends to introduce the book into his Society will be furnished with an assortment and allowed a credit—Kinne on the Types, &c. &c.—Kinne on the Sonship—Codman's Hymns and Prayers, for Family Worship—Flint's Surveying—Collyer's Lectures—☞Henry Kirke White, 2 vols. Corrected edition, with copperplates—Whitman's Key—Royal Convert—Evangelical Primer—Wilbur's Biblical Catechism—Hymns for Infant minds—Carey's, Collins's, Brown's, and Scott's FAMILY BIBLES, an extensive assortment, varying in size, paper, and binding, from one dollar to sixty four—Morse's Geography and Atlas—Cruden's, Butterworth's, Taylor's, and Brown's Concordances—Bigland's View of the World—Luther on Galatians—Clark's Travels—Campbell on Four Gospels—Macknight on the Epistles—Newton's Works, various editions—Cowper's Life and Works.

DATE DUE

CPSIA information can be obtained
at www.ICGtesting.com
Printed in the USA
LVHW011832190723
752911LV00005B/93